WHERE NIGHT IS DAY

A volume in the series

The Culture and Politics of Health Care Work

Edited by SUZANNE GORDON and SIOBAN NELSON

A list of titles in this series is available at www.cornellpress.cornell.edu.

WHERE NIGHT IS DAY

The World of the ICU

The World of the ICU

JAMES KELLY

ILR PRESS
AN IMPRINT OF
CORNELL UNIVERSITY PRESS
Ithaca & London

First published 2013 by Cornell University Press
Printed in the United States of America

Library of Congress Cataloging-in-Publication Data

Kelly, James, 1948–
  Where night is day : the world of the ICU / James Kelly.
    p. cm.
  Includes bibliographical references (p.).
  ISBN 978-0-8014-5168-3 (cloth : alk. paper)
  1. Intensive care nursing—New Mexico.   2. Intensive care units—New Mexico.   I. Title.
  RT120.I5K45 2013
  616.02'8—dc23   2012038924

Cornell University Press strives to use environmentally responsible suppliers and materials to the fullest extent possible in the publishing of its books. Such materials include vegetable-based, low-VOC inks and acid-free papers that are recycled, totally chlorine-free, or partly composed of nonwood fibers. For further information, visit our website at www.cornellpress.cornell.edu.

Cloth printing   10 9 8 7 6 5 4 3 2 1

For Loren, my true companion

CONTENTS

INTRODUCTION

You may never get to Big Sur or drive the Going-to-the-Sun Road in Glacier National Park or see where Hemingway lived in Key West, but the odds are that, one day, you will lie in a bed in an ICU.

I've been an ICU nurse for twelve years. I came to nursing late in life, after getting a BA in English just as the ten-year time limit was running out at UMass, having a little arts-and-crafts business, helping with the U-Pick at Hicks Orchard in Granville, New York, getting married, honeymooning at Sugarloaf campground in the White Mountains, studying theology at a Benedictine college, being a waiter in Vermont at the Wilburton Inn and then at the Dorset Field Club. I graduated from Castleton State College in Vermont in 1998 with an associate's degree in nursing two years after my wife graduated, passed my Boards in June, and we packed everything we owned on the tops of a red '94 Jetta and a yellow '84 Saab and drove across the country on I-80, then down to Albuquerque and our first jobs at what was then St. Joseph's Hospital.

On my very first day I walked into the ICU on the eighth floor of St. Joe's and saw a row of patients in small windowless rooms, flat on beds; some unconscious, some with their arms flailing, some with their hands tied down; some half naked; surrounded by machines and tubing; the smell of urine, sweat, feces, fear. Almost my very first thought was: What had these people done in life that they should be made to suffer this way?

The ICU seemed a world apart.

Walter Benjamin wrote that "philosophy is a struggle for the representation of a limited number of words which always remain the same." *Illness* is one of those words. Disease is the known world, mapped on the organs, rendered visible by autopsy, conquered by medicine. Illness is the new frontier.

Illness is said to have changed, to be postmodern, biocultural, a spiritual journey of self-discovery. In *Close to the Bone*, Jean Bolen writes that illness is a soul experience that brings us close to the essence of who we are: "Illness is a source of personal meaning and wisdom that can transform life and heal us."

Both nursing and medicine talk about the world of illness and the experience of people who are ill. Nursing less so. Medicine is more like a chorus, a symphony of voices; nursing, occasional solos. Nevertheless, they both talk about their role in understanding the world of illness, ameliorating suffering, healing, the very nature of their practice.

Medicine is what Jean Lyotard calls a "grand narrative." Medicine dominates the subject of illness like a colossus. Illness is the lost birthright that medicine says it has rediscovered. The history of medicine was not only a rise but also a growing away from the world of illness. Arthur Kleinman writes, "One unintended outcome of the modern transformation of the medical care system was that it drove the practitioner's attention away from the experience of illness." Physicians themselves write of how the world of doctor and patient grew distant, silent; how, with the turn to science, medicine forfeited the spiritual, humanistic qualities it possessed earlier and focused only on disease—a biological entity. Books like *The Wounded Storyteller*, *The Illness Narratives*, and *Narrative Medicine: Honoring the Stories of Illness* declare that the biomedical model has changed, that it is now the task of medicine to give voice to the silent world of suffering, to uncover the meaning of illness, to heal as well as cure.

Caring is considered by many to be the essence of nursing. Jean Watson, the architect of the philosophy of caring, writes that not only does caring distinguish nursing from medicine but the future of both medicine and nursing belongs to caring more than curing. Caring is moral and spiritual, in contrast to the technical skills and functional tasks of nursing. Caring is said to create a shared world for the nurse and the patient.

Medicine's theory of illness reflects its own social history: its elimination of competition, the embrace of disease theory, its accumulation of power, the increasing distance from the patient. Medicine sees illness the same way it sees disease: as something to be diagnosed, interpreted, as requiring medical intervention.

Nursing still lives in the shadow of medicine. Nursing theory is often distorted in the attempt to emerge from that shadow. Nursing, though, does have something that medicine does not, the thing medicine believes it lost and maybe covets: closeness to illness. A privileged proximity to the world of illness.

This book examines the concepts on which these perspectives are based—empathic knowledge, transpersonal caring, the meaning of illness, the silence of suffering. The world of illness may be different from that seen by either nursing or medicine. It may not be visible, but it is not hidden; it may not be articulated, but it is not unknown to the ill. It's not a mystery; it doesn't require interpretation. But it does not readily offer itself to our understanding. I use the works of James Agee and Michel de Certeau as metaphor and example.

In 1938, James Agee was commissioned by *Fortune* magazine to go to Alabama to write about the people who were the poorest of the poor in America: the southern sharecropper. Agee struggled to write the book. He found the world of the sharecroppers more complex than he had anticipated, more dignified. He felt that words would obscure what was already difficult enough to give appropriate clarity and intensity to and said that, if he could have, he would have shown the world of the share-croppers by doing no writing at all, but just through photographs, fragments of cloth, bits of cotton, lumps of earth. The book's title, from Ecclesiastes, is *Let Us Now Praise Famous Men*.

Writing about everyday life, the French philosopher Michel de Certeau described ordinary people as "unrecognized producers, poets of their own affairs, trailblazers in the jungles of functionalist rationality."

Nursing has a unique relationship to medicine: intimate yet subordinate, aligned yet dependent. In the ICU, they come as close as possible without touching. The teaching hospital makes doctors. They go from medical students to interns to residents to attendings. They begin as acolytes and leave as priests of health. This is described as an epic journey. Nurses witness it every day. How doctors are shepherded, nurtured. How they learn skills: "See one, do one, teach one." Becoming a nurse isn't like that. It isn't a journey. This book examines the relationship between doctors and nurses: how doctors sees nurses, how nurses sees doctors, how they are alike, how they are different.

A theory is often less the truth of an object than the reflection of a self-image, how a profession wishes to be seen. I look at the history of medicine, of medical education, and the growth of nursing to see that image. I try to see it through the words of medical historians like Paul Starr and Charles Rosenberg, doctor-writers like Ellen Rothman and Bernard Lown, nursing scholars like Jean Watson. And through my own experience.

This book is grounded in the day-by-day, hour-by-hour rhythm of the world of an ICU in a teaching hospital in the heart of New Mexico. It takes place over a thirteen-week period, the time of the average rotation of residents through the ICU. It begins in September and ends at Christmas. The patients are mostly poor. Hispanic, Native American, Anglo. The days are twelve-hours long. Unless the patient is so sick that one-to-one care is needed, an ICU nurse has two patients. The rooms have their own valence. They draw you to them, back and forth, all the day long. They call to you like the Sirens called to Ulysses.

At work I carry a clipboard. I write down the patient's past history, why he or she came in, the diagnosis, what happened during the course of the stay. I use it to keep track of what we did, what needs to be done. I organize it by systems, one page for each patient. As I was writing the book, during the day I wrote down conversations, events. The next day, or my first day off, I would rewrite the notes. And I would try to remember other things that happened that I couldn't write down. Some things—a death, unimaginable grief—write themselves in your soul and are always there. I've changed everyone's name, most of their ages, left out some things, so that they would be unrecognizable to themselves and to others.

WHERE NIGHT IS DAY

1

THE VOYAGE INTO THE SEA
OF CRITICAL ILLNESS

There is no night in the ICU. There is day, lesser day, then day again. There are rhythms. Every twelve hours: shift change. Report: first all together in the big room, then at the bedside, nurse to nurse. Morning rounds. A group of doctors moves slowly through the unit like a harrow through a field. At each room, like a game, a different one rotates into the center. They leave behind a trail of new orders. Wean, extubate, titrate, start this, stop that, scan, film, scope. The steep hill the patient is asked to climb. Can you breathe on your own? Can you wake up? Can you live?

Day is procedures: bronchoscopies, lines, taps, chest tubes. Day is traveling: MRI, CT, to dye the blood, radiate the organs, look inside the body. Then the plateau of the afternoon. Post-ops. A heart comes out. In the evening, the families. Then night to knit the raveled sleeve of care. Nights are quieter. But there are admissions, codes. The lights are always on. In the day you make progress; at night you keep them alive. Until day.

The ICU could be said to have begun in 1854 on the Fields of Scutari during the Crimean War. Of the 1,650,000 soldiers who fought, 900,000 died. Most died not from wounds but from cholera, typhus, dysentery. Florence Nightingale traveled with thirty-eight nurses from England, separated out the critically ill patients into a Monitoring Unit, and reduced the deaths of hospitalized patients from 40 percent to 2 percent. It may have begun in 1928 at Johns Hopkins Hospital, where Walter Dandy created two two-bed rooms for craniotomies and critically ill patients for the first twenty-four hours after surgery. Or in 1952, when Peter Safar, who invented mouth-to-mouth breathing, CPR, and the mannequin Resusci Anne, opened a six-bed Urgency & Emergency room at Baltimore City Hospital.

The ICU is pure medicine. The patient is a network of systems. Nine: neurologic, cardiovascular, pulmonary, gastrointestinal, genitourinary, integumentary, renal, hematologic, endocrine. Systems are the language, the code of the ICU. The progress notes in the chart are organized by systems. When they round, the residents present by systems. Nurses give report to each other by systems. For a patient to be in the ICU, a system has to fail. The principle of the ICU is actually simple: single-organ-directed interventions to support failing organ systems. A ventilator for the lungs, dialysis for the kidneys, a balloon pump for the heart. Death is indexed to organ failure. For every organ that fails, your chance of dying increases 20 percent. If more than two fail, you have MODS, multiple organ distress syndrome. MODS is unique to the ICU, like saguaros to the Sonoran Desert. MODS was discovered in 1973 and is sometimes called the disease of medical progress.

The ICU is pure medicine but like the hospital in general, it is a nursing world. The intensive care is intensive nursing care. Florence Nightingale's Monitoring Unit meant moving the most severely injured soldiers to beds nearest the nurses' station. Walter Dandy's neurosurgical unit had a trained nurse in constant attendance. Medicine comes and goes. Doctors come, write orders, leave. You find an order in the chart: Avelox 400 mg q day. In the afternoon, they are gone from the unit and, like a tide that goes out and leaves behind exposed coral reefs, what is left behind is the eternal terrain of the ICU: nurses with patients.

It is seven o'clock. The room where we get report is long and narrow, the size of a small trailer home. The two kitty-corner doors at each end are closed. The blinds are drawn. Outside, the western wall of the Sandia Mountains is in shadow. The streets of the city, with their Spanish names—Candelaria, Osuna, Lomas—are filling with cars. The room quiets when the night charge comes. It feels as if beyond the drawn blinds, the closed doors, is a storm and this room is a refuge.

"Bed One," Kate begins, "Bed One is . . .

. . . Cory Granger. Fifty-one-year-old patient of Critical Care and Neuro. Chest pain while up in the mountains, hiked out. One hundred percent occlusion of the right coronary artery. Stented in cath lab. Was on a heparin drip after and had an intracerebral bleed. He's got a left hemiparesis. He's been hot: 39.7 temp. He's gone from 40 percent to 90 percent oxygen on a nonrebreather mask. He's going for a CT this morning. He'll get sick before he gets better.

Bed Two. Dakota Yazzie. She's Hopi. Forty-two. New admit. Occipital bleed. Probably nonoperative. She's awake, alert. Moves everything. Left visual deficit. Room air. She had her CT this morning. Neurosurg hasn't come by yet. She might go out.

Bed Three is Valentín Sanchez. Sixty. He's from Guadalajara. Came up to visit his family. Presented in the ER with weakness, weight loss. Was on Med-Surg. Went into respiratory distress. Came to the ICU. Emergently intubated. They're ruling out TB. He's on propofol for sedation. Big family. They want a conference today.

Bed Four. Leroy Guzmán. Fifty-two. Found down, unconscious. Hit his head. Status post craniotomy for a subdural hematoma. No deficits. He's a drinker. Extubated yesterday. Nasal cannula. He's still withdrawing but not getting much Ativan. Restrained. His wife calls in the afternoon, totally drunk.

Bed Five is Nancy Vigil. Forty-nine. She came from Española for a higher level of care. Sepsis, renal failure, afib. Heart rate was in the two hundreds. They put her on a Cardizem drip. She converted to sinus rhythm at twelve thirty. She spiked a temp last night, 39.2. Pancultured: blood, sputum, urine. She's vented. Propofol's at thirty. Stage-two decub on her coccyx. Chest X-ray shows a pneumonia behind the cardiac silhouette. She's sick.

Bed Six is open.

Bed Seven. Lena Begay. She's from the Jicarilla Apache Reservation. Twenty-eight-year-old patient of Internal Medicine. Idiopathic pulmonary hypertension. End-stage. Awake, alert. Flolan drip at four. She made herself a DNR/DNI. She's very sweet. She's a mom. Two kids. Her family's all here.

Bed Eight is James Cushman. Fifty-six. Came in with upper-GI bleed. Scoped and banded. Went septic. Unresponsive. Hypoxic. ARDS. Lots of comorbidities. No family. He needs to die.

Bed Nine is Ricky Lucero. Ricky Boy. Twenty-one-year-old patient of Neurosurgery. Fell, was hit, or was thrown from a vehicle—take your pick—big, deep laceration on the back of his head. Restless, agitated. Extubated himself in CT to everybody's horror. He follows a couple of commands. He's on mannitol q six hours. Nasal cannula two liters. He took off his cervical collar. His C-spine's not cleared yet. If he doesn't paralyze himself, he can go out. He's a little *lloron*. His mother never leaves the room.

Bed Ten is Carolyn Britt. Meningitis. She was exposed to it in her dormitory. Was started on Cipro but stopped taking it. Go figure. She came in with a classic presentation: confused, fever, stiff neck. Trached two days ago. CPAP since four o'clock this morning. Doing okay. They're going to try her on a collar today. Awake. Alert. They had to take off both legs below the knee. It was going after her kidneys. She's seventeen.

Bed Eleven. Code name Tucson. Found down in the desert. Dehydrated. Acute renal failure. Rhabdo. CKs coming down. He's still intubated. He's on Levophed to keep his systolic pressure above ninety. They've got it down to two micrograms a minute. Normal saline's at two hundred to get his kidneys going. He gets fentanyl and Versed as needed for sedation. He's a little guy but he's wild when he wakes up.

Bed Twelve. David García. Alcohol, IV-drug history. Status post hiatal hernia repair. His stomach was in his chest. They nicked his esophagus. Got repaired. But he had a GE junction tear, so his esophagus is not connected to his stomach. I'm not making this stuff up. He's got three chest tubes, a jejeunostomy tube, a Jackson-Pratt drain, and a nasogastric tube to drain that we are not to touch. They're going to connect everything later. He's on a vent. Fentanyl drip.

Bed Thirteen. Maria Leyba. Sixty-four. GI bleed. Cryptogenic cirrhosis. Came in through the ER. Third of four units of blood going in now. She's a frequent flyer. She'll be scoped today.

Bed Fourteen. Peter Richardson. Sixty-eight. Motor vehicle accident. Fender bender. Came in with right hemiparesis, facial droop, drift. CT showed a large basal ganglia tumor. He's going for a biopsy today. He's still a full code. There's an abdomen in the OR. Four may be able to go. The ER is empty."

When she leaves, Kate leaves the door open.

Sue is the day charge. "How many nurses do we have?" She bobs her head as she counts around the table. "Eight nurses, thirteen patients. I'll be free. Who's back?"

Assignments go quickly, as though at an auction. A hand lifted off the table, a nod. Lori pushes her chair back. "I had Seven and Eight."

It's between Kay and me. She looks at me. "I don't care."

"You decide," I tell her. She takes Five and the admit. I get Two and Three.

Lacy is the night nurse. She has Sanchez. "This guy came to the ICU on the fourth. Yesterday. He was admitted on the second for shortness of breath. Went to the floor. Crumped. Sorry. Let me start over." She looks at handwritten notes on a yellow piece of paper folded in half. "He was admitted to the floor, went bad, came to us, and got intubated. I've got him on propofol and fentanyl. He doesn't do anything. We need one more sputum to rule out TB. I don't know what they plan on doing. He desatted last night so we bumped his oxygen to seventy from fifty. He's not making much urine. His creatinine's climbing. He might need to be dialyzed. He's got a femoral line. He's got a big family and they're all here in the waiting room. I think there's a thousand of them. Good luck with that. Questions? I'm back."

Nights are long. Some of the nurses sleep, in turns, on the one couch in the lounge, so in the morning the room has a trapped, tangy human scent, or they rest their heads on the white patient blankets on the roller tables where we chart outside the rooms. You can see a trace of their profile like a petroglyph. It must be a jolt at seven o'clock, the day shift coming at you like a car with its high beams on.

We call the bedside report a handoff. It can be good or bad. Things get left out, forgotten. It's like you're standing on one side of a crevasse and you have sand cupped in the palm of your hand and you're going to pass that sand to a person on the other side. Every twelve hours this is done and what happens is that the sand slips through your fingers and there is less and less each time, like when they came in, how many days on the vent, you need to check all stools for blood.

I find the history and physical in the chart. It's typed on blue paper. The progress notes are yellow. Everything else is white. *Past medical history: diabetes, hypertension. Was vomiting blood—coffee-ground hematemesis—for two weeks, abdominal pain, 40 pound weight loss, positive cough and fever. Admitted to the floor with a differential diagnosis of aspiration vs mass vs community-acquired pneumonia vs TB.*

And then the trapdoor in the floor of the hospital opened—respiratory distress, unresponsive, transferred to the ICU, gets intubated, they do a pulmonary angiogram to look at his lungs and the dye wrecks his kidneys.

He's like a pebble crack in your windshield that spreads and spiders until the whole glass is shattered but still there and all you have to do is touch it and it will crumble into pieces. Because we're ruling out TB, I have to put on a special face mask—it looks like a duckbill—before I go in. He looks much older than sixty. His flesh is loose on his body and thin like the skin of rotten grapes. Like it would rip if you touched it. The bones of his face are sharp under his skin and his cheeks are sunken. There is a creamy haze over his pupils. Cataracts. His pupils are pinpoint from the sedation. He doesn't do anything when I pinch his trapezius or press my pen into the nail bed of his finger. He's riding the vent. He's on sixty-five of propofol. Propofol's a sedative-hypnotic. We use it in the ICU because it has a rapid onset and a short half-life; you stop it and ten minutes later they're awake. It's white. It comes in a glass bottle. Some nurses call it the milk of amnesia. He's completely snowed. I cut the drips in half.

Mateo, the respiratory therapist, is at the door. He makes a face at having to mask up. Mateo's heavy, with bad knees that make him wobble when he walks. He lives out by Airport Road in a big double-wide. He's divorced but still lives with his ex-wife. They live at opposite ends of the house. They say he was wild, a gangbanger, when he was young. We need a sputum, I tell him. Mateo puts a bullet of saline into the tube before he slides the suction tube down Sanchez's throat. It makes the guy cough violently but Mateo gets thick tan stuff in the trap. He lifts it into the air and looks at it like a wine taster examining a cork. "That'll work."

Dakota Yazzie in Two had come in yesterday evening. The post-call resident is with the day resident looking at her chart. The post-call's name is Lucas. He's a big guy, maybe twenty-eight. Beefy. He looks like a high school football player. The day resident is a woman. She's flipping through the chart.

"Why is she on bicarb? You usually don't need to treat low bicarb in DKA." He says they checked it twice, with an arterial blood gas and then a venous.

"It doesn't matter. It corrects with rehydration." She asks him if he ordered an EKG and a chest X-ray. "I'll write for them," he says.

After they leave, I look in the chart. There's no history and physical yet, just the first day's progress notes: *Had presented at the Indian Hospital in Crown Point with nausea/vomiting for two days, right upper-palate pain that progressed to a right retro-orbital headache; was hyperglycemic in the 500s with probable diabetic ketoacidosis so was transferred to Gallup; CT there showed right occipital intracranial hemorrhage, 28 x 34 centimeters with no midline shift.*

Then she came to us. If you're sick, they move you along to a higher level of care. We're the highest level of care. We're the ICU for the state of New Mexico.

She's alone in the room, awake. When I introduce myself, she looks past me as if at someone standing behind me. She doesn't say anything. She has a wide face, high cheekbones. She doesn't have a headache. She can hold her arms out straight without drifting. I ask her to smile and then stick out her tongue and she does and then smiles after that as well. She looks like Annette Funicello. I ask her if she knows who she is. She laughs. "I know my Mouseketeers." She says she can't see the diamonds on her wedding ring. It looks like it melted. Her pupils are equal, dark like all her features, dark like starless nights, but tracking to the left she can't see. Her voice is calm, though, when with my finger off to the side she says, "I don't see it." I know it starts with an *h*, but I can't remember what it is.

Two residents are outside the room hunched over the chart.

"Who are you guys?"

"Neurology," one says.

"What's the word for a deficit in half the visual field of both eyes?"

One of them pulls a piece of paper from the chest pocket of his white coat. "Homonymous hemianopsia. I'm just doing a rotation. I'm in general surgery." There are other groups of doctors in the unit. They hover outside the rooms looking at charts the way hummingbirds feed in mid-air, always in flight. "We'll be by to see her later," the other one says.

Rounds is starting. The Medical team is outside One. In the middle, older by far than any of the residents, is Fowler. Fowler and Morgan are the two attendings. Murphy is the chief resident. The Good, the Bad, and the Goofy, Michelle calls them, although Murphy isn't really goofy; it's just that he wears nursing scrubs with funny designs because his mother is a nurse and he wants to show that he's on our side. I have about ten minutes before they reach my patient.

"Can you check blood with me?" Dana has Bed Ten, the meningitis girl. She looks small, smaller where the blankets below her knees drop off and lie flat against the bed. At first you see she has a cute round face with her hair in pigtails with paintbrush tips below elastic bands like Pippi Longstocking and buck teeth with a space between. But that's where the look-alike ends. Her skin is moist and colorless and sprinkled with acne from the steroids. Her central line is an internal jugular and juts from her neck as if someone is tugging at it, raising the skin into a little tent. So she won't pull things her hands are wrapped in gauze and look like boxing gloves. The drain sponge under her trach collar is mangled and wet with thick yellow mucus like Jell-O.

"We're just going to give you some blood, sweetie," Dana says to her. The girl raises her eyebrows and her eyes widen. "It's all right." She can read her face. Dana takes her a lot. Some nurses do that, take the same patient again and again. We check the numbers quickly. The medical record number, blood type, expiration—wristband to paper, paper to bag. "Your mother called. She said she loves you," Dana tells her. The girl makes a guttural sound that makes the mucus on the sponge shiver.

A man and a woman are in Dakota Yazzie's room. They didn't call to come in but people slip in all the time. The man is standing under the TV, which is on struts high on the wall, and stops punching the station buttons to shake my hand and introduce himself, in a soft voice, as Terrell. He is wearing a gray T-shirt with lettering about a basketball tournament. His hair is combed straight back in a rakish way. The woman is seated. She's wearing a maroon sweatshirt with a dream catcher logo over a flouncy skirt that goes all the way to a pair of black single-strap ballet shoes. She is obese. Everything about her is huge except her hair, which is thin and permed into tight ringlets. Resting on her chest on separate chains of different lengths are two silver crosses. She looks up at the door suddenly. The team is here.

Fowler leans toward a western style even though he's from Chicago and went to medical school at Northwestern. He wears a thick leather belt with Texas Gold Star conchos, bolo ties, and sometimes real cowboy boots. He's patient with the residents and generous. The residents are different from Fowler and not just because they're younger. It's like those waterfalls you can buy where the water flows down into a container and that container fills up and the water flows down into the next container. Somehow the water in Fowler doesn't seem to be flowing down. There are seven residents. They all wear white coats. They stand in a tight circle.

The hospital is like a two-way mirror. On one side you see yourself reflected and you think it's all for you. What you don't see but what sees you is the world on the other side. The world on the other side is teaching. The teaching hospital is a kind of workshop that makes doctors,

where they are put together, assembled, polished, made sure they are in working order, put through tests to make sure they're up to it. They're their own solar system, orbiting each other, balanced by their own gravity, whirling through the hospital.

Medicine is collegial in a way that nursing is not. Doctors call themselves a "team:" the ICU team, the Medical team. They never criticize each other in rounds. The progress notes say things like "Appreciate Dr. So and So's comments"; "Thank you, Dr. So and So, for the consult." They rotate through the hospital—ER, ICU, Med-Surg—climbing the ladder rung by rung. Nurses are alone most of the time—in a room spiking a bag, titrating a drip, charting at the desk. Alone like a person ice fishing on a frozen lake. You almost never see a doctor alone.

Lucas has already begun: "Denies weakness, no sensory deficits, no family history, no meds, never seen a doctor." He's reading from notes on loose four-by-six-inch pieces of paper that are also stuffed into both pockets of his white coat and is standing not in the middle but maybe a foot into the center. "Has a three over six systolic murmur, one son, married, one weekday drinks heavily and takes several days to recover." They all laugh at this with smirks and titters. They look alike, the residents, like a cluster of ripe cherries, plump, full, smooth skin glistening with dew. Even Fowler says, "Why am I not surprised?" I look into the room; the curtain is half drawn but the door is open. "That sounds familiar," he says. "Any visual changes? HH?"

"I didn't notice," Lucas says. He looks down at his notes.

"She has visual changes," I say.

"What about drugs?" Fowler asks.

"Cocaine."

"Keep going."

"She denied problems, no history of falls, she was in minor DKA. Her glucose was three ninety." He stops. Fowler is bent over the computer bringing up the labs.

"I gave her bicarb," Lucas says.

"Her gap was closed," Fowler says. "You wouldn't give her bicarb. Her sugar's not that high. What's her A1C?"

"It's not back yet."

"There's no urgency," says Fowler. "Okay," he says, getting them back on track. "What do we need to do from a medical point of view?"

"I gave her hydralazine for hypertension."

"Wrong. Neuro likes to use beta blockers. Hydralazine can vasodilate, increase intracranial pressure. Neurosurgs like a short-acting drug. Something you can take away. Did you put her on half normal or start NPH?"

"No."

A female resident has the CT up on the computer and has turned the screen to show the other residents. Her hair is cut boyishly with one side jagged like a serrated knife. It makes her look like that kid doctor, Doogie Howser. She's small; she's sitting on my chair that's like a swivel bar stool with one leg tucked under her the way small people can do. The lettering on her jacket is a blue cursive that says "Internal Medicine."

"This location is not consistent with a hypertensive bleed," she says. On the scan, which looks like an old black-and-white movie and is a view from top down, even though they lie flat in the scanner, in the lower left corner, what should be gray is a white spot as big and soft around the edges as the butter pat you get in a restaurant.

In the room, Fowler asks her if her head hurts.

"Some."

"How long?"

She shrugs her shoulders.

Terrell is standing by her next to the bed. Maybe because she's so quiet he starts to talk as if to be helpful and says how she had tried to unlock the back not the front door of the car and then had been driving and turned left way too soon. They're all standing behind Fowler, who has gone only as far as the foot of the bed.

"Do you have any medical problems?"

"No."

"You've never seen a doctor?"

"Never."

It's like she is from another planet, a planet of the poor, the outcast, the invisible. Come here, live in a catacomb of your own language, your own way of life, until illness drills a hole into it and the light of the world is on you.

"I do have a murmur. My grandmother wouldn't let me run around."

"Let's get an echo," Fowler tells Lucas. He looks at Dakota Yazzie. "We're going to do what's called an MRI. It will give us a better picture of your brain. How's your vision?"

"I can't see to the outside."

Fowler leaves the room first and the residents follow. They move down the hall together, as if they were all in a revolving door, toward Sanchez's room.

Two surgical nurses walk by, slowly, looking in each room, strolling, as if they were shopping in a mall. "Where's our patient going?" one of them asks. They're wearing thin blue surgical gowns, open in the front, and soft blue surgical caps like spun candy.

"Six," Sue says. She helps them pull the bed out of the room. "What are we getting?"

"From the Indian Hospital. Open abdomen."

"How long?"

"Twenty minutes. Thirty. They're still closing."

It's clear Fowler doesn't know Sanchez because he winces when he hears the renal failure was from the contrast for the angiogram. A thin olive-skinned guy is presenting. He's sharper, more confident than Lucas. Wherever he is from, he's not from the United States, and most of the residents are not. The quickness has passed to the world, to Asia, India.

"So, one," Fowler says, "we have respiratory failure. Two, we have acute renal failure. Is ID involved? Let's get them involved." One of the residents picks up the wall phone right away. "What did Renal say?" he asks.

"That he's improving," a resident says.

"Let's get a cortisol level." He pokes a finger in the direction of olive-skin guy. "See if Pulmonary wants to bronch him. This guy's sick. This is what you want. This is good pathology."

The unit is quiet. Rounds over. Now they go look at X-rays, CAT scans, have a teaching session somewhere. In the hospital you're not just in your bed, in one room; your body is in your bed, your blood in the lab, your lungs in X-ray, your brain in CT, your history in Medical Records. They'll come if we call, if we need them. They'll round again in the evening. For us, day begins again.

Nursing is like that six-degrees-of-Kevin-Bacon thing where every actor in the past thirty years can be connected to him. Everybody knows a nurse: your mother was a nurse, your cousin became a nurse, your brother married a nurse. My best friend in high school—Timmy Walsh—his mother was a nurse at Tobey Hospital in Wareham, Massachusetts. I was an orderly at Cooley Dickinson Hospital in Northampton, Massachusetts, for the six years when I left UMass without getting my degree until I returned and got it. It was the same hospital where in 1964 Ted Kennedy went after his airplane crashed and his pilot was killed. Cooley Dick is a few miles north of Smith College. Five years ago, after my mother died, my sister began sending me things randomly like items from a shipwreck washed up on shore at different times of the year. She sent me all the editorials from when I was editor of the Gateway Gazette. *Then she sent me a hundred copies of a black-and-white photograph of Ted Williams and Babe Ruth standing on the steps of a dugout at Fenway Park shaking hands that my father was going to sell and get rich. Then she sent a bronze cast of my baby shoes. She sent me my senior yearbook. There were 126 kids in my class. There were pictures of me. There was a picture of me on the basketball team. A picture of my game-winning shot from the baseline against Rockland High that knocked them out of the Tech Tourney. They threw rocks at our bus as we drove home through their downtown. A picture of me with the editorial staff of the paper. As president of the Key Club. Under my senior photograph is the caption "Tallest" and "Done Most for the Class." On one page is a picture of a group of girls. Half are seated in chairs and half are standing behind them. They are the Future Nurses of America. I didn't recognize any of them.*

The bed is still gone from Six. Kay has the room ready. On the roller table are two packages of red-dot electrodes, a pulse ox, a blood pressure cuff, an IV start kit, some saline flushes, a thermometer, a flashlight. A two-channel pump on the IV pole. Neat, ready, like a room at a bed-and-breakfast where they have a chocolate and maybe a flower on the bed and a little guide to the area. The rooms look scarier empty because you don't know what you're going to get and then the chaos of admission, getting them all hooked up, someone telling you how much blood they lost, what the vent settings are.

There's family in Sanchez's room. Three women and two men. One of the women, about his age, could be a wife. A man her age. The others children probably. They look scared.

"Habla inglés?"

They shake their heads or look down except one, who could be a daughter, who says, "Yes."

"I'm his nurse. Enfermero."

"How is he?" she asks.

"He's the same. Stable. Not better, not worse."

She turns to the others. "Estable, no mejor no peor." They surround the bed and stare down at him. The muscles of his face are starting to move like a kitten under a blanket. Thawing out from the sedation.

"The nurse yesterday said we could talk to a doctor this morning."

"Okay. I can arrange that."

"Podemos hablar con el médico esta tarde. Gracias. Do you know what time?"

"I don't." Suddenly he wakes up. His arms rise and they fly away from the bed like birds driven off from roadkill. Everything is up, heart rate, pressure. The vent is honking. His eyes are wide and fill his shrunken face. Now he feels the tube in his throat and twists his head from side to side. It must be a shock that you're not dead but alive and where were you?

"Mr. Sanchez, you're okay." I grab his arms by the wrists to keep him from the tube and put my face above his so he can see me, but his eyes are flying around the room. Looking for a way out. "Does he speak English?"

"Yes!" "No!"

"Está bien. Tranquilo. Está bien. Está bien," I say to him. One of the younger men is against the wall crying. I give Sanchez thirty milligrams of propofol off the pump and watch the drug smooth the features of his face, like a hand smoothing a blanket to flatness. Before he sinks back I say to him, "Mueve los dedos," to get a picture of his brain before he disappears behind the clouds.

They come back to the bed slowly, as though it was a fire that had been put out but could reignite, and hold his hands and stare down at him almost with reverence. Strange. Such a beat-up old guy. Wasting away for years probably. They talk to him and stroke his arm and wet his lips with a washcloth and I have to tell them to stop that and explain about oxygenation, rest, how he needs his strength to recover and that there will be time for that but for now they can be here but they should sit quietly. That they can love him quietly and there will be a time later when they can touch him and talk to him. Families resent this usually, but they go and sit in chairs, some of them putting a pillow under themselves before they sit. Except for the woman who speaks English. She looks early twenties. They watch her when she talks. A reed through which they can breathe the English air above them. She looks at the old woman in a chair. "That's his wife. It's because he loves her so much that he's trying to stay. Do you know when the priest is going to come?" I tell her I'll call.

"El sacerdote se acerca." They all nod. Everything she says in Spanish goes around the room like an electric current.

"We only allow two visitors at a time."

"Sólo dos visitantes se les permite en un momento," the woman says to her flock. They go blank like they don't understand.

Dakota Yazzie's eyes are closed but she's not sleeping. I have to do neuro checks on the hour. I think I would close my eyes too if I was in the ICU. She has a beautiful face. Black hair. The part in the middle as clean and straight as the narrow dirt roads that disappear off the highway to distant pueblos. Skin the glow of the desert at dusk. She is so quiet, so still, that when I talk to her I whisper. I take her through a quick assessment—tracking, grips, drift—to see if there are any changes. I move my finger to the left of her face.

"I don't see it," she says and closes her eyes again.

The woman in the chair is holding a small leather book with worn covers in her two hands in her lap. The crosses on her chest are clean and bright.

"Are you her mother?"

"I adopted her," she says. Then, "Not really. We're just close. My own mother died when I was young."

"I'm sorry. Of what?"

"Of liver." She points down toward her stomach. "Drinking. My father died of the same."

Terrell then asks me if I'm from Boston and then nods his head at Patricia when I say I am. "I like the Celtics," he says. "Bird. McHale."

"Parish," I say, and from the bed Dakota says, "He's the one they call Chief," and we all laugh at that. Parish. A black, seven-foot-tall NBA chief.

Terrel is trying to put a disc into the DVD player and asks me if I can help him with the DVD and I say that stuff is beyond me.

"Jim likes that Lawrence Welk music."

"Who do you like?" I ask him.

"The old stuff. Van Morrison. Bob Seger." His voice is strained from the angle his head is forced into.

"Help me, Jimmy." The screen is snow, the sound like letting air out of a tire.

"You're on your own," I tell him.

Lori is walking the Flolan woman around the unit, something you almost never see in the ICU. She's a walky-talky but can't go to the floor on a Flolan drip. Lori has her arm hooked in hers and is watching the woman's face while the woman is watching her own stockinged feet as if wondering what they're going to do. She's twenty-eight with two kids. She has idiopathic pulmonary disease, which she will die of. Her mother died of asthma at forty. I pretend to look at my chart when they go by. She wasn't feeling well and went to a clinic. By the time she got there she was blue and they flew her here. Had made herself a DNI, had seen what happened to her mother and knew she would never get off a ventilator. Her boyfriend had come to town and found a job. You have to have taken some course in Flolan to be able to give it, so I'll never take her. She's wearing two gowns, one on the front and one on the back, and the little gray hospital booties that have skid strips on the soles.

The first time we drove out west was a vacation in June 1996. We took I-25 south from Albuquerque, then down through Silver City, where Billy the Kid spent his childhood, and then to the Gila Cliff Dwellings. We were driving to Tucson. Loren had her shoes off and her heels on the dashboard. She was reading the *Rough Guide to the Southwest*. The distant mountains were purple and the farther mountains paler and paler, fading away like sound would look if you could see it. A thunderstorm far away like in another world. Something interesting she would read aloud. We had crossed the border into Arizona when she told me to look over to the left. She said those were the Sierra Madres. She said Geronimo had lived there. We were both silent for a while. When we were past them she read from the guide. His real name was Goyahkla. His final battle with the U.S. Army was thirty-seven Chiricahua Apache against five thousand soldiers. Only eighteen of the thirty-seven were warriors, the rest women and children. It ended when he surrendered for the fourth and final time. He was never a chief. He had special powers. He could walk without leaving a trace. Before a battle he painted the faces of his warriors himself. He rode at the head of Teddy Roosevelt's inaugural procession in 1905. Lori and the woman walked around the unit twice; the second time the woman walked by herself holding on to her IV pole with the Flolan drip.

Fowler calls. He wants blood cultures on Yazzie. "I think we should do them. She has that murmur and might have some vegetation. And include fungal." I tell him the Sanchez family says they've never talked to a doctor.

"I don't believe that." He pauses. "I'll be there around five."

Kay's patient comes out just before noon. Mateo is leading with the vent. The same two OR nurses now with blue masks untied and hanging under their chins like wattles and the anesthesiologist who is bagging him. We help hook him up like a pit crew at a NASCAR race. A-line, EKG, suction. His eyes are still taped shut from the OR. He's big, Native American, looks young, has a little goatee.

The anesthesiologist tells Kay, "This is Edward Maestas. He's still paralyzed. I didn't reverse him. I gave him eighty of rocuronium, twelve of Versed. He got two liters of Lactated Ringers. They took out one and a half liters of pus. Estimated blood loss two-fifty." He waits for a blood pressure, an oxygen sat, a temperature. They leave, the OR nurse saying, "His mother is in the waiting room."

The Pulmonary fellow is here to bronch Sanchez. After medical school, and after residency, some of them go into fellowships in a specialty. His head is shaved, so it's hard to say how old he is. His face is reddish but his scalp is white. I can see the roots of his hair under his skin like you can see bugs that die in a fluorescent light or seaweed underwater. He has large eyes and looks with his glowing scalp like a jack-o'-lantern.

He puts in a bite block and threads the soft tube into Sanchez's lungs. On the monitor it's like spelunking, looking through caves, around passageways. "Look at that," he says. "That's bad. It's narrow. This guy's been sick for a long time."

The door opens and Fowler leans into the room holding a mask to his face. 'How does it look?'

"He's got bronchiectasis."

Fowler grimaces and leaves.

"What causes that?" I ask.

"Chronic disease."

We need the cultures from Yazzie. Terrell and Patricia have gone to lunch. "I need to draw some blood from your arm," I tell her. Her eyes are closed but her skin is drawn to her eyes like a purse string. "Are you having pain? I can give you something for pain." She nods her head. I give her two of morphine into her line. The room is quiet without Patricia and Terrell. Putting on a front for all the time they were here. Must be frightening, your vision going like that. Opening the back door. Having to leave home, the reservation, come all the way to Albuquerque. Could be a hemorrhage. Could be a tumor. Could be nothing. Could be the end of your life as you know it.

After a bit, I put a tourniquet on her arm but no veins appear. I sit in a chair facing her and let her hand rest on mine. It's almost one o'clock. The day half over. Our hands are still. Her eyes still closed. I think this must be nice for her, to be alone, to feel my hand under hers, the touch. I watch the clock move past one, feel the day push itself over the crest and begin the slide toward evening. I stroke the inside of her arm with the tip of my index finger. Tap where a vein should be. Come out. Come out. Sometimes you can see the blue run of a vein deep in the skin like a skinny river that had carved itself deep into a canyon. The tourniquet finally tricks out a vein above her wrist.

"Little stick," I say, and then stop talking to her at all, she is so quiet. I think she wants it to be with her eyes closed and being so still that she is not here, is somewhere else, maybe in a car driving with Terrell, so I don't say anything so she can be not-here for a little while.

When she needs something, Kay sticks her head out from her room. Her cheeks are flushed against her short blond hair. "I need a four channel. More saline. I need some ten cc syringes." The room was filling with machinery: two poles of IV pumps, the vent lit up like a dashboard. Like she's building a ship plank by plank. I can see his heart rate on the monitor at the nurse's station. 148. 153. 158. Like a spring flicked into vibrating that doesn't slow down, keeps speeding up. She comes out of the room. "His temp is a hundred and two four."

"Was he cultured?"

"In the ER."

"Should I call?"

"Don't call. He's been cultured. You can give him Tylenol."

"He's got a bad liver," she says.

"Cool him with a blanket. Ice him and cool him."

Her voice is shaky like she's standing on a platform at a train station and a train is going by. I know how she feels. Before my wife and I were married, we were house-sitting for a writer at a big farmhouse in upstate New York. He was rich and was sailing around the world in legs. The first leg, he went to Panama and wrote a book called *Fever Coast Log*. This time he was on his way to the South Pacific, Borneo or somewhere, with his girlfriend. There was a typhoon. Either they turned the wrong way or the typhoon did. It overtook them. The boat broke up. They were in the water; she was in his arms. She was telling him to hold on to her. Wave after wave came. She slipped away. She died. It feels like that sometimes. Wave after wave coming at you as you try to hold on. We say the ICU is eleven hours of boredom and one hour of terror. When I first came to the ICU, an older nurse, Richard, who was tall and generally quiet and reminded me of Chief Bromden in *One Flew over the Cuckoo's Nest*, one day in the lounge looked at me and said, "Don't get the fear."

Patricia Benner says expertise in nursing is a function of experience: the ability to see the "likely future." I try to do what Bill Walton did. Bill Walton said that the night before every basketball game at UCLA he would play the game in his mind, the whole game, so that everything that happened, every shot, every rebound, he would have already seen it. I would get my assignment and I would think, Okay, this patient has this and this could happen and if it happens I'm going to do this and this. Because you're afraid that if that thing happens, you'll freeze. You'll get the fear.

The MRI scanner is a narrow tube. Putting a patient in is like watching your hand disappear into a glove or a knife into a sheath. Before we go I ask Dakota Yazzie if she wants something to help her relax during it. She shakes her head. We watch from a different room. We can't see her face. We can't hear the pounding noise. The image of the brain goes from nothing to everything like a sped-up view of a flower blossoming. "There it is," says the tech, pointing to a white spot on the screen. "We're done." On the way back I tell her she did good.

It's almost four and Terrell and Patricia are in the room. Terrell comes out to talk to me. He's grinning.

"That was a long lunch."

"We went to the casino." He seems happy. Now I see that he's older than I thought he was.

"Which one?"

"The new one. Cities of Gold." He's rocking a bit and smiling. He's teasing me.

"Did you gamble?"

"I won eight hundred dollars." His smile is wide. We could be two buddies who bumped into each other outside Ortega's on the Plaza. I put my hand out flat up. "Let me have some of that."

He shakes my hand instead. "I'm giving you some. I'm giving you some of my luck."

"Do you gamble much?"

"Usually the machine takes my money but today it just kept coming up."

"Where are you staying tonight?"

"We got a place at the Rodeway Inn off I-40."

I know it. It's off Lomas. Inexpensive but clean.

"Do you think she might go home tomorrow?"

"Not tomorrow. Maybe in a few days. Depending on what the MRI shows."

Father Martin is outside Sanchez's room. He's wearing priest garb with a short-sleeved shirt. He's old but with a full head of white hair.

"I need three minutes," he says.

When he enters the room they gather around the bed swiftly, like filings around a magnet. Father Martin makes the sign of the cross. Their hands fly in front of their chests and the women finish by touching their fingers to their lips. They know what to do. He opens the Bible. As one they bow their heads. No one has spoken. When Father Martin does speak, he speaks in Spanish and they all repeat what he says and every sentence has the word *Jesus*, which they say with an emphasis that raises it above the level of the other words. Father Martin says the patient's own name, Valentín, in a voice that seems to vibrate the air in the room as though he's Jesus calling forth Lazarus. He reads from the Bible again in Spanish and then he's done. Just about three minutes.

Labs are back on Sanchez. His creatinine is better, down to 2.9. He's starting to make more urine. His kidneys are coming back. He's breathing a little on his own. The Renal docs come by and say they're not going to dialyze him. The attending writes a short note: *Renal failure improving.* Maybe he'll turn the corner, get to go back home, back to his big family, back to Guadalajara.

The conference room is called the Harriman Room. It's narrow, with dark-patterned institutional chairs and couches surrounding the small empty center. The light is soft, yellowish, from half-moon globes in the middle of the bare walls like mushrooms on the bole of a tree. We keep it locked, and I think if I were brought into this room to talk with a doctor and the door closed behind me my first thought would be, bad news. I know Fowler doesn't believe that no doctor has spoken to them. We think families lie all the time. A female resident is with him.

Sanchez's family is already there. The wife, three daughters, two sons, some husbands and wives, aunts, uncles. Soft as it is, the light is better than the rooms in the ICU; the wife looks older, the boys younger. The impression from the elastic of the TB masks is still visible on their faces. The translator is a hospital housekeeper in her twenties; she gets extra money for doing this. Her badge says *Marta*.

Fowler speaks first, "Me llamo Dr. Fowler," and then asks, How long has Mr. Sanchez been sick; how long has he had diabetes?

"Cuánto tiempo hace que está enfermo? Cuánto tiempo hace que tiene diabetis?"

The woman who speaks English doesn't answer, but the other daughter, who hadn't spoken in the room, does, in rapid speech. Somehow the translator is the right wire, the right connection.

"Vino de Guadalajara a visitarla hace tres meses y no se sentía bien. Los hijos trabajan en Arizona. Por qué está tan enfermo?"

"He came up from Guadalajara to visit her three months ago and wasn't feeling well. Why did he get so sick?"

"People who wind up in the ICU usually get sicker."

"Las personas que acaban en la ICU por lo general se ponen más enfermas."

There's a little delay like on TV when the anchorperson is talking to someone overseas and when he's done with the question the person he's talking to just stands there for a few seconds. It seems too as if there are more Spanish words than English. The Spanish seems richer, vibrant.

Fowler turns toward the housekeeper. "Tell them we aren't sure what's wrong with him but we're treating him with antibiotics and we're helping his breathing with the machine. We gave him blood when he needed it. If I think it doesn't look good, I'll tell you. Right now, we think he's going to be fine and leave the hospital. But there might be a time when we have to decide what to do. We have to think what he would want. We're not there yet. I won't lie to you. I promise I'll tell you if that time comes."

When Marta finishes, Fowler looks at the wife. "Do you have any more questions?"

"Tienen más preguntas?"

They lower their heads. Several of them murmur, "Gracias."

We lag behind as they leave. I thank Fowler. Not every attending would come to a conference but would let some resident stumble his way through it. We watch the family turn the corner. Fowler turns to me. "Where do the sons work?"

"Phoenix. Miller Brewing Company. "

"We need to get them back to work so they don't lose their jobs."

I look into Yazzie's room. Dakota is sitting up on the side of the bed facing the wall. Terrell is on the other side of the bed, behind her. He's kneading her back, moving his arms slowly. Her eyes are closed and her head moves languidly like a sunflower in full bloom. The room is evening dark. Patricia is in the chair. A little tribe. A tribe of their own.

In 1907, a Dr. Duncan MacDougall weighed patients just after they died and said the soul weighed three-quarters of an ounce. The brain weighs three grams. Medical school is four years. If there is a unit of measurement in nursing, it's twelve hours. Half the day. Long enough to drive to Phoenix. To drive to Needles, California. To Death Valley. To El Paso and back. Long enough to eat three meals. Long enough that families go and come back and say, "Are you still here?" Sometimes they think you work all night. Lori says, "It's a long day but a short week." But it's a long day.

I walk the unit. We moved from Boston when I was nine to Cape Cod to a beach town whose population would swell like a bore tide after school ended until Labor Day when the summer people left. In the summer, the small cottages would be noisy at night with cookouts, drinking, radios carrying the Red Sox game from Boston, too many cars for the dirt driveways. In the fall I would walk home on now-empty streets past these dark cottages, windows shuttered, their wicks dampened.

On the unit we've kicked out the families. Only the back wall light is on in most rooms. They're like those cottages, the wick of life dampened. You wake up in the morning in the stream of life and something bursts, breaks, stops, and you're ladled from that stream and dropped onto a barren rock. End of the shift. In the gloom of Kay's room, the lights from the pumps, the monitor, the vent glow like a ship becalmed in a harbor at dusk being readied to set sail on a long voyage. The IV poles are like sails rigged for the wind, ready for the voyage into the sea of critical illness.

Sanchez's room is empty. They left him with a folded washcloth on his forehead and washcloths on both sides of his face, so his face is shrouded like a nun's. Next to his face is a plastic rosary of beveled pink beads attached to the pillow with a safety pin and a picture of Jesus the size of a baseball card. This Jesus has a crown of thorns that look like barbed wire. Little droplets that aren't sweat but blood because they're red drop down his face. Sanchez looks like the picture on the card. Gaunt, suffering, waiting for the blessed end. Before the end of the shift I turn him again, fluff him up.

I go into Yazzie's room for a last set of vital signs. Terrell and Patricia are still in the room. They've settled on the Discovery channel. The screen is showing wild horses running in the desert, wheeling in a pack over low hills. The horses are each differently colored and you can see the muscles under their smooth skin. A woman's voice is narrating. She sounds young. Now the screen shows lupines, then distant rolling desert. Then back to the horses. The room is darker now. Terrell is standing close to the bed. We all watch the TV. No one speaks. Dakota says, "His mane is up." The screen had shown a young foal in the herd.

"What do you mean?" I ask.

Without taking her eyes from the screen, she says, "He's young. It's coming out." Wild horses under the wide western sky running over the desert, wheeling, turning as by a hidden message over sage, juniper, coats shiny, unsaddled. I stand and watch with them long enough to feel I've slipped into their world, trying to be as quiet as they are, long enough that I feel that at the same time they're unaware of me they know what

I'm doing and don't mind but it's like balancing on a beam and after a moment I lose my balance and leave them and the room watching silently.

I usually don't say good-bye, just give my report and leave, but I stop at the door of Yazzie's room. "Good luck. I'm off for three days."

Terrell comes toward me. "I hope I never see you again."

"I hope I never see you too."

He puts his hand out and we shake. "Thank you," he says. And from the bed, like the upward drift of smoke from a campfire: "Thank you."

2

DIAGNOSIS, DIAGNOSIS, DIAGNOSIS

Before there were hospitals in America there were almshouses. An almshouse was for alcoholics, prostitutes, blacks, the insane, the aged, the syphilitic. Ezra Stiles Ely, a newly ordained Presbyterian minister who decided to preach in New York City's almshouse, described it as a place filled with the "depraved and miserable of our race." Hospitals were to be different. They would be for the worthy poor, for people who had no family or were away from home: seamen, urban workers, widows. The first hospitals were in ports and river towns. They had more to do with charity than with medicine.

Physicians had little impact on the internal world of the hospital. The hospital was more like a large home than an institution, the patients a family. Even today, the hospital is called "the house." The staff lived in them; the healthier patients helped in nursing the sick, washing and ironing, cleaning the rooms. Therapy was rest, warmth, and a good diet. Patients could be there for years. Hospitals were something Americans who were better off did for their countrymen who were worse off, not a place they would ever think of entering. You entered one if you had no family or were unlucky enough to become sick away from your family. They were regarded with dread. In Medical Inquiries and Observations, *the physician Benjamin Rush called them sinks of human misery. William Buchan said the best that could be hoped for was that they would disappear. The first American hospital was Philadelphia's Pennsylvania Hospital, founded in 1751. In 1873 there were 178 hospitals in the United States. They were as few and as scattered as are today's nuclear power plants. A person could go his or her entire life without seeing one. A rural doctor might never even have been inside one. Many Americans did not know they existed. Today there are more than nine thousand. They have over a million beds. From I-25 in Albuquerque just before the exit for Central Avenue, the old Route 66, you can see four: the Heart Hospital, Kindred, Presbyterian, and Lovelace. Five if you count closed-up Memorial, the old psych hospital. The one you can't see is the University of New Mexico Health Center, a mile away but, with its new Children's Hospital and parking garages and critical care towers, slowly marching toward the interstate. Some are so big you need a GPS. They have gourmet coffee carts. Mary Hitchcock in New Hampshire has a Papa Gino's. Oregon Health Science University sits on a hill over Portland like Transylvania and shuttles employees from below by buses. It has nine ICUs.*

The night nurse is a traveler I haven't met before.

"Cushman, James. Fifty-four. Past medical history, alcoholism, question of hep C, organic brain disease, whatever that means. Came in on the twenty-eighth vomiting bright-red blood. He was scoped. They banded five varices. Was getting blood but there was a problem with the transfusion. He went into DTs. He crashed on the sixth. They paralyzed him to help his oxygenation. We're using Nimbex. He's maxed on Levophed at twenty. They don't want to go any higher, vasopressin .02. They want a systolic blood pressure greater than ninety-five. He's on pressure control ventilation, rate of twenty-two, 100 percent. I'm not suctioning much out. He's got a rectal bag. He's not making any urine."

"Lines?"

"Lines. He's got a right femoral central line and a left femoral a-line. His mouth is bloody but I just did oral care. He's bleeding. All I've done is keep him alive. He's got sores on his mouth and his groin. Contact isolation. They think it's herpes. He's a DNR. No compressions. No electricity. Chemical code only."

"Family?"

"An eighty-year-old uncle in California, a brother in Idaho."

"The brother's power of attorney?"

"Yep. His heart rate is down. I think he's wearing out. We were feeding him through a Dobhoff, but his belly was so distended I stopped. He's got an OG that I put to suction. I got a thousand ccs out in one hour. Active drinker. No transplant. He's a day bath but I did it this morning."

"Thanks. Where are you from?"

"Reno."

Two doctors are looking at the chart, the older one through glasses on the tip of his nose. They're wearing white coats. All the doctors wear white coats. The coat of the older man is knee length; the younger one's ends at his hip. The white coat is the robe of medicine. In *On Call*, Emily Transue writes, "Medicine is a secret society with its own language, codes, and symbols. One of the subtle but powerful codes is found in the hierarchy of white coats."

"Are you ID?" I ask them.

"We're GI." They sit at the desk outside the room. The older one says to the younger, "He's infarcting his liver from hypotension. Ischemic hepatitis." He turns to me. "Have they contacted the family?"

"Just an uncle and a brother."

"What they should really do is quit. We'll sign off," the older one says.

They leave together, walking close, shoulder to shoulder, looking at a patient list. They probably spend the whole day together. Physicians nurture like that, older to younger, like kangaroos do when the baby spends nine months in the pouch. The newborns are the size of a lima bean. They're called joeys.

Sometimes it's like starting a book at the tenth chapter and having to go back to see what happened. Before the crisis—before someone left, cheated, died.

The ER note says, *Arrived by ambulance, vomited 300 ccs bright-red blood.*

Medical ICU attending notified. Transfusion stopped secondary to antibodies in his blood.

Then the progress notes:

9/6: Grade 3 esophageal varices; one at 5 o'clock w/ clot and actively spurting blood; 5 bands placed; Hemostasis achieved.

9/8: Had emesis w/ blood clot and bright-red blood; also stooling x 6; states he feels better but still has stomach pain; decreased mental status secondary to organic brain disease, encephalopathy, increased ammonia; blood pressure improving w/ fluids; transfused 4 units w/ improving H/H.

9/10: Transferred to ICU; Intubated and paralyzed for tachypnea, hypoxia, severe agitation. Question of delirium tremens versus hepatic encephalopathy.

9/12: GI note: critically ill w/ hepatorenal syndrome, s/p GI bleed, now septic shock; Acute respiratory distress syndrome; Liver enzymes not consistent w/ shock liver.

9/14: Neuro: sedated, paralyzed; Renal: anuric and creatinine rising. Condition grave; profound shock secondary to sepsis, have been able to contact brother; states pt. wishes no heroic measures, no CPR.

In the room is not the person who had said he was feeling better or who was improving with fluids or was agitated and difficult to intubate. Instead, around his mouth is a halo of sores and blood, oozing as though someone had crushed strawberries on it. His lower lids are turned out from all the fluid, like pockets turned inside out. His skin everywhere is weeping, sticky as anisette and with a sickly sweet odor that has turned the white chux under his arms yellow. The only sound, the only movement, comes not from him but from the ventilator, the rise and fall of his chest from the twenty-two breaths a minute from the machine. Someone has labeled the pumps by writing the name of the drug on one-inch tape on the doors: Nimbex, Versed, fentanyl, insulin, Levophed, vasopressin. I find the button on the Nimbex pump and press it off.

One thing that makes the ICU the ICU is drugs that infuse into the body. We call them drips. We can raise blood pressure with Levophed or dopamine. We can lower it with Nipride or esmolol. We can make the heart contract harder with dobutamine. Make it slower with Cardizem. We can sedate them with Ativan, erase their memory with Versed, take away their pain with morphine and fentanyl. We can paralyze them with Nimbex. Drips can save your life but they can also kill you. You can get cyanide toxicity from Nipride. You can lose toes from Levophed. Drips are almost the heart and soul of ICU nursing. You have to know them inside out; you have to be unafraid.

In rounds, the residents look up labs and X-rays while Fowler and one of the residents drift into the room. "He looks yellow," Fowler says. "Is he on pressors? Is he being fed?"

"No," I tell him. "His residuals were high. He's maxed on Levophed but we could go higher on the vasopressin."

"How much fluid is he getting?"

"Maintenance of two hundred. Total? About two seventy."

"What's he on?"

"One hundred of fentanyl, twelve of Versed, and ten of Nimbex," the resident says. The resident is Miller. Everyone calls him by his last name. He's short, a cute guy.

Fowler asks Miller if he wants to stop the paralytic. Miller is clutching his sheaf of papers as if they could blow away. He turns to me and says, "We can wean the Nimbex." I don't tell him it's off. We don't always tell them what we do. They order the drips but we titrate them, move them up and down. It's like they may start the car but we decide what gear we want to be in.

The other residents have come into the room. Fowler walks to the bed, puts his hand flat on the patient's belly, and pushes down. He doesn't glove up. "This isn't ascites. His belly's soft. It's shock liver. It may be herpes, but he's got shock liver. What did GI say?"

A resident looks through the chart for their note.

"That he has ischemic hepatitis. It's not herpes hepatitis."

"He's infarcted his liver. But it may be herpes. How are his coags?"

"His INR is five point two," someone says."

Clotting is a complicated process. It would be like having to turn on all the lights in your house one by one before any of them would go on. It's called the coagulation cascade. There are thirteen proteins called clotting factors. The liver helps make them. If any one of them is missing, your clotting time is prolonged: you bleed. The INR is one of the measurements of clotting time. It should be 1.

Fowler takes a deep breath. "We're not going to give him any FFP. It would be a waste and some teenage kid would come to the ER and we wouldn't have any. Let's give him some acyclovir in case he has herpes. Wean the Nimbex. Let's give him some vanco." Fowler turns to me. "Has the brother called?" Most of the team has gone to the next room. Miller is writing in the chart.

"If he calls, you can page me," Fowler says.

❖ ❖ ❖

I have to bring the chart to the secretary and spike a bag of Versed and by the time I get to my next patient, the resident is finishing the history. The resident is from India. Her name is Shreya. She talks in a musical way. Her lower lip is plump as if stung by a bee.

"She binge drinks four days a week." The patient is a young woman named Jamie Driscoll. She's a sophomore at the University of New Mexico. Her mother found her unconscious and an empty bottle of Benadryl.

"How many days in a week?" one of the resident asks.

"Twenty," another says, and they all laugh.

"The mother got right in my face," the Doogie Howser girl says. Her name is Kristen. That's what Fowler called her. She puts the palm of her own hand up to her nose as if her palm were the mother's face. "Why didn't you lavage her?" She imitates her with as shrill and as mean a voice as she can in the unit.

"How does she know that?" asks another resident. "Is she a trauma nurse?"

"Probably from her own overdose."

"You can see why she left home at eighteen."

"Okay," Fowler says, down to business. "How does Benadryl work? Why do we get sleepy?"

"We don't know a lot about the receptors," Kristen says. "We don't know a lot about the system."

"We don't know how it affects the central nervous system. Right. But we do know that it blocks neurotransmitters. It's a first-generation antihistamine. It blocks H1 and H2 receptors. It inhibits reuptake of serotonin. It's also anticholinergic. It inhibits parasympathetic nerve impulses by blocking acetylcholine in the receptor cells. You can get ataxia, photophobia, flushed skin, urinary retention. What are the cardiovascular effects?"

"Long QT," one of the residents says. "Tachycardia."

"Right. How is it reversed?"

"Physostigmine."

"Mydriasis. How are her pupils?"

"Huge," I say. They were. They were six millimeters, almost filling the iris. She wouldn't open her eyes at first and twisted her head to the side when I put my fingers on her eyebrows. Even though her voice was just a whisper, there was a little sarcasm and meanness in it, like something caked on the bottom of a pan. She's pretty only in that way that all the young are pretty and when they get older stop being pretty. She has blond hair with roots that are coming out darker. She's very thin. The blood pressure cuff on her arm is the tiny pediatric size. She's twenty-one. She supposedly took seventy-five Benadryl. The nurse in report said she "kinda follows commands, she's not crazy."

"The thing is, it can reabsorb," Fowler continues. "The kidneys play a big role in the excretion of Benadryl. Urine output is key. A slow rate and the drug will back diffuse from the distal tubules into the blood. It'll be a second pass and she'll overdose again. And the pH of her urine is important. Benadryl is a weak base, its pKa is five. Renal excretion of an acidic drug increases in alkaline urine."

"What's her pH?"

"Six point five."

"That's good. Let's keep her output greater than one hundred. Okay stay alert, watch it."

As they leave, Fowler turns to Shreya. "Has Psych seen her?"

"I'll write for it," she says.

The residents are in the hospital to see disease. The more exotic the better. Osler said the three most important things in medicine are diagnosis, diagnosis, diagnosis. They have a saying: "If you hear footsteps, think zebra." I once had a patient with lines on his fingertips like red crayon that turned out were Osler's nodes and apparently rare and a flock of residents appeared to look at them like it was the Shroud of Turin. They have shortcuts. Cholinergic overdose has an acronym: SLUDGE, for salivation, lacrimation, urination, diarrhea, GI cramps, emesis. Anticholinergic overdose has a saying: "Hot as a hare, dry as a bone, red as a beet, mad as a hatter." Medicine seems like a different world. They have a way of talking to each other that they call "roundsmanship." They have their own jargon, words like *scut, pimping, gomer*. Simone Weil called life "here below." Nursing feels like a "here below" and medicine an above of knowledge, learning, repartee you can see but can't enter.

I could see what the resident meant by the girl's mother. When she sees me, she flies at me like a bird hitting a windshield. She has wide, unblinking eyes, a scared look that doesn't change when I tell her that her daughter will be all right, that we're just going to watch her today. It's as if a long time ago a sound like thunder startled her but the sound has never ended. Her hair is an odd no-color pulled back into a ponytail but so tight over her scalp that it looks painful, and her skin has a dead shine like the scales of a fish on the shore. I ask her if the father is around. He's around, she says, but he's disabled, an alcoholic. He had been riding a bike in '97 and was hit by a truck. "I never see him. I could, but I don't." She looked to the other side of the unit. "He was in a coma in this hospital. For five weeks. I don't like doctors."

At one time the land of illness was a kind of medical Pangaea—doctors and patients spoke the same language, had the same view of disease. Knowledge was a bond, not a barrier. Care was mostly in the home. There was no difference between household medicine and hospital treatment. Women stored medicinal herbs just as they stored preserves. Americans were avid readers of medical manuals and books. William Buchan was a member of the Royal College of Physicians of Edinburgh. His book, Domestic Medicine, *was written in everyday language—which meant no Latin words—and was reprinted thirty times in the United States. It had two sections: the causes and prevention of disease and the symptoms and treatment. He wrote what probably most Americans believed: "Everything valuable in the practical part of medicine is within reach of common sense."*

Cushman's brother calls. He has a slow voice but the slowness seems not drugs or alcohol, just the sound of having been beaten down, tired. Fowler comes right away. Most doctors you have to drag to the family and even then they'll lie and say something about hope, chances are good, home for the holidays.

"He's very sick. His liver is bad. We're doing things to keep him alive that are not making him better." The brother must say something because Fowler is silent for a minute. Then Fowler says, "You can call later and talk to the nurse." He turns to me. "I didn't want to encourage him to come down. There's nothing he could do."

I realize it's a question. "I think that's the right thing. He seemed kind. He had a kind voice."

Driscoll's urine output is slowing down—85, 60, 30 this hour. I call Shreya and she tells me to give her a 500 cc bolus of saline.

A bruise, new, the size of a half-dollar, has appeared just below her eye on the knoll of her cheekbone, with petaled edges the color of wisteria. She won't talk. I sit her up and tell her to take deep breaths. She's like a rag doll. Sometimes you can't get or they won't give you a history, so you have to guess what happened. Last year, that girl from Santo Domingo they found by the side of the road unconscious. Just fourteen. Two days later on the inside of her thighs two perfect shapes appear. Thumbprints. The FBI came because everything on the reservation is federal.

Sandy has the two rooms next to mine. "What would you do?" I ask her and she tells me first to call the social worker and then to keep the boyfriend away and call Security if I have to. She says it without hesitating, like she knows. She has a son who lived with her last year but is now back in California with her parents. She never mentions his father. She wears jewelry that she makes herself, mostly beads. She has her hair done really pretty these days in a brown-gold color that reminds me of turning maple leaves in the fall in Vermont. She has the tiniest scar running straight across her cheek.

I find new notes on Cushman's chart. The doctors leave orders, notes like traces—scat, paths—of animals in the forest you know are there but never see.

ID: 1. Multiple organ failure; sepsis w/ profound shock; 2. End stage liver disease; GI bleed w/ varices secondary to alcoholic cirrhosis.

Renal: Acute renal failure w/ end stage liver disease; possible hepatorenal syndrome; even heroic measures won't help; hypotensive and deteriorating; will sign off.

Sign off. Doctors aren't really interested in death. They're interested in disease. We may die from disease, but dying isn't a disease. When it looks like death, doctors start to leave, one by one, like people leaving a room, closing the door behind them, so eventually it's only you and the patient. And a slow, sad voice in Idaho. It feels as though he's all alone. Blown in by the wind. Making him a DNR. Deciding against dialysis. No one to wonder, ask questions, protect. I could do it—call Case Management, the ethics committee—but it's too late. All the lights are green, the train is picking up speed, and everyone just wants to get out of the way. Specialists call medical doctors fleas because they're the last to leave the dying patient.

The sister, the brother, and the boyfriend are lingering outside Driscoll's room. The boyfriend is tall and thin, with black hair. Good-looking. He's wearing low-slung jeans, unbelted, and a white T-shirt tucked in. They look awkward, lost, no adult to guide them in what should be an adult world. They stare as if looking at their own fate, their own fate refracted through the broken glass of the girl's life. I tell the boyfriend he has to leave, that we have to rule out domestic violence, an altercation. His face takes on a look of such shock that right away I know it isn't true. "I would never do something like that."

The sister has gone into the room and pulled the chair next to the bed. I have to go almost right next to her to check the girl's blood sugar.

"Is it high?" the sister asks me. "Mine's high, one thirty."

"That's okay. Are you diabetic?"

"No, but my mother is. Since five years. Her eyes hurt all the time terribly. She can't see without glasses. The doctor says it's glaucoma but she can't afford the medication until she qualifies for Medicaid."

"Diabetes can cause eye problems."

"She doesn't know that." Her voice is excited like this is good news. "Can you tell her that?"

Her name is Melissa. She has straight blond hair tied back like her mother's. She is thin, too. A tattoo on her back. She's pale.

"Are you okay?"

"I had a rough night last night."

"Rough how?"

"I had a fight with my boyfriend and I left. He was drunk."

"Did he hit you?"

"He hit me once. I left."

"You know, you can't let that happen. There's never an excuse for that. Do you know that?"

"He's an alcoholic. He was molested as a child. His mother is drunk every day."

"That's no excuse. Are you all right?"

"I'm all right."

"What does he do?"

"He's a chef."

"That can be a rough lifestyle if you drink."

"He killed someone in a car accident. He's paying restitution."

She talks to me the whole time I'm in the room. As I leave, she says, "Can she have some Jama juice? She loves Jama juice."

I'm charting outside Driscoll's room when Kevin, one of the respiratory therapists, ducks behind my computer.

"You missed," Kevin says. He's talking to Mateo.

"Jim knows I got you. Tell him."

Kevin and Mateo are playing a game where they try and sneak up and shoot each other. Kevin points his index finger at Mateo and cocks his thumb. He makes a sound like *choo*. Mateo bends backward, his arms outstretched so the shot will miss him. He does it in slow motion like Keanu Reeves in *The Matrix* but he weighs about 250 and has those bad knees. I wonder if any families can see them.

"Jimmy, why are Mexican men so short?" Mateo says to me.

"Don't know."

"Because when they're young, their mothers tell them when they grow up, they have to go to work."

Pharmacy comes by and orders a renal dose of vancomycin for Cushman. "We'll start it now and check a level in two days." She could be about thirty. Four years of college. Four years of pharmacy school. She has square-jawed attractiveness and an accent that could be Dutch or just midwestern. She's wearing an ankle-length skirt and a short-sleeved blouse. They don't have to wear scrubs. They don't need to go into the room. They start at a hundred grand a year. Look at the creatinine, figure out the dose. Two days. It's like she's dropping a penny into a well she thinks is a wishing well but is really just an old dead well with scum at the dark bottom but I let her think that. There won't be anything to check in two days.

The brother calls again. "This is Patrick Cushman."

I told him there's no change. "Are you close?" I ask him.

"Yes. There's just been the two of us for a long time."

"Where are you?"

"In Idaho." It was as though he was a man used to being asked questions and answering just the question.

"Where in Idaho?"

"Sun Valley area."

I know were he lives. We once drove east through Oregon into Idaho and then to Sun Valley. We hiked in the Sawtooth Mountains. Stanley, just north of Ketchum, is almost every day the coldest place in the country.

Ernest Hemingway killed himself in Ketchum, "blew out his brain pan," my friend Kim says. His grave is in a cemetery near the downtown. People leave pennies and cigars on the gravestone.

I look into the room at Cushman through the meshed window. I imagine Patrick as a heavy man with a big sad face. His hair is dirty, uncombed, thin. He has a beard. He's sitting in a big easy chair. He's wearing a heavy flannel shirt over another shirt. His pants are cuffed but still too long, the edges frayed and black from dragging on the ground. Just the effort of talking on the phone exerts him.

"I don't think I'm going to come down. I'm disabled. I live in a subsidized apartment. I'm running out of minutes on this calling card. I'm surprised it hasn't run out yet. Let me give you a number. My two roommates are always here."

I tell him it's okay, that there's nothing we can do and that we've done all we can.

"You'll call me if anything happens?"

"I'll call you."

Cushman's INR is 6.8. I call Fowler. I can tell he doesn't want to give him anything but it would look bad. "Give him two FFP. Give him some vitamin K too. Did the brother call back?"

"I talked to him."

"He's okay with everything?"

"He understands."

Jamie Driscoll's mother is standing outside the room. She seems to want to talk. I ask her what Jamie is like, if she's always been so quiet. The mother doesn't say anything about Jamie but then starts to talk and says she herself was originally from Charleston. Her first husband committed suicide when she was twenty-three. She was three days from giving birth. She's had hepatitis C since 1970. She doesn't know how she got it. She had shoulder surgery in 1970. She took interferon for a while but it stopped working. Now she has cirrhosis. Her skin, I thought. She's not on the transplant list. "I have to quit smoking and I haven't done that. I have lost some weight. I'm not sure I want it." Her mother was dialyzed for five years. "She went from five foot six to five foot three. She got a kidney. She didn't get health. She died ten years later." She was homeless for a while. "I was Section 8. but they raised my rent. I lived in a motel, cars. Jamie stayed with friends. I'm disabled. My son tells me I should get a job, that it'll help Jamie if I look responsible. She's tried to kill herself twice. She couldn't get help because she has no insurance."

"She's thin."

She turns on that high-beam glare again, her face up close the way it scared Kristen. "They were both bulimic in high school. They were throwing up and running. Everybody thought it was great. But it was for the wrong reason. Their ribs were showing. They hid it. I caught Jamie and made her stop it. She has a lot of credit card debt. She's an impulsive spender."

"Melissa said Jamie's suicidal."

"What did she say?"

"Things like she'll be driving too fast and Melissa will tell her to put on her seat belt and she'll say, 'No, what do I have to live for?' That she binge drinks four times a week."

"I tried to get her help. The last time she was supposed to get insurance through her job and then she could see somebody. But she didn't qualify. It hasn't been easy for me. I've tried to do the best I could."

For a moment the anger leaves her face and she seems sad and older, her eyes not looking at the room or at me.

"Was there ever anything you wanted to do in life?"

"Have a stable family. That's the one thing I always wanted."

Michelle is standing outside her room; she calls my name. She holds her arms straight out in front with her hands in fists and then pulls them in toward her. She wants help boosting her patient. She's a traveler from Mobile. She can look wild: rich, strawberry-blonde hair, southern accent, bright scrubs. When someone is doing something she doesn't like she'll say, "He's getting on my last nerve." If you ask her where she's from, she'll say LA, for "lower Alabama."

Her patient is the woman who was beaten up. "Now she says her foster children are doing it," Michelle says. The woman has slid down on the bed so her legs are between the front and back side rails, dangling but not touching the floor. She's tiny, almost too small for the bed, like a button too small for a buttonhole. She has two black eyes that are perfect circles as if someone had drawn circles and colored them in with black crayon. Her gown is up. Her pubic hair is stubble. Above it is a tattoo of a red rosebud. She is so skinny her stomach is sunken into a valley. Michelle is not very tall herself but we get on either side. "Okay, Susan, we're going to pull you up now." She's as light as a bag of leaves. She has little tattoos everywhere—names, flowers—but some of them are bruises.

On the table in the lounge is a copy of *The New Mexican*. A headline says, "Three Killed on I-25." Saturday was Zozobra in Santa Fe. They have things here they don't have back east. The rodeo in June. Indian Market in August. The Pueblos have feast days that are open to the public when the Indians chant and dance all day in traditional attire. You can't take pictures and, at lunchtime, someone will just walk up to you and invite you into his or her home. Easter, thousands of people walk to El Santuario de Chimayo, on the High Road to Taos, where they believe the dirt in the chapel is sacred, and the room is full of crutches, canes, and walkers.

Zozobra begins the Fiestas de Santa Fe, which celebrates the retaking of the city in 1692 by Don Diego de Vargas after the Pueblo Revolt of 1680. Zozobra is a stick marionette, fifty feet tall, chicken-wired together. He's also called Old Man Gloom. In Santa Fe, in the weeks before Zozobra, the stores in town have tin cans where you can write something sad or bad that happened to you, some little piece of gloom that you want to forget, and they put it at the feet of Zozobra, and then at Fort Marcy at dusk, and there are thousands of people there, they burn him. All the worries and troubles of the previous year are burned in the flames.

The three dead were all teenage girls. Their pictures are next to the headline. In the pictures they're smiling. They look like the pictures you take for your yearbook. One has braces. They were all from Pecos. Two were cousins. They crashed near the city near a roadhouse called Bobcat Bite. The picture is of a Forester in the grassy median with the front end caved in. To the side of the Forester is a wooden cross with flowers and pieces of paper. They're called *descansos*, the Spanish word for "resting." Where they mark is not where someone is buried but where the person died. I never saw one back east. When we drove out west we saw them in Utah and in South Dakota. They're everywhere in New Mexico. Two of the girls were eighteen, one sixteen. They were on their way to the festival that ends all sorrow.

Melissa is carrying a dozen yellow roses on long stems. "As long as they're not in soil," I tell her. The more I see her the more I think she looks like her mother.

Sometimes I think how the world looks to the poor. The Doppler effect is that the sound coming toward you sounds different from the sound going away from you. The world looks different to the poor. If you're wealthy, the world is coming toward you, the sound rising, the road straight, flat, the sky clear, you can see forever; to the poor, the world recedes from you. You come out of the womb, find the road, and grow away toward your own life. But the poor hit traffic, construction. A detour sign takes you off the main road. It gets dark. You can see in the distance the lights of other cars on the road you want. You're driving parallel to it. It begins to rain so you lose even the light of the stars. You wind up heading back in the direction you came from.

Melissa shakes my hand when she comes in. She has pinprick scars in the hollow of her cheeks. Sharp edges of bones you shouldn't see. Bulimia, drinking, drunk boyfriend, like an underground mining of the soul that will someday leave the surface of her life thin as an eggshell. She is with another girl, her roommate. The girl is carrying a handful of DVDs. There's a rhythm in the world—classes, a part-time job, coffee at Starbucks—that they must leave to come here.

When the mother returns, the roommate has gone. Melissa is sitting next to the bed with the top of her head against the side rail. I can't see her face. Her hair is down. Longer than it looked in the ponytail, it hangs straight like pouring rain. I can see she is crying by the way her hair moves then stops, moves then stops, the way you know a snake is moving under leaves.

The ICU can be a lot of doing. Admission. Intubation. Codes. Codes are a lot of doing. Codes are like dust devils. The land spits them up, they take form, they whirl across the prairie, and they're gone. There are tasks. Hanging bags, titrating drips, turning, meds, labs, calling, procedures, calling, putting things in, taking things out, waking them up, then when they wake up helping them eat a bite at a time like little kids. Nursing is heavy with tasks—with doing—but there is also a lot of not-doing. The not-doing is watching. Years back, nurses whose responsibility was to watch the critically ill at night were called watchers. There can be long stretches of watching, waiting. You watch the monitor, watch the vent, watch the urine output, the heart rate, watch the chest rise and fall, their skin, their pupils. A doctor may be the gatekeeper to health care; a nurse is the catcher in the rye, watching, so patients don't go over a cliff.

The mother asks Melissa if she wants to say the rosary. Melissa doesn't raise her head and takes so long before she nods that the mother says, "We can say it to ourselves." She sits in a chair on the other side of the bed. In her hand is a string of beads the color of pink lemonade. She is in profile. She closes her wide eyes and lifts her head at an angle like when you're trying to remember something. Then her lips begin to move soundlessly and quickly in a sure rhythm and her fingers caress the lemonade beads, turn them, and let them fall one by one.

There's a crowd outside Kay's room. Maestas, the young one with the goatee, survived the night. Some of the ICU team. Fowler. Cardiology. The surgeon. ID. One of the ER docs. They're all here to see him. The surgeon is Dr. Cohen. He was a resident a few years ago. He's young and some of the nurses know him. He asks Kay how the boy is. Kay is sitting looking at notes and then writing in the chart. Written on the palm of her right hand are numbers—vital signs, labs.

"Not good," she says. "His heart rate is up. His systolic is eighty-two. His respirations fifty."

"He's septic," Sue says. She's standing next to me. We go in the room with the doctors.

"His liver looks good," says the ID guy. "His ammonia's not too high."

"He's not making urine," Kay says.

"How many organs are failing?"

"Kidneys. Heart. He had an MI. Lungs."

Fowler turns to Kay, "Let's give him some albumin. Squeeze that boy."

The ER doctor is looking into the room. He's a young guy with short blond hair. The ER docs wear cobalt-blue scrubs that make them look like pilots.

"You saw him in the ER?" I ask him.

He nods. "He was supposed to go back to the clinic. I kept him."

Jamie's brother has come back with someone who turns out to be the father. He is smaller and shorter than his own son and with an allover slimy sheen as if someone had lifted him out a vat of 10W-30 and a grin like he's here to pick up an award. He stops where I'm sitting. "What'd she take?" His voice is low and gravelly, the sound tires make when they hit a stripped road.

"Benadryl." I look to see if he knows what that means. "The body has a fast-and-slow mechanism. Benadryl stops the slow." A sweet, decaying odor comes from him, from his dirty lank hair, from the sheen on his black jeans. He's wearing sunglasses. "It has the effect of speed."

"White storm," he says and grins as if we're playing Jeopardy! It's an old meth term and fixes him in the seventies, where he must live, and he really is kind of a child, a friend to his own son. It is the son who wears the grave expression and leads the man into the room.

For the first time Jamie's face forms an expression. The father doesn't sit but instead stands next to the bed. The boy likewise doesn't sit and stands close to his father. She looks up at him and says something. He leans over probably to hear her. A long ponytail gray as a possum stretches on his back. He has black cowboy boots with the heels worn down. Which kid isn't his? If she was three weeks from birth when her mother's first husband killed himself, one can't be his. The boy standing close. Jamie actually talking. It must be Melissa. Jamie and the boy his.

After just a few minutes he says, "I gotta go, kiddo." He puts his hand out over the rail and Jamie lifts her arm, thin as a twig, with a drooped little hand at the end, and in the air between them they shake hands. "I'll see her when she gets out," he says as he passes me, and the boy and he leave, and in the oval of air between his skinny bowed legs you can almost see a little horse.

Michelle helps me bathe Cushman. The fluid swelling his body has pushed his tongue out of his mouth so it lies next to the tube. It is as hard and dry as a worm dead on the sidewalk. I moisten it with Surgilube and push it back into his mouth. Soak up the fluid thick as fondue that has collected in his ears. Wipe debris from the canthus of his eyes, his nares. He's like a cabin in Colorado you're opening up after a long winter.

"I'm going to shave him," Michelle says.

I stop everything—the Versed, the fentanyl. Take down the balloon and pull the rectal tube. Comb his hair. Getting him ready. Someone once said about death, "The first night is the hardest."

Michelle has left a tuft of hair in the hollow of his chin. I'm looking at it. "A soul patch," she says. She nods her head twice. "That's how God will lift him up to heaven."

They round again at five o'clock. In the morning they were tightly bound, focused, presenting the patients. Now they're loose, straggling. Going off. Some of them are already on to the next patient. One of the residents is saying to the Pulmonary fellow, "That's because you're a liar," and they both laugh. Fowler comes by. He looks into Cushman's room. "Stop everything. Don't extubate him but stop everything."

Jamie is awake; her arms are raised, her fingers picking at the air. She's staring at them like a child looking at a mobile. Fowler is watching her. "That's classic anticholinergic," he says. "We'll keep her overnight. She can go in the morning. If they need a bed tonight she can go."

Medicine wasn't always taught in the hospital. A hundred years ago entrance requirements for medical school were lower than for high school. Teaching was by lecture alone. A term lasted sixteen weeks. You would get a degree to practice after the second term no matter how you did academically. You could graduate without ever examining a patient.

William Osler founded the teaching hospital. If Hippocrates is the father-god of medicine, William Osler is the Saint Paul. He is one of the four physicians who began Johns Hopkins Hospital. He is eponymous throughout medicine. Osler's nodes are raised tender nodules on the pulps of fingertips or toes and are diagnostic of subacute bacterial endocarditis. Polycythemia vera is known as Osler-Vasquez disease. There's an Osler's maneuver, an Osler syndrome, an Osler triad. He wrote the essay "Aequanimitas," about coolness and presence of mind under all circumstances. At Hopkins, Osler established the full-time, sleep-in residency program. He insisted that residents see and talk to patients.

"I desire no other epitaph," he said, "than the statement that I taught medicine in the wards."

3

NURSING ISN'T A JOURNEY

Doctors haven't always had the esteem, power, and authority they have today.

A professional journal in 1869 described medicine as the most despised of all the professions educated men could enter. Paul Starr writes that in the nineteenth century, the medical profession was "generally weak, divided, insecure in its status and income, unable to control entry into practice or raise the standards of medical education." The medical profession shared the terrain with domestic medicine and lay healers. Indian doctors were highly regarded; Cotton Mather wrote, "They cure many times which are truly stupendous." No one was just a doctor. The Sweet family of Rhode Island were famous bonesetters from the seventeenth to the twentieth century. They practiced part time; they were also farmers, mechanics, laborers, and fishermen. In eighteenth-century Virginia, a Dr. John Payas sold not only drugs but also tea, sugar, olives, grapes, anchovies, raisins, and prunes. Jean Pasteur was described as a surgeon in his obituary but a wigmaker in his will.

I have two young men today. Most of the young are traumas or ODs. Timothy Lawson is twenty-two. He was diagnosed with ALL, acute lymphocytic leukemia, in October last year. Had chemotherapy and radiation but still got metastasis to the hip, leg, pelvis. Was admitted first to Memorial down south in Las Cruces near his home. Then mets to the head. Air-flighted to us for a higher level of care. On the way he began to bleed—from his mouth, his rectum. When he got here, they did an endoscopy and it showed severe erosive esophagitis, radiation induced. I look at his labs: white count 1.8, H and H 8.4 and 23.4, platelets 36. Chemo kills.

The Oncology note from the day before is hurried, in large script: *22 YO presumptive ALL, diffuse tumor, spinal compression. Head CT seems not to indicate skull infiltrate. Lesion biopsy may be indicated to r/o tumor foci vs inflammatory response, no stools, quiet, slept.*

No one in the room. He's so tall his feet stick out of the sheet and almost touch the footboard. He could be six four. I don't know the difference between ALL, CML, and AML but I do know ALL is the worst. There's no hope. I ask him if he's having any pain and he says "ten" in a whisper, but angry. He must have been asked that a hundred times. He doesn't open his eyes. He's got a patient-controlled analgesia pump, a PCA, where he gets one milligram of morphine an hour and can push a button and get one milligram every six minutes. And he has a fifty-microgram fentanyl patch on his arm. He's pale, thin. His hair is spotty from the chemo. Scabs are scattered on his head like ice floes. There are dried flakes of mucus on his lips, like candle wax. A porta-cath on the right side of his chest where the chemo goes.

It's quiet in the room. Like the quiet before a basketball game back in high school, sitting on the wooden bench in the locker room before going up the two flights of stairs to the gym, the bleachers full, the noise. The steep hill of the morning. The window from Four opens up to the bays for ambulances coming to the ER, but the blinds are halfway down and drawn. On the lower half of the window are three pieces of white printing paper from the copier with the corners attached to the glass with silk hospital tape. They're covered with photographs. Three of the pictures are with two girls who look to be his sisters. Three people at a table in a restaurant leaning together so their heads almost touch. Four young boys in baseball uniforms with their arms around one another's shoulders. The uniforms say "Eagles" and they are each holding up an index finger. A picture of him and his mother wearing white cowboy hats standing next to a big saguaro cactus, which means it must be near Tucson.

Families do this, they nest in rooms, feather them with memories. They leave and you find notes taped to the wall, cards on the roller tables, a scapular in the pocket of the gown, a rosary on the pillow.

On the cork bulletin board are handwritten notes.

"I love you cousin. May God help you. Better days are a head. I hope to see you soon."

"To Timmy. You have to get better soon so we can tear the town up."

"Son: Grab the bull by the horns and tell it you're coming home soon. I need my happy side back"—there is a happy face drawn here—"I'm with you and you're with me. I miss you—your ugly sister."

A medical student is presenting Lawson. Fowler calls her Anna. She reads from her papers. "Twenty-two-year-old man with ALL, esophagitis.

Afebrile. Hemodynamically stable." She gets some things wrong. She says he's on a Protonix drip when it had been discontinued. She says "FFP" when she means "platelets" because they're the same color. She leaves out things.

In the room, Fowler asks him if he has any pain, nausea. He palpates his abdomen. Outside he says his hemoglobin has drifted eightish. "Let's tank him up with two units. Who's seeing him?"

The student says Heme/Onc. "They want a biopsy. Neurosurg."

"What about GI?"

"They signed off."

"Why?"

"The EGD showed only esophagitis and there was nothing for them to do."

"We need to biopsy the scalp lesions. It could be ALL. It could be melanoma, an aggressive cancer. It could be hematologic. What does Neurosurgery say?"

"They want to do an MRI."

"Anything else?

"We're not feeding him."

"Let's give him another day. I don't want to drop any more tubes into him."

"Pain," I say.

Fowler looks at me.

"It's not controlled."

"What's he on?"

"Morphine PCA and a fentanyl patch. It's not enough."

"Call Heme/Onc. We'll let them manage it."

"Good job, Anna," Fowler says. He looks into the room again. "He's an unlucky kid."

Doctors are prolific writers. Every rung of the ladder is chronicled: medical school, internship, residency. Every specialty has its bard—Richard Selzer on surgery, Oliver Sacks on neurology. Between 1965 and 2010, more than sixty books about medical education were published. They tend to be about the emotional experience, the drama, of becoming a physician. A review of Residents, *by David Duncan, describes the world of the doctor as having a peculiar code of heroics, self-denial, and stress.*

White Coat *is the story of Ellen Rothman (Ellen Lerner Rothman; she marries another doctor at the end of the book) and her four years at Harvard Medical School. The* Chicago Tribune *describes* White Coat *as a "clear picture of what it takes to make the journey to physicianhood," one woman's transformation from a terrified first-year medical student into a confident, competent doctor.*

Nursing isn't a journey like medicine. Medicine is transformative, an odyssey to selfhood. Doctors talk about mountains, abysses, struggles, scars. They have guides like Dante had Virgil. Annie Dillard says that when they are ten years old, children wake up and find themselves here. "They wake like sleepwalkers, in full stride, in media res, *surrounded by familiar people and objects, equipped with a hundred skills." Nursing feels like that. One day you're a nurse, you're in a hospital, wearing scrubs, suctioning someone on a ventilator, deciding how much to go up on the Levophed. School was kind of a prelude and you do get better, you learn things, get more comfortable. But nursing isn't a journey, there's no nursehood.*

Edward Maestas is awake. Someone has angled the bed toward the TV, and he has the remote in his right hand. He is actually not that young; he is thirty-four. Along with the goatee, he has long eyelashes and wire-framed glasses. He looks like a scholar. The TV is on. He squeezes my hand, follows my finger, shakes his head no to pain. In between, his eyes go to the TV. He is calm. I don't know if I would be that calm. Lying there almost flat, day after day, the vent hissing, the pumps, like going off the road into a ditch and being trapped. He's doing better. Still on the ventilator, but down to the lowest oxygen and breathing on his own. His blood pressure better, the Levophed off, the dopamine only at three. But he's still not making any urine. The night nurse said, "His kidneys are fried."

This is his fourth day in the ICU. That he is still alive is surprising. I look at the first day's flow sheet. All the drips he had been on, vital signs every fifteen minutes, Kay's handwriting jittery, like somebody writing a letter on a bus. I find the history and physical:

Edward Maestas is 34. He has rheumatoid arthritis and was on Naprosyn and Embrel. These were stopped in July because of swelling. Somewhere around that time he was placed on Lasix. Over the past six weeks he has had increasing shortness of breath, cough, and some edema. He has been followed by the pueblo clinic. He was told he had an enlarged heart. He was started on diuretics but there was no improvement. He also has a history of alcoholism. Had been in recovery but eight months ago relapsed. He has been drinking some these past months. The patient's mother lives in Algodones. When he started drinking and became ill about four months ago he moved back with her. The mother brought him to an appointment at the clinic on Wednesday, 2 days ago. He was weak and dyspneic. He was found with ascites and had a 4 liter paracentesis. He was transferred to this hospital yesterday for further imaging and evaluation. The ER doctor felt strongly he should be admitted. He had emergency surgery. Additional abscesses were found. He remains intubated and on pressors. He is critically ill. He is now oliguric with a rising creatinine and rising potassium. The patient wishes to be fully resuscitated should that become necessary. Recommend emergency hemodialysis.

There is a note from Cardiology: *I do not know anything further that can be done for this young man. Further inotropic agents are not likely to be beneficial. His prognosis is poor. About the only possibility is that he will recover from his sepsis and the workload on the heart will decrease and we might be able to obtain some sort of improved cardiac functioning and compensation. At the present time there is no sign of this occurring.*

Somebody has already written the assessment/plan for the day:

1. *sepsis: improved; wean off dopamine; only at 3*
2. *cardiomyopathy: consider digoxin*
3. *renal failure w/ increased potassium*
4. *abdominal abscess*
5. *stigmata of critical illness*

The stigmata are the marks on his toes. Each toe, except the baby toes, is the livid blue-black of storm clouds. The cyanosis is from the Levophed's constricting distant vessels and shunting blood to vital organs. It raises blood pressure but they lose toes, fingers. Someone has marked them with a black Sharpie so each toe has a unique squiggly tattoo. They use the word *stigmata* a lot. Stigmata of endocarditis for the splinter hemorrhages under the nails. Stigmata of liver disease. It's from Saint Paul's Letter to the Galatians: "I bear on my body the stigmata of Jesus."

It was as if before, he had been drowning; now he had been towed to shallow water, the shore in sight. Breathing on his own. His blood pressure holding. Dialysis for his kidney failure. Still some storm flags, though; his creatinine, his white count both up.

He may be in shallow water, but a riptide could suck him out to sea again.

Timmy Lawson's mother comes in right at eight, when visiting hours begin. Her name is Violet. "Call me Vi." She puts her big leather bag on the floor and a bottle of water and a book on the table. She's wearing blue jeans, a wide leather belt, a leopard-skin top with roses, a necklace with a golden heart. She wears those fake aviator glasses and her hair is not white but whitish, the color of old snow. Her lipstick is very red.

"I love you," she says to him and kisses his knee just above the compression stockings that cover his calves; he opens his eyes and smiles. I think it was Goethe who said the saddest thing in the world is to be standing on a shore while your beloved sails away. The saddest thing in the world really is when your child dies. The book is called *The Haunted Mesa*, by Louis L'Amour. I recognize the cover. I've read that, I tell her. She smoothes the blankets over his chest and manages to get his feet covered. She pulls a tube of Chapstick from her pocket. She twists it open.

"It's okay," she smiles at me. "They told me I could use this."

Oncology is here to see Lawson. The attending looks like an English professor. He's wearing a corduroy jacket and readers that sit low on his nose. A resident and a pharmacist, a tall, older woman, are with him. They go into the room to talk with his mother. "We need to biopsy these lesions. If we know what it is and we treat it with the right drugs, his pain will be better."

Outside, the pharmacist says, "We should hold the bowel regimen because of his GI bleed."

"What about his pain?" I ask the attending. "They want you to handle it." He looks over his glasses at the pharmacist.

"We'll leave it as it is," she says. "We need to let his serum level build up."

I look up ALL. Disease is everything to doctors—Osler told his students to "immerse yourself in illness; live with it; breathe it; be jostled out of your nightly stupor thinking of nothing but illness. You must wrestle with it as Jacob in Genesis wrestled with the angel; only then will you be fit to spend the rest of your life eye to eye with it"—but they never really talk to us about it. It says ALL is common in childhood, with a peak at ages two to five and then another peak at age fifty. Eighty percent cure rate in kids and sixty percent with adults. Prognosis drops with mets to the brain or spinal cord—which is what he has. Undertreated, Fowler said. They're from Carrizozo. Way down south of Albuquerque and then east. Maybe it's like what they call a food desert where there are no supermarkets, just convenience stores and fast food, but it's a medical desert instead. Unlucky kid.

The General Surgery docs come and do the biopsy. When they leave I find a single black suture in his scalp. Vi is reading in a chair by the window to keep the room dark. I ask her what he did before he got sick. We talk quietly. She said he worked as a waiter, went to a community college. He didn't know what he wanted to do. I look at the photographs on the window. The sisters, she tells me, are at the Marriott. "We can't afford it but it's nice and clean. We're all in one room." I repeat the CBC: his platelets are up to fifty-three but his hemoglobin is down to six and his hematocrit twenty-three. His blood should be thick, like minestrone, but it's more like a broth.

In Maestas's room are his mother and his two sisters. The mother and one sister sit in the chairs. The other sister stands by the bed. We allow only two at a time but he is so sick I pull the curtain halfway. The sister has the remote in her hand and is changing the station. Maestas is watching the TV stations flick by. They could be at home. The sister wears athletic clothing: baggy blue knee-length basketball shorts and a football jersey with the number 33 on the back. They each have short, square bodies. When the family speaks to me they speak English. When they speak to each other they speak the language of the pueblos, Keres.

"How is he?" the sister in the chair asks.

"He's stable."

"Is he getting that dialysis today?"

"Tomorrow."

She says something to the mother in Keres. The mother is quiet. He had moved back in with her. Driving him up to the clinic.

"What pueblo are you from?"

"San Felipe."

The interstate between Santa Fe and Albuquerque—I-25—goes through four pueblos. When the state wanted more money from casino gambling, the tribes threatened to put a tollbooth on the highway. Only Sandia and San Felipe have casinos. Sandia's casino is new. It's just north of Albuquerque, at the foot of the mountains. It's enormous. At night it looks like a spaceship hovering in the desert. Sandia has a hotel, a golf course. San Felipe is twenty miles north of Albuquerque at the end of a long road that disappears from sight and goes from gravel to dirt to the pueblo. The casino is small. Next to it is a Travel Center with cheaper reservation gas, and behind it a racetrack that never gets used. Truckers sleep overnight in the casino parking lot. It doesn't have a golf course or a hotel; what it does have though, which is even better, the first thing you see at night, coming down from Santa Fe, on the top of the roof of the casino, is a ring of pretty pink lights like rosettes of cake frosting.

"He's going to be okay?"

"He's sick. But he's young." During rounds, Fowler said he was turning the corner.

"How long will he be on dialysis?"

"It could be months. It could be temporary. His kidneys can return. He's young," I say again. They seem to relax. The sister has picked *The Price Is Right*.

Doctors come by all day. Renal to check the dialysis schedule. Cardiology. ID. Cohen comes in to look at the incision. The dressing is held together by Montgomery straps that you can untie. We're changing it every two hours.

"What could happen?" I ask him.

"Two weeks could pass. Maybe it will seal over. Looks like he's slowly crawling out of a hole. He's a save."

In Joan Didion's The Year of Magical Thinking, *her daughter, Quintana, is admitted to the ICU at Beth Israel Hospital with septic pneumonia. "She had been admitted to the ICU on Christmas night,"* Didion writes. "She was in a hospital, we kept telling each other. She was being taken care of. She would be safe where she was." People think of the ICU as a haven, as shelter from the storm. But it can be a race against time. Line infections, pressure ulcers from lying in bed,*

pneumonia from the ventilator, abdominal bleeding from stress. Some-
times it feels like we're not really saving them but Jake braking on a
steep downhill, slowing ourselves down so we don't go off the road
before we reach the bottom.

Vi finds me in the unit. "He's breathing faster. His heart rate is up." I had told her we can control pain in the ICU. That we have powerful drugs. No one should be in pain. It was like a promise.

The pharmacist has a small office next to Bed Fourteen at the end of the unit, like a caboose. She sits with her back to the door at a computer going through the orders.

"You need to give it more time." She doesn't turn around.

"Do you want me to call the attending?"

She brings up the profile of Lawson's meds. "You can increase the basal rate to three milligrams an hour and two milligrams every ten minutes."

We have to take him for an MRI. I bring extra morphine with me. We'll have to move him to the hard MRI table and back. It'll be like taking a stick to a cooling fire, his pain will get so stirred up. Be flat on his back for half an hour. I go to MRI with a big transport kid named Paul who changes his wavy hair from loose to his shoulders, to a po-nytail, to cornrows—"It takes three hours"—and who jokes that he's not Hispanic but Samoan. When we get there the vital signs don't come through. When I go in the room to fix the blood pressure cuff, his head is deep in the MRI tunnel and even though we had put spongy things in his ears, the pounding jackhammer noise must still get through but he gives me a thumbs up. Outside I just watch his stomach move up and down to be sure he keeps breathing. The tech, sitting down, shakes his head as the images come up. "His spine looks bad. Abnormalities everywhere."

The sisters and Vi are all in the room when we get back and hook him up again. Vi comes to the bed. "Hi, honey." I tell her he did good. They surround the bed. The sisters are big girls and strong looking. In New England you find huge granite boulders alone in fields. They're called erratics. They were dropped there by the glaciers as they receded. They remind me of them. Big solid girls from the country. The MRI showed a concave bleed in the right frontal area. Most of the time they ask what it showed, but she doesn't ask as if she knows the news would be bad news and it would come when it came.

Just before the end of the shift they tap Maestas's chest for some fluid they saw in the wall of his lung on the morning chest X-ray. Murphy sits in the chair and talks the resident through the procedure. Murphy tells him where to cut, how far in to put the drain. They get only fifty ccs off.

"Did he really need that?" I ask him after. I know the residents have to-do lists when they rotate through the ICU. They need to put in arterial lines, central lines, intubate somebody.

"We thought it would be more."

It's six thirty. Most of the families have left. The same ER doctor comes by, the one who kept him. I tell him how it's going. What Cohen said about being a save. He doesn't go into the room, but looks in.

"The mother?"

I nod.

He puts his hand out and we shake. "You guys do a great job up here."

"Thanks."

4

ONE MORE DAY

Paul Starr describes the history of medicine as an epic of progress, as a century-long march from an only sometimes respectable trade to a sovereign profession, to a position of cultural authority, economic power, and political influence: "Medicine went from a relatively weak, traditional profession of minor economic significance to a sprawling system of hospitals, clinics, health plans, insurance companies and myriad other organizations employing a vast labor force."

If, in the nineteenth century, doctors swam side by side in a sea of bonesetters, nostrum makers, homeopaths, botanic practitioners, midwives, cancer doctors, inoculators, and abortionists, in the twentieth century they alone emerged from that sea. Gone were the other paths to becoming a doctor: the apprenticeship, the house pupil system, the private summer schools. The hospital metamorphosed from a place of dread and exiled human wreckage into a citadel of science; from charity to a business; from patrons and the poor to professionals and their patients; from the periphery to the center of medical education and practice; from a sleepy domicile for the deserving poor into a bastion of scientific medical care. Medicine was hospitalized and the hospital medicalized.

You have to walk by the waiting room on the way to the unit. It's never empty. There's always somebody in it, day and night. Maybe a late admission but often either people who look Hispanic or Native American from Gallup or from a pueblo too poor for even Motel 6 or the Super 8. The couches are designed so you can't lie down on them. They're short, with a wooden arm in the middle. There are nine people in the room. All of them are sleeping. Two are sleeping on the floor in opposite directions, their heads on pillows almost touching, as though it's one person in a mirror, and covered not with hospital blankets but with quilts of bright reds and purple trapezoidal shapes. Navajo. The others are slumped in chairs, legs splayed, heads resting on pillows, mouths open, some with the white hospital blankets pulled over their heads against the recessed ceiling lights that never go off. The low rectangular table and the two round ones are covered with nearly empty bags of Doritos and popcorn and bigger white to-go bags from Arby's and boxes that say KFC and Big Boy sodas with straws sticking up from plastic lids. The TV is on with no sound. There's no switch for the overhead lights and no windows and there's no door they can close against the world and no darkness they can retreat into.

I take Lawson back, along with a GI bleed coming from the ER.

In report, the night charge said Lawson's mother was "on edge." I find Lawson flat on his back. The fitted corners of the sheet above his head have popped off, exposing the blue mattress, as if he were an injured bird on a shrinking ice floe. His eyes are closed but the lids are clenched, his long body and the white sheet twisted like a phone cord. His heart rate 125. No night. Vi is in the big blue recliner that doesn't go all the way flat and is really for getting patients out of bed, especially the hearts, getting them going again. "He's been awake and in pain all night. The nurse only came in once." She's a little angry, but it's more like she's keeping tabs on things, sizing people up, remembering who's who and what they did. Frontier justice. Something real "West" about her, her and the sisters. Code of the West. Old things, like after you pass someone on the trail, don't look back at the person. It implies you don't trust him or her. Always fill your whiskey glass to the brim. Don't wave at a man on a horse, as it might spook the horse. A nod is the proper greeting. And they don't wave out here; when a man in a car knows you, he lifts his index finger off the wheel. That's it. That's hello. And then things like honesty are absolute; your word is bond.

Pharmacy comes right after I call. It's the same woman. I tell her I'm going to call Fowler to manage the pain. She says we can change him to Dilaudid. "Tim," I tell him, "We're going to give you a different medication. It's more powerful. You can push the button every ten minutes now and you'll get more pain medication." He nods his head, but he only lives for his mother. When the Dilaudid comes down, I give him a two-milligram bolus. A nursing bolus. If they say give five hundred of normal saline, we might give a thousand. That's the small print in the contract they don't read.

The sisters come back midmorning. "We don't stay all night. We're wimps." They try to get Vi to go back to the hotel. They like the Marriott. The beds, the Jacuzzi. When one says *Jacuzzi* they look at each other and laugh. The sisters are reading a menu. One looks up, finished. "Get me a chimmy." She writes something on the paper in the window. "Should we tell him?" one whispers. "They mean the Red Sox lost," Vi says. Later I hear one tell him, "Manny hit a home run."

We don't discuss his code status with Vi. We could even ask the boy, but we don't. It's understood that we're doing everything. Only if you look at the pieces can you have hope: white count, temp, heart rate. The whole is death. It's the dream of cure.

In early times, physicians had no diagnostic skills beyond what they could see, maybe touch. Cure was rare. Early hospital records often failed to record a diagnosis. The treatment for tuberculosis was opium and lies. Then science flowed into medicine. There was the germ theory, which led to a better understanding of disease, which made diagnosis more accurate. Between 1873 and 1905, microorganisms were discovered in conditions from relapsing fever to anthrax to syphilis. Vaccines were developed against rabies, typhoid, and bubonic plague. Every disease would have its magic bullet. Medicine would become the curing profession. But disease didn't vanish. It seemed to disappear but then it came back. They called it the "restless tide." Still, people in the hospital dream the dream. The unit's busy. They're wheeling in an ER admission, an overdose. He's covered in soot, like a chimney sweep. The ER nurse is talking. The ER nurses are young, thin, tough. They're like rodeo riders. "He threw up the charcoal on the way. The nasogastric tube came out. His mother is craaaaaazy. She's outside yelling. 'Don't give him any drugs.'"

We're getting a trauma from Taos. Sue is opening the doors in Nine. "They're on the roof. He's got a systolic of fifty-five. His last crit was seventeen. He's intubated. Call Murphy. Intubated. Jesus. Call Derek and tell him to bring a vent. Tell Murphy he needs to come right away."

Lawson's mother reads constantly. Magazines. Books. She has her feet up on a chair. When I need to get by, she apologizes even though I tell her it's all right. She's easy to talk to. She's almost part of the unit. She stays at night, sleeping in the recliner, a white hospital blanket over her. She knows everyone by name. She's friendly with the housekeepers who mop the floors and the guys who change the trash barrels. "It was quiet yesterday.

Dana told me I couldn't say that." The word *quiet* she whispers. "I could say it was peaceful, or it wasn't busy, but I couldn't say that."

In early hospitals, nurses were drawn from recovered patients. At the Pennsylvania Hospital, a Mary Falconer who died in 1805 was "3 years a patient, near two years Matron, and about 18 years a nurse in the house." We come from the same soil. The families, their stories, their guilt, fear, recrimination, their hopes. Their lives echo in ours. Divorce, mistakes, the rough road. Charles Rosenberg wrote of the early hospital, "Society reconstructed itself within the hospital. At least two subcultures coexisted within the hospital: that of the patients and attendants who cared for them, on the one hand, and that of the hospital's lay trustees, medical staff and superintendent. The recruitment of the medical staff guaranteed a maximum social distance between the doctor and patient."

I ask her about the picture of Lawson in the baseball uniform. "I tell him how he's going to be in the big leagues some day and take care of his mother," she says. "He's cool under pressure." I know how much she loves him. Every time they left the ICU, Joan Didion's husband, Gregory Dunne, would whisper to his daughter, "More than one more day." The phrase is from the movie *Robin and Marian* where Audrey Hepburn, as Maid Marian, says to Sean Connery, who is Robin Hood, "I love you more than even one more day."

A different neurosurgeon today. A short man; he is African American. He's talking to Michelle and some student nurses. "What's the difference between a ham sandwich and a blow job?" Some of them laugh. He looks at a small woman in whites, Asian. She says, "I don't know." He puts his arm around her and says, "Let me take you out to lunch."

Michelle says, "What goes in pink and hard and comes out soft?" Nobody guesses, so she says, "Bubble gum."

"As a black man, I resent that," the neurosurgeon says.

He brings the CT up on the computer screen. "They won't get the diagnosis they expect. He's got a subdural." He says to the resident, "There's brain, skull, blood." He puts his index finger on a small white area on the right side. Blood. "We'll have to watch this."

"Can you talk to the family?" I ask him.

"There's nothing to say. There's no change."

Medicine does seem like a path that some see and others don't, a fruit on the tree you can pick or not pick. Ellen Rothman says, "I first thought

of applying to medical school at the end of my sophomore year in col-
lege but didn't make up my mind until the middle of my junior year."
She originally planned to major in the classics and follow that with a
career in law, "preferably constitutional law." That changed when she
took an introductory course in biology for her science requirement. She
loved it. She wrote on political and social issues for the Yale Scientific
Magazine. *She prepared for a career in medical ethics. In* What Patients
Taught Me, *Audrey Young says she "first imagined becoming a doctor in*
the foggy swirl of high school in suburban Seattle, where my peers were
the children of lawyers and physicians." She set off for Berkeley "feeling
intellectual resonance for medicine where many students entertained at
least evanescent thoughts of becoming a doctor." Even when I worked
at Cooley Dickinson, I never thought about becoming a nurse. I was an
English major. I was reading Joyce and Beckett. I was young. Working
in a hospital was one of those jobs you have before you begin your life,
like when you hike in the White Mountains and you have to walk two or
even three miles in the woods before you reach the real trail, before you
start to climb.

We became nurses late in life. We were living in Minnesota. I was
studying theology at St. John's. Loren was taking courses at the sister
college, St. Benedict's. We weren't as young then. Life began to seem like
the sound of doors closing or of hallways too long to walk. We moved
to Dorset, Vermont. Loren decided to go to nursing school. She went
to Castleton State College then worked at Rutland Community Hos-
pital then at Mary Hitchcock in New Hampshire. After she graduated
I went to nursing school. We moved from Dorset to Pittsford. There's
a sign on Route 7 when you enter Pittsford saying, "Welcome to Sun-
shine Village." We left Vermont the summer I graduated. Loren drove
our red VW Jetta and I drove a 1994 rust bucket SAAB. We had ev-
erything we owned on top of the cars. Loren's father gave us two-way
radios. We called ourselves Uly and Lope for Ulysses and Penelope. We
could listen to the truckers. We were only separated once and that was
on the bypass around Cleveland. We saw the Badlands at dusk. At a
rest stop in Missouri a man with long black hair asked me if I knew
how far away Wichita was. He pronounced it Wi-chee-tah. In Raton we
stopped for gas next to four kids with shaved heads and thin as knives
in a long, white lowrider. We arrived in Santa Fe on July 4 and stopped
at a fast-food place, Sonic, on Cerrillos Road, parked in one of the
pull-ups, and the sky opened and more rain than I had ever seen in my

whole life flooded the streets, and cars crawled single file on the camber of the three-lane road. It was a monsoon, the first of the summer.

A child comes into the nurses' area, where she shouldn't be. "Have you seen my daddy's rosary?" She's cute, stocky. She's smiling. She looks maybe seven or eight.

"How old are you?" Sue asks her.

"Thirteen. I'm small." She's wearing a shiny Green Bay Packer football shirt with the number 4 in front.

"Which one is your dad?" I ask.

She points to Bed Two. He's a prisoner. Tried to hang himself on a TV cord. He has a terrible CT. Anoxic injury. I can see him coughing violently, his face bright red. His wife is by his side. There's a guard sitting in a chair in the corner even though the patient's not going anywhere but to a nursing home for the rest of his life. They've already done a tracheostomy and put in a feeding tube. The feeding tube is called a PEG. They go down through the esophagus into the stomach, make an incision, and pull it out through the skin. It's a little rubber thing. He'll never be able to feed himself. When they say about a patient, "Trach and PEG Wednesday," you know it's over.

"Let's go find your daddy's rosary, sweetie." Michelle takes her by the hand.

"You like Brett Favre?" I ask her.

She turns her head. "Who?"

Kevin, the respiratory therapist, comes out of Bed Six.

"Can someone help with an a-line?" Kevin's a big guy, maybe six four. He's from back east too, but he's from New York.

"What's wrong?"

"She needs another pair of eyes."

It's Maestas. The a-line is a catheter in his right radial artery that gives you real-time blood pressure. The waveform is red. The numbers are 54/25. Lori pulls the blue pigtail on the transducer and a crisp wave appears with two spikes. "It looks accurate." I look down at him. He's awake, his eyes open under the glasses. He's staring right at me, as if he's wondering what's going on. His heart rate is 140. There are four of us in the room.

"He just had four liters of fluid taken off, thirty-six from dialysis and four hundred from the tap," Colleen says. She is standing at the side of the bed, looking at the monitor.

"They tapped him again?"

"He does this after dialysis, his pressure goes soft," Dana says. Everybody in the room has taken care of him. You feel like you know him. "He'll bounce back."

"What's he on?"

"Levophed."

"Crank it up. You're giving him a bolus?"

"OK," she says.

We leave, but it isn't more than four minutes later, the time it has taken us to drift back to our own rooms: "I need help!" It was like a yelp. Like if you stepped on a dog's tail. It was Colleen. Tina already has the crash cart in the room, has ripped off the plastic lock, pulled opened the med drawer.

Dana is standing next to the vent, bent over, her arms locked in CPR. He's off the vent. Kevin is bagging him.

"Do you want a board?"

"It's in CPR mode. It's like a rock beneath him."

Dana is moving like a piston. The a-line is spiking in rhythm with the compressions.

"Can somebody move these lines?" Kevin asks.

"We need drugs."

"Atropine or epi?"

"Epi."

"What happened?"

"He just crashed." Colleen is ducking under someone's arms to get to his IV and give the drugs. You can barely see her through arms and legs and lines. Just her voice like a bird hidden in a tree.

"Epi's in."

"Do you feel a pulse?"

"With compressions."

"Open up that saline."

"Is somebody recording this?"

Morgan is here. "Stop CPR. Let's see what he's got."

The a-line spikes go lower and lower then the line flattens.

"Continue CPR," Morgan says. "Give him a milligram of epi and an amp of bicarb."

"Epi and bicarb?" Lori is recording on a clipboard. "That's two epis."

"Let's switch," I tell Dana. We rotate like dance partners.

I find the groove of his sternum and push down. I feel bones crack in his chest like twigs crack under your feet in the forest.

A pharmacist is in the room. 'Do you want an epi drip?'

"We have Levo going," Colleen says.

"Thanks, we don't need it. Stop CPR." Morgan says.

We look at the monitor. Ten seconds. "Keep pumping."

Two ER doctors come into the room. They come to codes, even to the ICU. One of them has a turban coiled like a fat snake on his head. He's young and white. A Sikh from the commune in Española. I've seen others like him at Whole Foods. Dressed head to toe in white robes. Some drive Toyotas, Hondas. The other doctor is the one who kept Maestas.

"Who's running the code?" the one with the turban asks.

"Dr. Morgan."

"We've got it," Morgan says. "Stop."

Now his pulse is ninety-four. The a-line is skipping along with peaked waves like full sails at the starting line of a regatta. His pressure is 102 over 68.

"The epi hit his heart," Kevin says to me.

Dana puts two fingers to the side of his neck. "Bounding carotid."

Kevin lifts the bag from his face. I hold my hands over his chest, my fingers still clasped. We are all still, as though someone is taking our picture.

"Okay," Morgan says. "Put him back on the ventilator. Let's get a gas. Let's get a bicarb drip. Three amps."

The ER doctors leave. Lori and I stand outside the room. "Is the family here?" I ask her.

"They're in the waiting room. The mother never leaves."

We can see Morgan putting in a chest tube that fills the atrium with blood. Now I remember Colleen carrying bags of bloody serum. I had asked her what they were. "We did a thoracentesis." I go in the shallow of the room. High on the IV poles are small bags of Levophed and Neosynephrine and inflated white pressure bags of saline.

"Call pharmacy and tell them we need that epi drip," Morgan says. "And let's give him four units of blood."

"We need to let the family in. They need to see this," Lori says.

"I'll talk to them," Morgan says. "Is there an air leak?" he asks.

I get on my knees to level my face with the chest tube. The columns of the atrium are almost full of bright-red blood. The chamber of blue fluid, like a picture of the Bahamas, is still. "No leak." I wonder what's going on. His pressure is falling. The epi is washing out. The atrium has about thirty ccs to go before it's full. The long tube from his chest is filled with blood. I'm next to Colleen. It was Kevin who called us in. I wonder how long his pressure was down. Some nurses will stare at a life-threatening arrhythmia like V-tach or oxygen saturations in the sixties and not believe it, not do anything. I say to Colleen, "I guess it was real."

"I guess so," she says.

Morgan is staring at the chest tube. There's Morgan, some of the residents—Miller, Lucas, Murphy—Colleen, Tina, Lori, Dana, Kevin, and me. Everybody is standing, as though at a wedding and the band is playing and one song has stopped and we're waiting for the music to start again because it's not over. Carvell comes into the room. He's the cardiac surgeon. I wonder what he's doing here. He's tall, thin, with pure white hair, and walks a little as if a wind is blowing him forward. He is supremely confident. He was in special ops. One time I saw him walk by two doctors who were talking about buying guns. He stopped and said, "You never call it a gun. It's a weapon." He raised his hand in the air and said, "This is my weapon," then grabbed his crotch and said, "This is my gun"; then, repeating the gestures, "This is for fighting, this is for fun."

"I need a Foley catheter with a 30 cc balloon," Carvell says.

Kevin is next to me. He whispers, "The resident hit an intercostal. He's bleeding to death."

"What's he going to do?" I ask him.

"Tamponade it."

Morgan must have called him. They say in a riptide you're not supposed to fight it but instead try to get out of it by swimming parallel to the shore, but we're just going right against it. You can kind of feel it, the strength of it.

"I need a sterile scalpel with a fifteen blade." He's not wearing gloves. It's like we're in a garage fixing up a beater.

Tina gives it to him from the crash cart. "Does someone have a flashlight?" He pulls out the chest tube and makes a bigger incision.

"I assume you went straight in," he says.

"He did," Murphy says. One of the interns or first years must have done it.

He threads the rubber catheter into the hole and inflates the balloon. He stands up, leans back, and looks at it.

"Will it work?" I ask him.

"It's bleak."

The music has started. Tina is doing CPR. Kevin is bagging again.

Carvell turns to Lori. "Do me a favor." He is speaking very slowly. "Ask the secretary . . . Where . . . the . . . hell . . . is . . . X-Ray."

"I'm right here," says a tech standing next to her machine just outside the door.

"Just an AP is fine."

The X-ray plate is wet when we pull it out, like something left out in the rain. He's dead. Blood everywhere. From where Morgan had gone in with the chest tube, little streams of blood from his mouth, nose. Trash all over the floor. Empty boxes of drugs, red epinephrine, light-purple atropine, yellow bicarb. A small lake of blood on the floor where Carvell had knelt. It's four thirty. He's naked. His huge belly jiggles with each compression. As though he's laughing at something funny. Limbs splayed. They never closed him, so his stomach is filled with the black foam of a wound-vacuum device like the pith of an avocado. His glasses are still on but that scholarly look is gone. I cover his genitals with a towel that's lying on the bed.

"Thank you," Colleen says softly.

There are more people standing and watching than doing things, like runners dropping out of a race. Lori is next to me. She makes a slashing motion across her neck with her hand.

"We need to stop," she says.

Carvell is watching the monitor. "I'd give it five more minutes."

At the door someone says, "Lab's on the phone asking if you want two more units of blood." No one says anything. No one says the thing we're all thinking: Let's not waste it. No one speaks.

"Get it," Carvell says.

Morgan says, "I think we should stop."

"Any objections?" Lori asks.

"Let's stop," Morgan says, louder.

"Any objections to stopping?" Lori says. The room is quiet. "Code called without objection at 1645."

The doctors stand off to one side. The room looks storm whipped, as though after a thunderstorm, branches down, wet leaves splashed on the pavement. The ventilator is off. The suction is still going. The monitor is blank. We take the bite block out and blood pours out. "I need some gauze," Colleen says.

"What did he come in with?" Carvell asks Morgan.

"I didn't know him well."

"Where did he perf?"

"Never able to find it."

The ER admission doesn't come up until after five. Her name is Mary Vigil. She's relatively young, 48. They still hadn't scoped her. The nurse said, "We've been flogging her with fluids; she's a frequent flier." She's a tiny woman, Hispanic, but her stomach and legs are huge; she's like one of those cardboard things you put your head in and it's your face and below you're Angelina Jolie or a hippopotamus. Her stomach is swollen, yellowish, hard as a summer squash. No chart, no history yet.

They float in like a message in a bottle and then you reconstruct their life. Sometimes we have three or four GI bleeds in the unit. Lori calls them the sad little tribe of alcoholics. It's always the same: blood, lactulose to get their ammonia level down, Ativan for the DTs, restraints, sometimes intubation if they get wild, coags out of whack, and then there's always that person who loves them, who comes in and sits by the bed for hours and hours. But we don't judge them, really. We had a guy who was drunk and hit a girl on a bike. Lori had him. Someone started to say something about him, what he had done, and Lori said, "I don't want to know. Don't tell me. It doesn't make any difference."

GI comes with their machine. The GI doc is Quinn. "We've scoped her before," he says. "Many times." He turns to the bed. "Hi, Mary." Then to me. "Give her fifty and two."

"We need to do a time-out," the nurse with him says.

"There's only one way in," he says.

We put her on her side, bend her knees up, and bring her hands together at her waist so she'll keep them there and not go for the tube. I run my fingers along her temple as you would to still a child. "I think I need a new diaper," she says. She has on a white plastic diaper that's Velcroed at the waist. There's stool dried on the back of her thighs. "I'll clean you up after."

"I'm sorry," she says.

"It's all right, we do it all the time. Don't worry. I'm going to put this block in your mouth so you don't bite down." Her eyes drift as the fentanyl and Versed hit her.

On the screen, the esophagus looks like a slimy cave. It looks too close, out of focus, like when you're taking a picture and your thumb is in front of the lens. Quinn zips in and out though.

"Can't find a site. She'll need an angiogram."

A young woman is at the door. I tell her I need to clean her up.

"I'm her goddaughter. I can help clean her up."

Maestas's mother is alone in the room. She's standing next to the bed. He had gotten sick. Moved back in with her. She drove him to the clinic. Drove him here. Lori and I can see her even though the curtain is almost closed. The sliding doors are closed. Both her hands are on his chest, palms down. Her head is moving. She's talking to him. Sometimes you have an illicit feeling, being a nurse, that you see things that are too intimate, too personal, things you are not meant to see or from just being in the presence of people who have to bear these things. To hear the way people talk to each other—"I love you," "You can do it," "I'm here," "Susie's coming"—the way they wordlessly hold someone's hand, the vigils they keep, the quiet ministrations, to see on their faces the ebb and flow of hope, the sudden premonition of the worst that can happen, how little they ask of us, how they insinuate themselves into the tiniest fold of the ICU, what they finally will have to live with.

James Agee said that when he was in the Gudgers's home he felt like a spy. It caused him to wonder what it was, what he saw, "that so freezes and abashes his ambitious heart." Later, alone in the house, after the Gudgerses had all gone to the cotton fields, he writes, "I am being made witness to matters no human being may see."

Lori says that Morgan told the family. That it was like TV. Someone had sat them on chairs in the hallway. Morgan had come out of the room shaking his head. She shakes her own head slowly side to side, eyes downcast, to show me. How the mother started to cry. That the ER doctor had come back. That he talked with Colleen for a long time. That he went into the room.

"They shouldn't have tapped him," Lori says. "He wasn't symptomatic." She has a big green book called *Principles of Critical Care*. She reads a list of pleural effusions that generally should not be tapped: congestive heart failure, hepatic hydrothorax, uremia, postoperative. Postoperative! Massive fluid resuscitation! She closes the book. "They killed him," she says. "We saved him and they killed him."

Vi and the sisters are sitting in chairs in a row facing the bed. I ask them if they want the TV on. They look at the TV as if they didn't know it was there. "No, we don't watch TV. We're workers." They both laugh. I tell Vi the plan was that he might go to the floor tomorrow and that they would start chemo there. The sisters had come back with white bags of burritos and chimichangas whose greasy fry smell fills the room like perfume. "We want you to come with him. We want you to be his nurse," Vi says. He's sleeping now. Two days of chasing his pain. But now he has much farther to go.

Mary Vigil's room is backlit. The head of the bed is up as though she's sitting in a chair. The goddaughter has left. She seems to be looking at the TV, nodding off, and then awakening. The straw-colored FFP and the red bags of blood are hanging on both sides of the bed. Suddenly she screams.

"Mrs. Vigil, are you all right?"

"I thought I was falling. I dream I'm falling."

"You're okay. You're in bed. You're okay. Are you all right?"

She looks at me with her child eyes. "I'm okay."

"You dream you're falling?"

She nods.

"How far do you fall?"

"I don't really fall, I float."

"So you don't get hurt?"

"No."

"Where are you when you're falling?"

"Different places."

"So you aren't afraid?"

"No."

"How long have you had this dream?"

"A long time."

Just before shift change, her husband comes in. The resident had asked me to call him when he came in. The resident asks him if he wants everything done, if he wants her to be intubated, get CPR, shocked. He says he does. He says it quickly. He's been asked this before.

Bed Six is empty, the room cleaned. The blankets pulled down neatly to the foot of the bed. A clean white sheet. The floor sparkles. The monitor lines are coiled and dangle through a loop in the IV pole like willow branches. The ventilator is gone. The pumps are gone. The voyage is over. Eleven hours of boredom and one hour of terror. "Don't get the fear." Colleen was slow to see it but it wouldn't have mattered.

Bob Feller pitched for the Cleveland Indians. He was a hunter. He said, Twenty-four hours before a storm, flies start to fight and rabbits go out to hunt. No animals died in the tsunami in Asia in 2004. An hour before it hit and killed 150,000 people, elephants could be seen running for the hills. Something happens before it happens. They get a little diaphoretic. Their eyes drift back into their heads. The peak pressures on the ventilator inch up; it's harder and harder to push the breath in. A premature ventricular contraction. Then another. Then another. You try to see it before the pupil blows, before the rhythm goes into V-fib, before it happens.

I'm sitting down to finish charting. Lori is standing next to me. She's holding Maestas's chart. She puts it in front of me open to a progress note. It's a poem.

Death be not proud, though some have called thee

Mighty and dreadful, for, thou art not so

For, those, whom thou think'st, dost thou overthrow

Die not, poor death, nor yet can thou kill me.

From rest and sleep, which but thy pictures be,

Much pleasure, then from thee, much more must flow,

And soonest our best men with thee must go,

Rest of their bones, and souls deliver,

Thou art slave to Fate, Chance, and kings, and desperate men,

And dost with poison, war, and sickness dwell,

And poppy, or charms can make us sleep as well,

And better then thy stroke; why swellest thou then;

One short sleep past, we wake eternally,

And death shall be no more; death, thou shall die.

"The ER guy," she says.

It's seven thirty. There is still light in the sky. Twelve hours is a long day. Being in the hospital, in the ICU, you almost forget the outside world. The windows are on the back wall behind poles of IV pumps, tubing, cables, maybe a vent, the blinds usually drawn, and even if they are open, the windows are small and the view onto nothing, and it's like you're under a bell jar that descends on you at seven o'clock and lifts up twelve hours later to let you out. People are coming in. Shift change. The spade of time turning the soil of the hospital. Everyone comes and goes by the back door into the employee parking lot; swipe your badge to end the shift then swipe again to open the door. Everyone wears a uniform. The housekeepers. Nurses. The maintenance men wear khaki. Transport guys wear hospital scrubs like the nurses. It's like being in an army. Two rivers trickling by each other. Everything else in the world shuts down at night: banks, schools, all the museums downtown, stores. The waiting room is full. Different people. Like they have their own shift change. Time-sharing the waiting room. A woman is standing facing the wall talking on her cell phone. Two young girls sit close together on the floor with their backs to the wall. One is texting on a cell phone. I swipe my badge. The door opens.

5

THE DREAM OF CURE

After its long, historic march, after the cure of so many once fatal diseases, medicine's journey ended, not in triumph, but in crisis.

Medicine seems to look back at its history as something it abandoned. In The Lost Art of Healing, *Bernard Lown writes that "medicine has lost its way, if not its soul. An unwritten covenant between doctor and patient, hallowed over several millennia, is being broken." The voice of medicine is elegiac, haunted by the feeling of something lost, left behind, forfeited, abandoned. Eric Cassell sees it as something "forgotten"; the doctor, too caught up in the role as the curer of disease, "forgot" the role as healer of the sick: "Modern medicine is too devoted to its science and technology and has lost touch with the personal side of illness."*

The history of medicine is a moving away—a long, slow retreat away from the patient, away from the country of the ill. Charles Rosenberg describes it as an inward vision: "That vision looked inward toward the needs and priorities of the medical profession, inward toward the administrative and financial needs of the hospital, inward toward the body as a mechanism opaque to all but those with medical training—and away from that of the patient as a social being and family member."

Earlier, the patient and the doctor looked on a common land. The world was visible, palpable: there was the pulse, perspiration, urination, defecation, skin. Things you could feel, smell, touch. There was a shared belief in the value of emetics, cathartics, diuretics, and bleeding. In the mid-1800s medicine began to harvest the fruits of science. In 1819 Laennec, having difficulty examining an obese patient, rolled some sheets of paper into a cylinder and placed one end to his ear and the other end to the patient's chest. Stanley Reiser said the stethoscope isolated physicians "in a world of sounds inaudible to the patient" and caused them to "move away from involvement with the patient's experiences and sensations, to a more detached relation, less with the patient but more with the sounds of the body." These were sounds the patient could neither hear nor interpret.

In 1850 came the ophthalmoscope, in 1857 the laryngoscope. The next wave of technology—the microscope, radiology, bacteriological tests, ECG—removed diagnosis even more from the judgment of the physician. Now, Lown writes, "compared with the sharp images provided by ultrasonography, magnetic resonance imaging, computerized tomography, endoscopy, and angiography, a patient's history is flabby, confused, subjective, and seemingly irrelevant."

Michel Foucault describes it as the difference between the doctor's no longer asking, "What is the matter with you?" and now asking, "Where does it hurt?" Pangaea breaks up. The world of medicine and the world of illness grow apart.

You could hear him moaning in the unit, the sound like the wail of a fire alarm.

"What's the matter? Are you in pain?"

"No."

"Why are you moaning?"

"It makes me feel better. Sorry."

"No, it's okay. Can you tell me your name?"

"Bernard Fleischer." He's a small guy with patchy white hair, the red scabs on his scalp like burn patches in a forest.

"Do you know where you are?"

"Home."

"No, you're not home. You're in the hospital. Do you know what month it is?"

"September. October?"

"Close enough. It's October. If you're having pain you need to tell me, and I can give you some medicine." They forget the month, the day, day or night. The borders of time dissolve. Joan Didion's daughter spent five weeks in the ICU at UCLA. She described the only memory she could summon as "all mudgy."

It's his third day in the hospital. He is the only Anglo patient in the unit. I look at the history: *Bernard Fleischer, 72-year-old male who presented with explosive diarrhea, in septic shock as well as with left lower quadrant abdominal pain, anemia. He was resuscitated with Levophed and dopamine, was started on Solu-Medrol and broad-spectrum antibiotic coverage. He did develop ventricular tachycardia and responded to medical treatment. He had a history of inflammatory bowel disease and subsequently developed severe Crohn's disease, for which he was hospitalized in the past. He was felt to have a perirectal fistula and now has chronic anemia. He has had coronary artery disease and had a myocardial infarction and stents placed.*

They skip him in rounds. "Surgery is following him," Fowler says. "Hot belly."

His wife comes in carrying a pitcher-type vase with flowers. She's wearing a man's-style tweed vest with big buttons and those pants they call culottes that cover her knees and then stockings for the rest of her legs and boiled-wool clogs for shoes. Clothes you would wear in New England.

"No soil," she says. "Can I play some music?"

"Sure. Softly." From a bag she pulls out a small CD player.

"He's a violinist. I stay. All the time."

"That's okay. But if I ask you to leave, you have to leave right away. Deal?"

"Deal. Do you know what time he's going to surgery?"

"I don't but I'll find out."

The flowers are nice—roses, daisies, lilies. She kisses him on his temple and then sits in the chair and pulls a ball of red yarn from her bag.

In report they said Vigil had been awake all night, crying, hallucinating.

She's sitting up in bed. Soft wrist restraints tie her hands flat on the bed.

"Mrs. Vigil. Hi. Do you remember me from last night?"

She starts to cry. She's looking at a space in the bed next to her. "This is my sister. She's my best friend."

"Why are you crying?"

"She has no fingers."

She looks at me, and then she looks toward the corner of the room under the TV. "That man over there is making a bomb."

Her ascites is worse. Her belly huge, hard as a gourd. Purplish bruises all over her body as if she had been smeared with rotten grapes. Blisters on her ankles and feet like leeches. She's on ten liters of high-flow oxygen. It's going to be hard to keep her oxygen up, her diaphragm pushing against that belly, as though opening a door against a hurricane.

"Help me boost." Michelle has a guy they're going to withdraw on. A towel is covering his eyes and a sheet is up to his neck so only the lower half of his face is visible. Nurses have different ways: some don't put gowns on them; some don't use fitted sheets; some put a gown just over their genitals. "We're waiting for his sister to arrive from Arizona. She called from the airport. We had to say a Buddhist prayer on the phone." She shakes her head.

"Is he more swollen than yesterday?"

"More swollen! His head's three times as big."

"From what?"

"From forty liters."

"Big drinker?"

"Unknown amount of beer a day. He was diagnosed with cirrhosis last year." We boost him up. "He needs to die. He needs a dirt nap."

The H and P, the history and progress, is in Vigil's chart: *The patient reports that at 11:30 last night she began vomiting blood. She persisted in having multiple episodes of hematemesis since then. Last night she fell down in the kitchen, it sounds like because of its being dark, and not because of any syncopal episode. She had a black, tarry bowel movement this morning. She has had sweats and chills since last night.* Her past medical history lists sixteen things, most of them from drinking—bleeding from the veins in the esophagus, then anemia from the bleeding, the ascites that fills her belly with fluid, falling.

In rounds, they say she's still bleeding. Her hemoglobin dropped to six and her hematocrit to twenty-one. There's no attending today. Murphy is leading rounds. Today, his scrub top is different—colored baby elephants with their tiny trunks uplifted and musical notes coming out of them.

"We're going to send her to Interventional Radiology for an angiogram."

"She's encephalopathic," I say.

"How bad?"

"Hallucinating."

"What's her ammonia?"

"Fifty-six."

"She's getting lactulose?"

"Q six."

"What about an Ativan drip?"

"She's not withdrawing. She doesn't drink anymore."

"What about Haldol? Let's give her Haldol one q six. We need to get her ready, so let's give her four of FFP."

Murphy goes into the room. "Hi, Mary."

"Hello," she says. She looks young, but she has two kids who look like they're in their twenties who come in and are very nice.

Murphy pulls down the blanket and lifts her gown. "I'm just going to touch your stomach, Mary." He takes the resident's hand and puts it palm down on one side. He puts his palm on the middle of her stomach. "Little pressure, Mary." She's watching him with saucer eyes. He taps the other side of her stomach. "Feel that?" he asks the resident. The resident widens his eyes like you would do if you felt a baby kick. "It's called a fluid wave," Murphy says. "The ascites transmits it." He pulls her gown back down. "We should tap her today. Let's get an ultrasound first." The intern stays behind to write orders.

"We'll do H and Hs q four and I ordered the angiogram," the resident tells me.

"You should do q six," I tell him. "Q four isn't enough turnaround time. And you have to call for the angiogram. It's doctor to doctor." We have to tell them things. It's like those switches they throw that route trains in the right direction; you have to keep them on the right track. You can't give Dilantin through a peripheral vein; chloride has more calcium than gluconate; what the maximum dose for Levophed is.

Surgery is outside Fleischer's room. "We're doing him later today."

"What's he got?"

"We'll know when we open him up."

"He's still on amiodarone."

"We'll let Cardiology handle that."

He moves the chart toward me. It's open to the consent form. "Can you witness this for me?"

Ellen Rothman's journey seems to be the four years of medical school. The first year she studies normal human physiology; the second year, disease. The last two are the clinical years. She rotates through Surgery,

OB/GYN, Pediatrics, Internal Medicine, Psych, ER. A big part of it is the Patient-Doctor course, a three-year curriculum where they learn how to relate and respond to patients and videotape their interactions. She receives her white coat the first day of orientation. In the beginning she looks forward to growing into her white coat. The coat, she writes, "signaled our medical affiliation and differentiated us from the civilian visitors and volunteers. My white coat ushered me into the foreign world of the patient-doctor dynamic." It was also a disguise: "It masked my youth. It masked my inexperience. It masked my nervousness."

She has a lofty view of medicine. She sees medicine as the ability to save; if she learns medicine's secrets, she will heal people from self-induced diseases, rescue them from their genetically predetermined fate, understand the human body, the enigma of life.

In the chapter "Naming," Rothman writes, "When I become a physician, I will determine the diagnosis for many people with many problems. I will provide the vocabulary for these people to describe what had gone wrong with their bodies. I will offer the words to explain how their bodies have outwitted them. I will give them a name. Through that name I will link them to other people whose bodies and minds have undergone a similar pathologic process. With the ability to bestow that name, I will carry the power to provide both identity and community."

Fleischer's wife is in the room all the time. I let her stay even during the one-to-three quiet time, draw the curtain across the door and tell her not to make any noise. "Quiet as a church mouse," she whispers, which sounds very New Englandy. She tells me they've been married fifteen years. She says he's a Renaissance man—he worked in finance, taught economics, played the cello, painted in pastels. He was diagnosed with Crohn's eight years ago and had developed bowel incontinence, which had made life difficult for him. She says Fleischer means "butcher," which is funny because he's the kindest man she's ever met. She reads books. She reads Tony Hillerman, Rudolf Anaya. She never sits in a chair unless it's near something—the roller table, the side of the bed—that she uses to help her stand. There's something wrong when she walks, a hitch, and her calves look thin as if she had polio, and she was in New England in the fifties when it happened. I would have had to watch her walk away to figure it out, but I don't and she never talks about it.

They come for him just before one. I take his hand. "You'll come back here in two hours. You're going to be okay."

"Thank you. You've been kind."

I tell his wife, "The surgeon will find you after."

Both my patients are gone. I walk the unit.

The two sisters are in Michelle's room. One is in a chair next to the bed. She has a book on the pillow and is reading aloud in a whisper into the patient's ear. She's wearing sixties clothing: a red Indian-style top with a string tie; yogi pants; black slipperlike shoes. She had walked in lightly skimming the ground like someone who was used to walking in an ashram.

When the father had arrived, the two daughters had shepherded him down the hall, one on each side. A small, frail man. Now they are all in the room sitting in chairs. The room is next to the stairwell and is one of the smallest in the unit. The daughter is still reading. They come to the ICU with fragments—books, memories, decisions—and make for themselves a spiritual structure, eclectic and idiosyncratic, to protect themselves, as if they've set up a tent in the howling winds of a desert.

Michelle comes out of the room with a lab printout: "His pH is seven point one six, PO2 fifty-two, CO_2 seventy-six, bicarb thirteen."

"When are they going to withdraw?"

She shrugs her shoulders. "The docs are getting on my last nerve."

Martha is in charge today. She's short, older. She's let her hair go white, like snow. "Did you call donor network?"

"What could he give?" Michelle says, "His organs are all bad."

"Eyes. You have to call."

Michelle walks away and hisses with a hint of backwater meanness, "You call."

Dana is talking to the wife of Four outside the room. Some families don't like to talk in the rooms even if the patient is on a vent and sedated, they won't even whisper.

"How is he?" the wife asks Dana. The wife is a small woman. She's probably in her early sixties but her hair is colored as black as a teen-ager's. The mascara has leaked, so there are smudges under her eyes. Someone should tell her. She's wearing those new shoes with springs on the soles. She has to look up at Dana.

"Very poor—we're concerned because he's not waking up and how long his brain went without oxygen."

The wife shakes from head to toe, as though an electrical current is going through her. The way hip hop kids dance, like something goes into their head, wriggles the length of their body, and comes out their feet. She's holding Dana's hand with one hand and her wrist with the other.

"He's a brilliant man. He was a biologist; he reads voraciously. He's disabled. He started drinking and I called his doctor. The doctor told him to make a list why he wanted to live and the first thing was 'I love my wife.'" She shakes again. Dana looks at me. They tell us everything.

"I'm sixty-five. I'm going to retire in two years. He had a hundred-thousand-dollar life insurance but they said he could do light duty so they canceled it. The paramedics asked about a DNR, did I want them to continue." She can't talk. She's trying not to cry. I can see her face, her jowls soft like a tarp sagging with rainwater, her black hair like a new frame around an old photograph, staring at life ahead, alone.

"You did everything you were supposed to do," Dana says.

"I felt I owed it to him." She shakes again.

Dana hunches down so now she is level with the wife's eyes. "You should only think about what happens from now on and never think about what happened or what you did ever again. You did everything right. You did. He deserves this chance. He would be proud of you."

"Thank you." She looks at her hand holding Dana's. "Did I break your hand?"

She goes into the room. Dana stays outside.

"What's the story?" I ask her.

"She found him down in the bathroom. She didn't go in right away. She doesn't know CPR. Three bottles of hard liquor a day. Troponin's high."

"What's he doing?"

"Not much. Opens his eyes. His ejection fraction dropped from fifty to about eighteen." She shrugs her shoulders. "Dead meat don't beat."

Mary Vigil is back from the angiogram. Her husband is sitting in a chair by the bed. He has one hand between the metal rails, holding one of her tied-down hands. Hard when you have to explain to them why they are restrained. That they might pull something out, try to get out of bed, hurt themselves. He has a thin, kind face. Wonder if he feels guilty about her getting so sick. End-stage liver is like a train picking up speed; you can see it in her body, ascites flooding her abdomen, veins wriggling on the surface, irises the color of rotting butter, ammonia bubbling in the brain, hallucinating.

A tech is here do an ultrasound. I ask the husband to step out.

"I'm going to turn you," I tell her. "Just relax and let me do it, then we're going to keep you like this for a few minutes."

"I couldn't hold it," she says. She starts to cry. The smell rises as though from a long-closed cellar whose door you opened. There's liquid stool under her and then flowing down the back of her thighs like candle wax.

"It's all right. When we're finished I'll clean you up. It's good that you're going. We're giving you medication to help you go and get rid of the ammonia in your system."

"I'm sorry. Do you hear that music?"

Afterward, I ask her husband when she first got sick.

"A year ago."

"How?"

"Drinking."

"You drank a lot?"

"Yeah, we would finish work and get a bottle."

"For how long?"

"Twenty years."

"You didn't get sick?"

"I got jaundice. I get my blood checked. We always thought I would get sick."

Dana taps my shoulder. "I'm going to CT with Six," she says. "Can you watch Four for me? They just put him on CPAP."

Fleischer's been gone three hours. His wife has already called the unit twice to see if he's back. That guy who went for an aortic tear last year, some secretary from the floor was his friend and had been there in the morning before he went. He had gone early, nineish. The room had been empty at lunch, then after lunch in the afternoon when there are no visiting hours, and then at three when there were visiting hours. The friend had come twice, then the third time saw that the room was still empty and left. I never saw her again. Just before shift change Martha had told me the guy died in surgery.

The pump is beeping in Dana's room. I add some volume to it. There are three people in the room in chairs. Low laughter. One says, "Can you do a reading?" The wife is next to the bed, leaning, so her shoulder is on the bed and her face close to her husband's on the edge of the pillow. On the roller table are pictures—a young man with a beard and long hair outside at a picnic table, another at a campsite. The man in the pictures is thin; by his long hair, bell-bottom pants, it's the sixties. The man in the bed is old, heavy, his hair white, his nose thick, spider veined. She is talking softly now. "I'm not going to let this go on much longer. Don't worry. I love you. You gave me a wonderful life. I love you." They do that. They say things like that. Like a gene of grief that lights up, and then they always say the right thing, the most beautiful thing.

The recovery room calls and says that Fleischer will come back on a vent. They did a colectomy and a Hartmann's pouch. Recovery is a burial ground for old critical care nurses. One of our nurses, Megan, works there now. She says how "cush" it is. They come out of the OR, you give them pain meds, wake them up, send them home or to the floor for one night. They don't even know they've had the surgery. She says they're like drivers who go into a tunnel and come out the other side and then ask if they've gone through the tunnel yet. The ICU is like a tunnel you go into and never come out of, or you come out and the world has changed.

People will come into the unit and say they're here to see so-and-so and you tell them the room and they come back and say calmly, "That's the wrong room, that's not him," or they'll walk into the room and take a step back as if they were hit by a blast of heat from an oven door they just opened. Hartmann's pouch is a colostomy. You can smell it right away. When Fleischer's wife comes into the room she stops, and when she stops her breath stops and goes back into her, but then she pulls a chair next to the bed, sits down, and finds his hand.

Michelle storms by with the crash cart. "They want everything done. She used the wrong language; she gave them an alternative. She said we can keep going." She means Shreya, the resident. Shreya is in Michelle's room. She comes out and goes up to the Pulmonary fellow. She looks concerned that she has done the wrong thing. I can hear her say, "Lactate's seventeen, bicarb drip." She opened a door she's trying to close.

They don't know how to talk to families. They don't know how to tell them it's okay to stop. Doctors will almost never tell the family the patient is dying. Nurses will. Nurses have little phrases. Dana says, "actively dying." Lori will say, "it's irreversible." When they ask me how the patient is doing and it's bad, I'll say, "You should prepare yourself for the worst." Some nurses will try and sell DNR orders. They'll ask, "Would you want to have chest compressions?" and they'll clasp their fingers together and move their upper body like a jackhammer, or, "Would you want to be shocked?" and pretend they're holding paddles onto a chest and then jerk their body like they got Tasered.

Martha is in the room. His heart rate is forty-eight and his pressure sixty-four over twenty-eight. Martha turns to Shreya. "I'm not getting a pulse." She has her weight on one hip and her head cocked at an angle. She looks irritated. Shreya has stones on the rim of her ear like a string of coral islands. The family is standing at the end of the bed frozen.

"Get the board," Martha snaps, "and start compressions."

Shreya asks the family to leave. "No, they should stay," says Martha. I know she's thinking, If they want us to pound on his chest and shock him, they should stay and see it. Martha turns to the father. "Do you want us to keep going?"

"I'm a doctor. I believe in doing everything. As long as there's hope." So that's it, I think. He's small, shrunken. His clothes hang on him like on a scarecrow. The daughter who was reading is behind me.

"We think he's dying. Do you want us to stop?" I say to her.

"It's up to him," she says, looking at the father. She looks frightened now and not the sweet Buddhist of earlier. The father is next to me. I put my arm around his back onto his right shoulder and feel bones under his old-man sweater like I'm diving and discover the water is shallow and rocky and draw him next to me. "Do you want us to stop? He can't recover. He can't come back."

"If that's what you think." His voice is tight. His only son, I bet.

"He's dying. He can have the last seconds of his life in peace."

Now Shreya says, "Do you want us to stop?"

"Yes," the father says.

The Buddhist daughter mouths, "Thank you" to me and with a fairy quickness is at the head of the bed again, leaning, her book open, reading into his ear.

After, the daughters give us hugs and are outside the room holding each other's hands, talking, even laughing softly. How fast, after someone dies, they can return to normal. Like a rack of balls scattered on a pool table and then back neatly in the wooden triangle. Sometimes it's what everybody wants: the patient, the family. Us. Death.

They're going to do a paracentesis on Mary Vigil. Liver failure backs everything up and the pressure pushes fluid into the stomach cavity. What they do is stick a needle into the abdomen to drain the fluid. Murphy sits in a chair in Vigil's room and talks the resident through the paracentesis. I don't have to give her anything, she's so weak. Her eyes are open, the irises yellow, pupils small black moons above a saffron horizon. Flat, her stomach huge, full of fluid as if her body had melted, as if her bones were salt crystals dissolved in the sea. Yellowish fluid pours out from the scalpel cut. They have to put a chest tube trocar into it and sew it in. Only so much you can do. Try to clamp them down with octreotide, give them blood, scope them, tie up the bleeders, watch them for a few days hoping they hold.

Michelle sticks her head out of her room. "Can you help me wrap him up?"

The rancid, fishlike smell coming off his skin makes us gag. He's swollen. His eyelids are golf balls. His scrotum sits on his closed thighs like a basketball.

"Why is he warm?" asks Dana.

Across his waist is a wide purple bruise like a sash, from where he had fallen and lain against the bathtub for three hours.

"Why is he so warm?" she asks again, with anxiety. We stop opening the shroud.

I put my hand on his thigh. He is warmer than any of us.

"The Bair Hugger," Michelle says. "He was hypothermic. We were trying to warm him up. The Bair Hugger was on," and we relax.

"You can't be cold and dead," Dana says. "You can be warm and dead, but you can't be cold."

Michelle slaps an ID label on his leg like he's a package. She lines the shroud along one side of the body and we roll it toward ourselves as she tucks it under.

"What did he do?" Dana asks.

"Musician."

"Successful?"

"He had his moments." She must have talked with the sisters.

We zip the shroud closed. A body in a shroud feels strange right away, even if you just closed it. You get startled by the feel of a leg or an arm that you just saw a minute ago. Frank is our tech. He's holding his index finger in the air. "Put your finger against mine. Now rub them like this." With the thumb and index finger of his other hand he rubs the outside of the two pressed fingers up and down." I do it. "Creepy."

"That's what they say death feels like. When you're dead and someone touches you, that's what it feels like."

We slide him over to the metal gurney and cover it with the fake top of forest-green cloth.

"What now?" Michelle asks.

"Call Security to meet you at the morgue."

Sometimes we'll say—disdainfully—"They want everything done" or "They don't get it." But it's not always their fault, that they're stubborn or unrealistic. Ordinary people dream the dream. It's medicine. Dr. Ira Byock wrote, "A strong presumption throughout my medical education was that all seriously ill people required vigorous life-prolonging treatment, including those who were expected to die, even patients with advanced chronic illness. It even extended to patients who saw death as a relief from the suffering caused by their illness."

When that dream does end, or they finally see through it, people understand and accept death in ways medicine does not. The book the daughter was reading into the ear of her brother was the *Bardo Thodol*. It is known in the West as the *Tibetan Book of the Dead*. It is sometimes translated as the *Great Liberation upon Hearing in the Intermediate State*.

Kahlil Gibran described death as "a little while, a moment to rest upon the wind, and another woman shall bear me." But Tibetan Buddhists believe that when you die, you don't have to come back; you can escape the cycle of death and rebirth. That at the moment of death, you see the Clear Light of Ultimate Reality, and if you recognize it, you get to stay there. It must be like going to heaven. But most people don't. They get pulled down, back into life.

What happens then is that the soul travels through different realms until it is eventually reborn. It can take forty-nine days. The soul misses having a body, so it becomes confused and frightened. It sees visions, angry deities. Someone reads from the *Book of the Dead*—whispers into the dying person's ear—to guide it through these realms: "O nobly born; Fear not. Flee not. Be not terrified; Be not fond of the dull smoke-colored light from hell." The soul is guided to rebirth.

The final words of the *Bardo Thodol* are "Let virtue and goodness be perfected in every way."

So at its peak, medicine was at its end; at the summit, it had lost its way; at its most effective, it had no purpose.

Medicine says different things about the crisis. It sees it as the need to go back. Arthur Kleinman said that physicians needed to return to their time as beginning medical students when they listened to the speech of their first patients with great intensity, with something approaching awe, with respect for hearing the patient's story in his or her own words, and with deep sympathy for the human condition of suffering.

In a farewell address to Canadian medical students, William Osler urged them to recognize the "true poetry of life—the poetry of the commonplace, of the ordinary man, of the plain, toil-worn woman, with their loves and their joys, their sorrows and their griefs. Amid an eternal heritage of sorrow and suffering our work is laid, and this eternal note of sadness would be insupportable if the daily tragedies were not relieved by the spectacle of the heroism and devotion displayed by the actors."

The way back begins on a path of distinctions: between disease and illness; between pain and suffering; between curing and healing. Illness, suffering, and healing replace disease, pain, and cure. Doctors would become savants of areas they had abandoned, lost contact with.

Despite their having left it behind, they speak a lot about illness. David Morris refers to "the country of the ill, the night-side of life. Everyone who is born holds dual citizenship, in the kingdom of the well and in the kingdom of the sick." He writes that postmodern illness is "biocultural," that the changing relationship between culture and biology has "reconfigured our experience of illness."

Illness is an "experience," a distinct way of being in the world. Illness transforms the everyday world; it changes our experience of time and space, of the body, work, relationships. "Illness," Morris writes, "is not something we can know inside and out. Illness is a fluid process that changes as we change, enigmatic, insubordinate, subjective. It captures bodies, minds, emotions, remains at its deepest level inaccessible to language."

Illness is said to have meaning. But the world of suffering is silent, the meaning of illness hidden. One way to discover the meaning of illness is to make a story of it, to make your experience a "narrative." The task of medicine now is to elucidate the experience of illness as it is "lived through" by the patient, to build a bridge to the experience of illness within the patient, to give it voice, to comprehend its meaning. Medicine enters the world of illness by empathy, orders the experience, gives meaning to illness, and restores the patient's humanity.

The biomedical model for medical care is incomplete. The experience and meanings of illness are now at the center of clinical practice. The interpretation of narratives of illness is the core task in the work of doctoring.

Healing is the lost birthright that medicine now seeks to reclaim. Bernard Lown writes that he saw medicine rise to an apogee of respect, amounting to adulation, and then watched it begin a rapid downward slide. "The rot will continue," he writes, "until doctors reconnect with their tradition as healers."

The pursuit of cure led medicine astray, away from the primordial gift of healing, as if science had laid out bread crumbs that medicine followed into a forest but lost its way back. Cassell writes: "As we briefly trace the development of scientific medicine, we shall see how the two functions of physicians, healing and curing, have become separated and how, at least in part, it is the overwhelming success of curing that has caused the breach." It is the healing function, eclipsed by medicine's curing power, that will lead to the resurrection of medicine.

But you can never go back: home again, youth, yesterday. Medicine may look back, but the trail is gone. There are no bread crumbs. And although it never left, it is nursing that inherited the world of illness.

6

NURSING: WHAT IT IS AND WHAT IT IS NOT

Florence Nightingale wrote Notes on Nursing *in 1859, fourteen years after she began taking care of the sick. It is subtitled* What It Is and What It Is Not. *It was written for women who had personal charge of the health of others, which would be "almost every woman in England." The book was not a manual to teach someone how to nurse or to teach nurses to nurse; it was a book of hints. Nightingale believed that "the very elements of nursing are all but unknown."*

What nursing was not, however, was certain: it was not medicine: "Nursing is recognized as the knowledge which everyone ought to have—distinct from medical knowledge, which only a profession can have." That knowledge, the very first canon of nursing, the first and last thing, without which all the rest you can do for a patient is as nothing, is "To keep the air he breathes as pure as the external air, without chilling him."

One hundred and forty-eight years later, in Our Present Complaint, *Charles Rosenberg, the historian of science and medicine, writes that, in its commitment to the person as a whole and not to a disease or organ, to care not cure, nursing has a structural—linked but subordinate—relationship to medicine. But, he writes, "nursing is by definition not medicine."*

Thirty years ago, nurses didn't carry stethoscopes, didn't listen to the heart, the lungs, the stomach. Physicians started IVs. Nurses didn't draw blood. Doctors pushed chemo. There was no defibrillation, no advanced cardiac life support with all the algorithms for V-tach, V-fib, asystole. Since then, a lot of what was medicine has drifted into nursing. Now nurses titrate drugs such as Levophed and dopamine that are like rocket boosters in the body, interpret arterial blood gases, decide what's artifact or arrhythmia, call the code, call the doctor, make decisions all day long.

Suzanne Gordon writes about how increased patient acuity, sophisticated treatment regimens with narrow margins of therapeutic safety, potent drugs, and complex intricate interventions have created a skilled, and largely unacknowledged, area, outside the traditional boundaries of nursing practice.

Bed Ten just died. She came over the U.S. border a month ago from Mexico, gave birth last week, and arrived last night in cardiac arrest. They coded her for almost two hours. They shocked her ten times. They're trying to convince the family to autopsy. The room is dark. When there's a dead person in a room, the room looks different, *feels* different, as though something has gone out, letters missing in a neon sign.

There are three residents outside the room standing shoulder to shoulder, so close the sleeves of their white coats touch. Jacobs I know, two others I don't. Their faces are shiny; light gleams off their glasses. Everything about them is trim; they're like a new ship with white sails: hair moussed, dark dress slacks, white coats. Their backs are to the door leaving the unit. Facing them are several men and women. The women are weeping softly into their hands. The men wear large black felt cowboy hats with brims that rise up like waves and curl back into the high furrowed crowns. They are wearing long-sleeved western plaid shirts with silver snaps and front pockets with flaps that are buttoned. Their jeans are clean and still blue with a pressed fold that runs down the length to boots that come to points as sharp as a woman's high heels. They wear black leather belts with silver buckles as big as doorknobs, polished to a shine. They are stocky men who stand straight, with big chests and thick thighs and their clothes fit them like skin without an inch wasted. They stand stone still, and the grieving women flow around them like fish.

Betty Robinson got a crush injury when a friend rolled a wheelchair over her toes. She waited three days to come to the ER, and when she came they were gangrenous. She's diabetic. Neuropathy. Diabetics can't feel things—cuts, chest pain, have heart attacks and don't know it. Maple trees in Vermont die from the top down; diabetics die from the toes up. The dates on the progress notes are like cairns that tell you where the trail came from and where it's going:

10/16: Pt. had vascular procedure and debridement and subsequently became incoherent, then unresponsive; hypotensive; bradycardic; transferred to the ICU and intubated for respiratory failure;

10/17: Transvenous pacemaker placed for symptomatic bradycardia; too unstable for cardiac cath; respiratory failure possibly secondary to MI vs pulmonary embolism vs flash pulmonary edema.

10/19: Now diagnosed with acute MI, troponin peaked at 48; worsening gangrene, cardiogenic shock; needs temporary pacemaker; acute renal failure; EEG shows global slowing, anoxic injury.

Sometimes you can't tell whether they're falling slowly to the bottom or rising to the surface. She's a huge woman, African American. She opens her eyes when I ask her to, squeezes my fingers, lets go. Long strands of black and gray hair on her chin like a daddy longlegs, little black moles on her face like those sprinkles on doughnuts called jimmies. She raises an arm slowly. Her gown lifts up. Between her legs, down the inside of her thighs are large open wounds. They have wavy pink borders like coral surrounding an island of eschar and look the way islands look from the sky. Her toes are like hot dogs that fell into a campfire. She has a gastric tube through her right nostril. It's to suction, to a little plastic container on the wall that has about two inches of dark brown liquid that looks fecal.

Outside Bed Ten, the residents and the family of the dead woman haven't moved.

Delma, one of the housekeepers, is here to translate. Jacobs says to her, "Tell them we'd like to examine her heart. It would be for research."

"Los médicos quieren examinar su corazón. Sería para la investigación."

One of the Mexican men says softly, "Cuánto se tarda? Queremos llevar su cuerpo de regreso a México."

"How long will it take? They want to get the body back to Mexico." The other men are quiet but their eyes alive.

"We can call the pathologist right now. He could be here in ten minutes. No more than three hours. Tell them we can find out why she died."

"Tres horas. Podemos descubrir por qué murió."

"Tell them we can do it right now. Tell them we have to do it right away."

"Tenemos que hacerlo enseguido."

Silence.

"It will help someone in the future." Impatient because time is of the essence. Death is the teacher and the enemy. Death the wind erasing footprints of the disease.

The nurse is Lynette. She's trim, a biker. She's been listening to it all. The men don't say anything. It's like the O.K. Corral before the first shot was fired.

"Tell them they can just say no," Lynette says.

The doctors all turn to her the way in sci-fi movies those dishes listening for sounds from space all turn at the same time.

"Se puede decir qué no," the housekeeper says.

"Qué va a pasar?" It is always only the one man who speaks. They look like vaqueros.

"They want to know what will it mean," Lynette says.

"We'll take her to a different part of the hospital, and the pathologist will make a small incision to examine her organs. We'll bring her back in plenty of time."

Silence. There's English, then Spanish, then long silences. No one moves.

"It won't help his daughter, but it might help someone else someday."

His daughter. One of the men is the father.

The father speaks, "Este médico puede venir inmediatamente?"

Jacobs can tell by his tone. "Sí, pronto. Call Brennan," he says to one of the residents.

I grew up in a mixed community. I found out later—just as I found out later when I went to college that my family was poor—that most of the blacks in my town weren't African American but Cape Verdean. They were Bravas, black Portuguese. Many had names like Barros, Almeida, Silva, Gomes. They came to Wareham to work on the cranberry bogs. Many stayed. They lived in two areas, Oakdale and Onset. Oakdale is just over the Wareham Bridge, and Onset is way out of town on a road white people called Hershey Highway. On the basketball team I played with Mikey Gomes, David Silva, and Carly Barros. Before a game, the cheerleaders in turn would step out alone and do a cheer with someone's name on the team; "So-and-so, he's our man if he can't do it . . . " and then the next cheerleader would come out and say someone else's name until everyone had been named and then all the cheerleaders would come on the court and say together, "If he can't do it, the team can."

A cheerleader would have the name of her boyfriend or someone she liked. Sheila Almeida had my name.

Betty Robinson's daughter calls and asks if she's had dialysis yet. I tell her it's scheduled for later. Her voice has a southern touch, slow, deep. "I'll be in tonight," she says. "Will you tell her I called?"

I look into the room through the tinted, wire-crossed windows. Betty's feet are on pillows to float her heels. Her toes are a pure black, the little toe twisted and gnarled like a tree scorched to black in a fire. On one page in the chart is a short note: *Gangrenosity followed by vascular; no active management; amputate when pt. better.*

In rounds, Morgan complains of problems placing Robinson into long-term care because of the military issue. The daughter is in the military.

"She's into the chronic stage." They all nod. They're tired of her. There's nothing to learn. She's sick but she's a puzzle all put together. "We need to get her to Vencor—or whatever the rehab hospital is called now."

"Kindred," one of the residents says.

"Is she breathing over the vent?"

I can see the resident doesn't know.

"She's breathing ten over. She's set at ten," I say.

"Trach and PEG tomorrow. Renal can schedule the dialysis," Morgan says.

They're about to move on, but before they do I say, "Her gas is good. She's alert. She follows commands. Do you want to try her on CPAP before you trach her?"

"She's not weanable," Morgan says.

"Why not?"

He looks into the room. "Poor protoplasm." Some of the residents snicker. "We need to have Case Management see her every day to keep the pressure on." A female resident says, "Maybe I can get her transferred to Internal Medicine."

"If you do that, that would be a miracle."

"She has an NG to suction," I say. "It looks fecal. She hasn't had a bowel movement in three days."

Morgan nods. "We don't want her to get a megacolon. She's at risk for that."

He says to the female resident, "You get her off my service and you'll be on my good side forever."

Terry Mizrahi studied the culture of residents and interns in a southern teaching hospital over several years. Her book is called *Getting Rid of Patients: Contradictions in the Socialization of Physicians*. The contradiction was that they hate patients. They call an admission a "hit." VA patients are "con men." Gomer means Get out of My Emergency Room. A patient who is not medically interesting, who is an alcoholic, who has a chronic or terminal illness, they would try to get rid of as quickly as possible, "turf" to a different doctor or team. Mizrahi wrote that the strongest factor in the socialization of residents—in shaping their beliefs and attitudes—was not the teaching of the attending, not interaction with patients, but their own peers, the subculture of themselves.

Ellen Rothman's journey begins with a five-day orientation hiking trip called FEAT, the First-Year Education Adventure Trip. Her classmates are all beautiful or handsome, gifted, privileged: "Alyssa is beautiful, a bold speaker with delicate gestures and soft movements. Kate, soft and warm. Remu was beautiful with golden brown skin, long, thick brown-black hair, the black of her pupil barely distinguishable from the rich brown of her iris." They have classes together. They are "ER addicts." On Thursday nights they all meet mostly in her room to watch ER. "ER around here wasn't an option," she writes. "It was an obligation. It was the experience of watching physicians, residents, and medical students deal with detailed medical information against a backdrop of complicated personal situations and ethical issues. Through the ER physicians, residents, and medical students—my classmates and I explored who we wanted to be and developed a paradigm for how we wanted to respond to our patients." When someone on ER says V-fib and they know that it means ventricular fibrillation, she sees it as "a moment of arrival symbolizing our induction into the medical community."

Dana comes up to me with a plastic tube. "Can you help me put in an NG in Five?" She says it in a sweet, little-girl voice. "You need to wear goggles." She hands me a thick plastic eye shield. "HIV," she mouths.

He's sitting in a chair. He's thin, cachexic. His head is weaving, like somebody nodding off in a classroom.

"Jason, we need to put a tube in your nose so we can give you your medications. I need you to swallow when I tell you." She gives me the tube. "It's already got goose juice." She squats so he can see her. "I'll hold his arms," she says.

I put it through his nose, there's a little resistance, and then it slides in. "You listen."

She puts the bell of her stethoscope on his stomach. She shakes her head.

"Jason, can you open your mouth?" I don't want to put my fingers in his mouth. I grab his jaw and pull down enough to see the plastic coiled like a garden snake behind his teeth. He starts to pee.

"Jason, wait!" Dana says. "Fuck." She grabs a urinal but he's holding his penis straight up so it's going all over his gown. Dana pulls his gown up. He's shaved down there. Even his balls. Strange. Like it's July and the trees instead of the leaves they should have are just naked winter limbs. Dana lifts his penis by the skin between her thumb and index finger and puts it into the urinal. "We need to put him in bed and do it." He's like a drunk you're trying to help walk. We have him under his arms. "Don't look down!" Dana kind of yells at him. In bed we flex his head and get it in easy. Dana looks down at him. His head is drooping like a sunflower. "I'm going to have to tie him down," she says.

They take the dead woman, but not in the cart with the fake top that lifts up like a magician would use to hide a person, but rather as though alive, with her head on a pillow and a sheet up to her chest. Karen has a nursing student from Santa Fe Community College today. The student wants to go to the autopsy. I wouldn't, but Karen lets her go. Karen is talking to her about preeclampsia and HELLP and telling her to see what the liver looks like. I'm trying to remember: HELLP has something to do with pregnancy and hypertension.

There's a man in Robinson's room. He's a short black man. He's dressed nicely, with a visor hat and khaki pants, a white short-sleeved shirt, a silver bracelet on his wrist. He's standing holding the bed rail, looking down at her. Her eyes are closed.

"How is she?"

"She's stable. They'll be taking her for a tracheostomy tomorrow."

"Does that mean she's getting better?"

"No, not really. But it does mean we can ventilate her easier. And it reduces the risk of infection."

He nods. He keeps his hands on the side rail and looks down at her, a kind smile on his face. "I won't be staying long."

"You're her . . . "

"Brother. Walter. There's five. There's me and her, we call her Bell or Bella, and there's Melanie, we call her Nell, and there's Pat. I've got a stepsister I've never met. My father remarried and had six kids."

"What do they call you?"

"Sometimes they call me Preacher. Sometimes they call me Duke. I was young and I had this pool stick"—he spreads his arms wide—"and I had 'Duke' written on the side. Sometimes they call me Old Man because I dressed like an old man when I was young. I lived in Texas for years. I came to Albuquerque with my sister after my lady friend died. We'd been together for thirty-nine years. I got out of the Corps in California and just drove right through to Houston. I was staying with her. You know how you meet a woman and you become more than an acquaintance. You become friends and you take up with each other. She was older than me. Sometimes she would refer to me as her roomer, her boarder. But we were together. It broke me up when she died. But we had thirty-nine years together. I was two months away from becoming a preacher. In the Western African Methodist Episcopal Church. Now that I'm back in Albuquerque, I'm going to the St. Augustine Church."

"Are you going to stay here?"

"I've taken an apartment in a place for the elderly right behind the church. I figure I'll stay here until she gets better. Albuquerque is like Houston. They tried to break into my car. You can't stop it. It's too much. The drugs. There's too much money involved. You can't stop it."

He's still standing quietly. He looks like a man with the patience to stand for hours without complaint or expectation.

Two of Michel de Certeau's students, Luce Giard and Pierre Mayol, were among the first to write about everyday life. They considered themselves "voyagers in the ordinary." Giard's work is called "Doing-Cooking," a study of what she called Kitchen-Women-Nation. It's about women preparing meals at home.

Giard discovered she lacked the tools to analyze everyday life: "We know poorly the types of operations at stake in ordinary practices because our instruments of analysis were constructed for other objects and with other aims. Our categories of knowledge are still too rustic and our analytic models too little elaborated to allow us to think the inventive proliferation of everyday practices."

So when Giard interviews the French housewives of Kitchen-Women-Nation, she decides not to ask them any questions, not to interview them, not to analyze them, but to just let them speak, to let them talk about their way of doing cooking. She discovers that "they are diverse, living voices that approve of, are moved, and remember themselves; voices that regret, answer, and contradict themselves. They are voices that talk simply about ordinary practices with everyday words, women's voices that talk about the life of people and things. Voices." She concludes, "That there remains so much to understand about the 'obscure heroes' of the ephemeral, those walking in the city, inhabitants of neighborhoods, readers, and dreamers, fills us with wonder."

The dialysis nurse has parked her machine outside Mrs. Robinson's room. It looks like a Zamboni. Walter is still standing by the bed. He lifts his head. "I've got to go get something to eat. I'm gonna get a cup of soup." He puts his hand on his stomach. He turns to the bed. "Someone will be coming in to visit. You're going to be okay"; then to me, "Nice talking to you."

The other place besides Recovery that critical care nurses go to die is Dialysis. For dialysis, they set the machine up, hook the patient to it, and sit there for four hours. The dialysis nurse's hair is Lucille Ball red. She has small, yellowish teeth, a gravelly smoker's voice. Her accent sounds southern. She talks while she sets up. "I'm not from the South. I was an army brat. We lived all over." She had been a VA nurse for thirty years. She complains about women in nursing. "They have agendas. Lots of men at the VA. Ex-corpsmen. They make great charge nurses, but they're lousy at ordinary care."

Dana asks me to watch her patient while she's at lunch. He's back in bed, the nasogastric tube in. "I untied him. Watch his hands. His mother and sister are here."

"What does HELLP stand for?" I ask her.

"Hemolysis, elevated liver enzymes," she pauses. "Low platelets. Do you mean the lady in Ten? Supposedly the cure is to give birth."

In the room, I ask the mother and sister to tell me if they're going to leave.

"Why?" the sister says. She has a droopy kind of face, wide and soft at the jawline; thickish hair flat against her face; sad eyes.

"He's encephalopathic," I tell her.

"We haven't heard that word before."

"It means an alteration in mental status. He might pull out the tube."

"Oh," she says. The words they hear. *Meningitis. Sepsis.* Like arrows sinking into their hearts.

Jacobs is back in the unit. The autopsy is over.

"Was it HELLP?' I ask him.

"No, her liver came after. Probably in a sequence of cardiomyopathy, shock liver, renal failure, pulmonary edema. We'll never know why."

Mary Vigil's husband and one of the daughters are in her room in chairs next to the bed. She's opening presents on her lap. Each present is a stuffed animal: a yellow duck, a penguin, a frog. The three of them are laughing.

"She's a para," Lori says. Lori has her a lot.

"What do you mean?"

"She can't feel anything below the waist. Ischemic cord. T3."

"Why? You mean like polyneuropathy? In report they just said numbness."

"No. Para. Like quad. They think it was the angiogram."

"Will it come back?"

"They don't know. She wants to go home. She says she just wants to go home for a day or two and then she'll come back. She promises. It's her birthday."

The dialysis nurse is pushing her machine from the room the way homeless people push shopping carts with all their stuff in it.

"Thanks," I say.

"You bet."

In Robinson's room there's a large woman whose hair is done up in tight cornrows wearing a loose, below-the-hips sweater over capri pants sitting in the middle of the three chairs. The daughter is standing under the TV; her finger has found the power switch and she's turned it on.

Their being here wakes up the room and the fact that it's dusk and you can see the soft glow of the conch-shaped light on the wall, which is on all day but you never really see. "What's your name?" she says. She's got a big smile on her face. She's a little out of breath.

"Jim."

"You work a long day."

I wonder if I had talked to her today. One of the calls this morning. Now I remember the phone voice. I did. She had asked how Mrs. Robinson was doing and said, "Thank you."

"Twelve hours. It goes by fast."

She nods but doesn't say anything as if she's thinking it over and could tell it was something you might say a lot but not believe.

"What's your name?"

"Chica. She calls me Chica. Don't you, Bella?" She raises her voice toward the bed. "She'll call me in the morning and say, 'Chica Lean, do you want to go to lunch?'" She's laughing. She's full of merriment. The daughter has found a show and pulled her chair to the bed. She's talking softly. "What are you thinking about, Mama? It's time for you to wake up, Mama."

"What does 'Chica' mean?"

"Short and fat."

"In what language?"

"Spanish." She talks to the bed but stays in the chair. "You got to get better. Help me lose this weight." She turns toward me. "She'll tell me, 'Stop eatin' that bread.' I love the bread. They want me to stop eating it."

"How much bread do you eat?"

"I'm down to two slices. I love the white bread. They want me to eat whole grain."

"You need to lose some weight."

"I need her to help me," Chica says. The figures on the TV are talking in flat, robotic tones. It's one of those animated shows, *The Simpsons* or *King of the Hill*.

There's a sudden *whoosh* from the bed. The endotracheal tube has popped off.

"I didn't do anything," the daughter says. She leans back and raises her arms in the air like when you surrender as I put it back, but she smiles a little, her teeth white and glowing.

"It's okay. It just happens. She's okay."

"She's in the army," Chica says. "She's going back to Germany." I look at the daughter and she nods. "Mama, you need to get strong enough to fly. We can chase Philly around the house."

"Jim, give me a shot in my arm." She has pulled up the sleeve of her sweater.

"You want me to punch you?"

"No! It hurts. A shot. The doctor wanted to give me a muscle relaxant, but I said no. It would make me go to sleep." I put one hand under the upper arm she's offering me. The soft flesh slides into my hand as she raises it. It's like holding a beanbag. I press two fingers into her arm.

"It hurts?"

"It's my muscle."

"You know I can't give you a shot. You need to lose some weight," I say softly to her.

"I'm tryin'. I'm cuttin' back on that bread."

"You need to walk. Are you walking?"

"I'm walkin' four blocks."

"You can do it. I know you can do it."

At the very beginning of Let Us Now Praise Famous Men, *even before he stayed with the Gudger family, James Agee had doubts about the whole idea of writing about sharecroppers: "It seems to me curious, not to say obscene and thoroughly terrifying . . . to pry intimately into the lives of an undefended and appallingly damaged group of human beings, an ignorant and helpless rural family, for the purpose of parading the nakedness, disadvantage and humiliation of these lives before another group of human beings, in the name of science . . . curious, obscene, terrifying, and unfathomably mysterious."*

The nursing student is back. She's excited, flushed like someone who has run a 10K or come in from a storm. She's tall, gangly. Her hair is short, a not-natural blonde. She arches her shoulders as if hearing a voice telling her to stand up straight. She's describing how they soaped the table to move the dead woman over, and moves her arms quickly to show how it made it easy, then she says they opened her, and she makes a cutting gesture on her own body from shoulder to shoulder and down to her pubic bone. She's describing the necrosis around the heart, how the left ventricle wasn't that enlarged. She's talking to some nurses and another student who is in the ICU today. They are looking at her like she's a teacher and they are her class.

I would not have let her go. I've never seen an autopsy. I've never seen organs harvested. What I have seen as a nurse I've seen in the course of day-by-dayness, over the years, like in basketball before a game we would tell each other to be patient, to "let the game come to you." Someone like her, a student, seeing that, it's like helicopter skiing, where you get dropped off at some high, unreachable point, without climbing, without the effort.

I'm sitting outside Robinson's room when Chica and the daughter leave. They stop.

"We're leaving. Walter will be coming back. You think of me, Jim."

"I will."

"I just have to lose one of these." She has a hand under a breast lifting it up. "They weigh a hundred pounds each." She laughs. They walk away. The daughter and she are holding hands, their fingers interlaced. They walk down the hall that way, through the doors and out of sight still holding hands.

George Orwell wrote, "Every institution will always bear upon it some lingering memory of its past. Hospitals began as a kind of casual ward for lepers and the like to die in, and they continue as places where medical students learned their arts on the bodies of the poor. The dread of hospitals probably still survives among the very poor. It is a dark patch not far beneath the surface of our minds."

The relationship between the hospital and the poor is older than the relationship between the hospital and medicine. If you look deeply into the hospital, you can see the past, that dark patch. The early hospital was a battleground between physicians and patients. Physicians saw patients in hospitals as the clinical material they needed to teach medicine and to learn more about disease. For their part, patients feared being experimented on while alive and dissected after death, feared that they would pay with their bodies for the board and care they received. Hospitals tolerated teaching but restricted access to the patients. Lay trustees were like levees against a hurricane. Eventually, the levees broke and the medical profession surged into the hospital: the hospital became a medical school. The poor were part of a contract they didn't know about and didn't agree to. In exchange for care they did not deserve or could pay for, they would serve as clinical material for younger physicians to hone their skills. The argument for teaching privileges echoed the argument for autopsy and would echo again in the argument for research and then for organ donation.

At the heart of the teaching hospital is an unsolved moral problem: by what right does medicine transform into an object of clinical observation a patient whose need or poverty has compelled him or her to seek assistance in a hospital?

Foucault put it this way: "But to look in order to know, to show in order to teach, is not this a tacit form of violence, all the more abusive for its silence, upon a sick body that demands to be comforted, not displayed? Can pain be a spectacle? Is it just that the illness of some should be transformed into the experience of others?"

7

CARING

One thing nursing has done is to try to separate itself from medicine. There are doctoral programs in nursing that teach the "science of nursing." Some of it mimics medicine. There's a "nursing diagnosis," a "nursing plan." An early theory was from Dorothea Orem, which says that we do for them what they can't do for themselves, until they can. It's the self-care theory. I like that. It's modest.

Early medicine and nursing were both modest. Florence Nightingale had little faith in therapeutics. She wrote that the physician could do little to alter the course of a disease. Nature heals. What nursing could do was to put the patient in the best possible position to be cured by nature. Medicine and nursing were both adjuncts to the healing powers of nature. It's only as time goes by that people begin to think that they're the ones who do the healing. In philosophy, it's called confusing the signifier with the signified; when you confuse what happens with something you've done.

The philosophy of caring was developed by Dr. Jean Watson in the 1970s, when nursing entered the academic world. Watson was a Fulbright Scholar. She is the Distinguished Professor of Nursing and holds an endowed chair in caring science at the University of Colorado in Denver. She is the founder and director of the Watson Caring Science Institute, whose motto is "We are the light in institutional darkness."

It is not a modest theory.

It is meant to define nursing but it is also a straight-arm to medicine: medicine cures but nursing cares. Empathy and caring are the cornerstones of nursing and distinguish it from medicine. Donna Diers writes: "Nurses observe, listen, test, assess, diagnose, monitor, manage, treat and cure. But above all, nursing is caring. The essence of the practice, and thus the knowing, is caring."

The philosophy of caring pretty much dominates nursing theory. It's like the theory of relativity. It wiped out other theories like the meteor that killed the dinosaurs. But it's not taught in nursing schools. And nurses never talk about caring. Never.

Watson says there are ten "carative" factors: attentive listening, comforting, honesty, patience, responsibility, providing information, touch, sensitivity, respect, and calling the patient by name. Watson says that caring is not just the core of nursing; it has replaced cure. "The future of medicine and nursing belongs to caring more than curing," she writes. Medicine represents "the outdated morality of treatment and cure. Caring is a moral ideal and end, cure is only a means, often a detour from issues of health and healing." Caring is the ability to focus on healing and wholeness, rather than on disease, illness, and pathology. Caring can be viewed as the nurse's moral ideal of preserving human dignity by assisting a person to find meaning in illness and suffering in order to restore the person's harmony.

The carative factors are also in contrast to nursing's "trim." The trim is procedures, functional tasks, the specialized focus on disease, treatment, and technology. The trim is more like medicine. Although the trim is important, Watson writes, nursing cannot be defined around its trim and what it "does" in a given setting at a given point in time.

But Watson goes further. She says caring has a spiritual dimension. Caring means that you can enter the life of the other person. Transpersonal caring conveys a concern for the inner lifeworld and subjective meaning of another. But it isn't a one-way street. The patient and nurse are partners in the healing journey; the person doing the caring and the person being cared for are interconnected. Watson says that in transpersonal human caring, the nurse can enter into the experience of another person, and another can enter into the nurse's experience; together they join in a mutual search for meaning and wholeness of being. Both are changed. What is learned in caring, Watson says, is self-knowledge. We learn to recognize ourselves in others.

The world Watson describes—empathy, sharing, knowing, meaning—doesn't seem like the world of nursing that we live. It feels like the scene in Samuel Beckett's Molloy where the character Moran hears someone say, "Life is a thing of beauty and a joy forever, a joy forever, a thing of beauty," and Moran thinks, "Smiles are all very nice in their own way, very heartening, but at a reasonable distance, I said, 'Do you think he meant human life?'"

The night nurse is Linda. "This is Helen Bardwell. Seventy-six. I got her at eleven last night. She came down from the floor. She was admitted for COPD exacerbation. She gets here with a pH of 6.9 and a carbon dioxide of 111. She had been on a heparin drip for a clot in her left leg. She's been bleeding all night. The first thing I did was turn off the heparin. I didn't wait for an order. She was DNI but the resident on the floor talked her husband into intubating her. It was Miller I think. The intubation was traumatic. I tried to put a nasogastric tube in, but there was blood everywhere. I put tampons in her nose. The resident here in the unit was an idiot. She couldn't get any lines in. We had to call Anesthesia. He was a MacGyver. The a-line is a twenty-two-gauge needle. Her pupils are unequal, left greater than right. I think that's new. They want a CT to rule out a bleed. She's in sinus tach about one fifty. She's got horrible bruising, paper skin. She's on steroids. We pancultured her last night. I bag-suctioned her and got thick, yellow stuff. Pulmonary, she's on assist control, rate of fourteen, 40 percent, five and five. Her urine output has been dropping steadily. I don't know." She shrugs her shoulders.

Right away the husband calls. I just have to say yes to everything he asks, "Yes, she's in the ICU, yes, she's sedated, yes, she's on a ventilator." His name is Arnold.

"I feel like I disobeyed her," he says. "I'm surprised she's still alive."

She's awake. An anguished look on her face, which is small and hollowed, her bones hard and visible, the way granite outcrops in the White Mountains. You could tell she must have been expressive and animated in life so now her expression is clear: terror. I bolus her with Versed. She has the stigmata of resuscitation. An arterial line in her groin. A big IV in the right internal jugular vein. A central line in her right chest just below her clavicle, blood floating under the transparent dressing like a Popsicle melted in its plastic. Band-Aids along her arms from failed sticks, the white tape securing the endotracheal tube digging into her face and around her neck like a garrote.

Miller presents in rounds. He looks tired. One side of the collar of his white coat is up. His hair is messed. He said he tried her on BiPAP but she couldn't tolerate it so he transferred her to the ICU and intubated her. Most patients can't tolerate BiPAP. It's a soft see-through plastic face mask. It attaches with black Velcro straps that go around your head twice. It pushes breaths in. It's loud. It's like a hurricane on your face.

"Wasn't she a DNR/DNI? Do not resuscitate. Do not intubate? She changed her mind?" Kristen—her last name I found out is Sawyer—is sitting legs tucked on the swivel chair again like ice cream on a cone. She takes my chair every time.

"I talked to the husband. I told him I thought it was reversible, something we could correct in a few days. I thought she was DNR, not a DNI."

"Wasn't she on a heparin drip?" Fowler asks.

"Yes. We stopped it. She was oozing blood. Her lines are"—he looks at his notes—"right femoral a-line, right IJ. She was a difficult stick. Looking at the physical exam"—he keeps clearing his throat and saying, "Excuse me"—"she has unequal pupils. I don't think they're new."

"She had a fever of thirty-nine," Miller goes on. "We cultured her. She was in sinus tach. I didn't know if the fever was causing the sinus tach or the sinus tach was causing the fever."

"How does sinus tach cause fever?" Sawyer is like a mosquito buzzing around him. But you can tell they have affection for him, he's like the runt of the litter.

Miller looks flustered. "It was a long night."

"I like fever causing sinus tach, but . . . "

"Her white count is sixteen, down from twenty-two."

"Insulin drip," Lucas jumps in with. It's like Miller is running out of gas at the five-yard line and Lucas is trying to push him into the end zone.

"Insulin drip. Started her on Vanco and"—he's holding the last sheet in his hands—"Cipro."

"Do you still want the CT?" I ask Fowler.

Miller is grinning like a guy who's just finished a triathlon. "I had a scary night," he says to Sawyer. "I was putting lines in a guy with a hemoglobin of three." He looks toward Bardwell's room. "She was scary too."

Fowler doesn't say anything, as though he's waiting for things to clear. "Let's go ahead and do it and then when the husband comes . . . "

Robert Zussman spent 114 days between 1985 and 1987 making rounds with medical teams, reviewing charts, talking with nurses, talking with families in the intensive care units of two major teaching hospitals he calls Outerboro and Countryside, which were really in New York and Boston. The book is called *Intensive Care: Medical Ethics and the Medical Profession.* At Outerboro, the nurses and doctors describe their work as torture. In what he says is standard black humor, they tell the "cheechee" story.

The story is that two missionaries are traveling in a tribal land and are captured by the natives. They're brought before the chief and the chief asks one of the missionaries, "What would you prefer, cheechee or death?" The first missionary thinks for a minute and then says "cheechee." When he says that, the entire tribe descends on him. He is tied to a pole, and each member of the tribe takes turns beating him with sticks and whips. Then a rope is tied around his hands to a horse, and he's dragged in a circle around the camp over rocks and stones that rip and shred his skin. Finally he's thrown over a cliff. The chief comes back to the other missionary, who has been watching this with horror. The chief says to the missionary, "Well, what do you prefer, death or cheechee?" The missionary says, "I never thought I would say this, but I would prefer death." The chief nods and says, "Yes, you may have death, but first a little cheechee."

The point is, death may be inevitable in the ICU, but before it comes, there must be cheechee.

Bernard Fleischer is back in the ICU. The progress notes say

1. *Post-op day 12 sigmoid colon resection;*
2. *Septic shock; resolving; remains on pressors;*
3. *Respiratory failure secondary to #1 and #2.*

At the bottom is a note. *Big picture: critical, cannot give wife a prognosis/endpoint; iffy for survival; moving to long-term vent; feel as do not expect rapid recovery. Plan PEG, trach. I told wife of above.*

It's surprising he survived. They opened him up and he had fecal peritonitis. They couldn't close him and he's gone back to the OR for two washouts and then a third time to have a drain inserted into his gallbladder. Then he gets a clot in his leg, gets anticoagulated with Coumadin, nobody checks his INR, it goes up to eight, gets an arterial bleed in his stomach that they have to go to the OR to sew up. Somehow he goes to Med-Surg for a few days but gets septic and back to the ICU and on Levophed again. His body is swollen and soft like a sponge, even his eyelids puffy like wafers in water; his gown, the sheet, the pillowcase all moist. The blanket wet over the incision a yellowish color like an animal had peed on it. He's on five drips.

I once saw Bela Fleck at the Lensic in Santa Fe play a song on his banjo by playing one string and then turning the tuning pegs to make the song.

That's what drips are like, up, down, on, off, constantly tuning the patient. But he's awake. He lies perfectly still. He opens his eyes when you ask. Turns his head for a temperature. Other than that, he lies perfectly still. I think I understand. If you're perfectly still, no one can see you. The way the rabbit freezes in my yard when he hears me, his ears straight up. Perfectly still. Safe. If you are still, you won't die. If you play dead, death won't see you. I think I would be like that. Be still. Be quiet. Let time pass and hope it ends.

Fleischer's temp last night spiked to 38.8. His white count up to twenty-two thousand. In rounds, Fowler says the CT this morning showed an abscess. "We'll get Surgery on it. He's going to need that drained," he says.

Before, Fleischer's wife had looked smart in the vests she wore, the knickers and clogs, her hair parted in the middle to just below her ears, but now she looks pale, unsteady. His children have come and gone and come back again. Supposedly in the Bible it says that God never gives you more than you can bear. And you hear people say it. I wonder if there's a weigh station in heaven like you see on the highway for trucks: does God weigh ovarian cancer, losing a job, even a flat tire, to see if it's too much, too much to bear, because when I tell her he might go back to surgery today, her shoulders sag just like a weight had descended upon them.

Whatever they believe, people know that this life is once, once only. This person once. Being here is everything, said Rilke. Time is real and fleeting. These hours precious.

Intensive Care: A Doctor's Journal *was published in 2000. It describes the experiences of John F. Murray as an attending physician in the Medical ICU at San Francisco General Hospital over a four-week period. It's sort of a user's guide to the ICU. When her daughter, Quintana, was in the ICU at Beth Israel with sepsis, Joan Didion kept a paperback copy of it by her bed. Toward the end of the book, Murray writes about the morning when he walks in on a code in the ICU. He looks through a window, and this is what he describes: "There is Dr. Ella Andrews on her knees; with her arms outstretched in front of her, one hand on top of the other, she straddles the body and rhythmically compresses the chest of a youngish-looking, disheveled man. The resident in anesthesiology, who has just performed the intubation, is pumping one-hundred-percent oxygen into the patient's lungs. The CCU resident*

places metal electrodes on the young man's chest to try to stimulate his heart. The patient is too acidotic but this is quickly remedied by injections of sodium bicarbonate and increased power in the bolts of electricity. Finally, a feeble pulse appears that is abetted by adrenaline and powerful pressor drugs."

Ellen Rothman arrives at the hospital on July 1. She has no idea how patient care is organized in the hospital but learns quickly: "Inpatient care was delegated to different medical teams, divided by specialty," she writes. "Each team consisted of between three and six residents and was responsible for the care of fifteen to twenty-five patients. A senior resident supervised each team, keeping track of all the patients and their care plans and helping more junior members solve clinical dilemmas. Interns, in their first year of residency, were the workhorses of the team, scheduling patients for tests, performing basic procedures, admitting new patients, and discharging those ready to go home. One or more staff physicians supervised the entire team and ensured that we did not make mistakes or miss potential problems. They were also responsible for teaching. This team structure was preserved in every specialty to train residents and care for patients."

There are 3.4 million nurses in the United States; there are six times as many nurses as there are doctors. Nurses are the largest employment group in the world. Suzanne Gordon writes that nursing may be the oldest art, but in the contemporary world, it is also one of the most invisible. She says doctors don't see nurses as involved in medical care. She quotes a surgical resident: "There's a kind of black box in our knowledge of what happens between the time we write orders and the time nurses carry them out. We just don't really know what nurses do."

I decide to wait on the CT. Maybe we won't have to put her through it. The husband comes midmorning. He's tall, about six three but bent. He's pushing a wheeled stroller. He's got Dumbo ears that come forward as if invisible hands are cupping them, a long face, and saggy flesh under his eyes. He sits in a chair against the wall between the dirty linen basket and the supply cabinet.

"How are you doing?" I ask him.

"I don't know what I'm going to do. Thirty-seven years. We were inseparable." He looks at the bed. "What's going to happen? She wouldn't want to be like this. She wouldn't want this."

"Do you want to sit closer? You can pull the chair up. I can lower the rail."

He shakes his head.

"We could take out the tube and make her comfortable. If she was unable to breathe, we would sedate her so she wouldn't suffer."

"I don't want her to suffer."

"Did she suffer before?"

"It was terrible. She was gasping for breath. That's the reason I agreed to this. I feel I was manipulated."

"We would make it so she wouldn't suffer."

"I would like that."

Two surgeons walk by. One is carrying a lidded coffee cup; the other is on his cell phone.

"It's not efficacious . . . Pretty close to the same thing, like which side of the ocean you're on . . . Most don't go to the neck . . . I would have just filleted the duct . . . Her problem is pancreatitis. Her gut's full of pus."

They stop at Fleischer's room. "We don't know him. Can you give us a geography of his abdomen?" I show him the incision; it's still open and packed with black foam with a tube attached to a vacuum machine hanging on the end of the bed. It's meant to bring blood to the wound and to suck out excess fluid. On either side of the incision are two plastic bulb drains. They're compressed to create suction. They're called Jackson Pratts, or JPs, and when they're full, they look like hand grenades. The gallbladder drain, the plastic colostomy bag with black liquid fluid like soy sauce. The stoma is dark with an ashy halo the way the moon sometimes has a halo around it on summer nights. One of them says, "That doesn't look good."

Outside they look at the chart.

"Why is he on Levophed?" the one with the coffee asks me.

"Septic."

"From what?"

"It's there in the notes. Abscess."

"His INR is five point eight. What are they doing to reverse it?"

"Vitamin K."

"That'll take forever. Today's Friday. We'll do it Monday."

Along the way, Rothman has experiences, epiphanies. In Patient-Doctor 1, she learns how to interview a patient. In Patient-Doctor II, she touches a patient for the first time. The patient is Tracy and she has amyotrophic lateral sclerosis. Touching a patient, Rothman writes, "introduced me to the power and intensity of the clinical touch but also reinforced the futility and failure." She feels the "ominous potential" of her probing hands.

She takes an elective course called Living with Life-Threatening Illness and meets Steve, who is dying of AIDS. She says she is "drawn to these dying people. I was taken by their struggle to be human and to be a better human in the face of their death."

She has a hospice rotation. It changes her: "I felt I was a different person from the one I'd been before the summer experience." Her patient, David, is dying of melanoma that metastasized to his liver. He dies. Her experience is that hospice is not only about dying. If it were, she writes, "it would be too painful. I learned that hospice was just as much about living as dying. The two processes were inextricable." From her encounter with dying "I felt I understood better the value of life."

She hates obstetrics: "I was appalled by women defecating in the birthing bed."

She loves pediatrics, loves the children.

At the VA she becomes depressed: "I fought back tears daily. There were no new admissions. I was sick of reading." After nine months, she becomes tired of the hospital, her enthusiasm and energy worn thin.

Fowler calls and asks me if Surgery had come by to see Fleischer. "Is that what they said? Is that what they said? We're going to do him today. Give him six units of FFP. I'll call Interventional Radiology. I'll have them do it. I don't want to get a call at *night* that he's dying."

Families go out for lunch or a cup of coffee, to make a phone call, come back, and something has happened. It can be that quick. We have to tell them, "We had to sedate him"; "We had to intubate him"; "He's going to surgery in fifteen minutes."

Fleischer's wife is alarmed. "I thought the other doctors wanted to wait." I tell her I think it's the right thing to do. I can't decide if Fowler meant he didn't want a call at night, or a call that he was *dying*. I think it was *dying*.

Two rooms down, outside Mary Vigil's room, Lori waves her arm to me. "Come say good-bye to Mary." They already have her on the bed to go to the floor. Along her side are plastic bags with her clothes. She's sitting up. Under the white blanket, her legs are still. Her husband is here. He's holding two small wooden jewelry boxes with the lids open. They're gold medallions of the Virgin Mary. "We make these," he says. He seems excited. One is on a chain, and he puts it around Mary's neck. "I had it blessed by a priest in Chimayo," he says.

"He made me a ramp," Mary says. She's smiling. Closer to going home. She looks so different from that first day. Her hair is combed. She has on lipstick. Happy. She seems happy.

The transport guys are here. "I think you have everything," Lori says.

The husband gives Lori the other box. "This is for you." He puts his arms around her. "Thank you," he says, and from the bed Mary says, "I love you, Lori," and one of the transport guys unlocks the glass doors and opens them wide off the sliders, and they get at either end and ease the bed out of the room, down the hall, and Mary Vigil gets to leave the ICU and gets closer to going home.

While I give the FFP to Mr. Fleischer, Peggy reads in a chair next to the bed with one arm through the side rail, holding her husband's hand. The book is in her lap, and when it's time to turn the page she does it with one hand and never lets go of his hand with the other. I saw another woman do that. It was with her daughter. She was sixteen. Something had happened to her when she was young and she had a shunt from her brain to her stomach to drain spinal fluid, but she kept getting worse and worse, in and out of hospitals, getting the shunt revised, experimental drugs, but fading away, like something left out in the sun. They hold their hands like that, as if save for that touch, they would float away; all that keeps them here is that touch, the hand that holds their hand.

When I lived in Amherst, Massachusetts, a friend of mine, Henry Lubin, was the chief dentist at the university. He was diagnosed with a brain tumor. He was forty-two. He was tall like me. He lived on a ranch in Leverett. He had horses, a beautiful wife, children. Everything. We were friends because we had children at the same school. Some days I would stop at the Cumberland Farms on the way to school and his Forester would be there and he would have his two kids strapped in the backseat. You could hear reggae music through the closed doors.

When he found out I was going through troubled times, he made me meet him every Monday for breakfast at a roadhouse café near the school. The tumor was inoperable. A month before he died, I took him to lunch at a Chinese restaurant in downtown Amherst that he liked. He spoke slowly, as if he had been outside in the cold and his mouth was numb. He told me love was everything, that he knew now that love was everything and that I should not forget that. Outside on the sidewalk he got dizzy and had to hold on to a light pole.

"Iffy for survival." There's a tipping point in the ICU. You can stay too long. Survival from critical illness is often determined by the number and severity of complications related to life support and monitoring interventions; a "race" between cumulative risk and gradually returning organ function. Chemo kills. Leave-'em-dead-Levophed. Medicine calls it the intensity-benefit relationship. The tipping point. VAP: ventilator-acquired pneumonia. Antibiotics and superinfection. The saving fluid that floods the lungs. The therapy that kills.

The promise of the ICU was that if an organ failed, you could support it until the person got better. Mortality dropped at first, just as it dropped initially with antibiotics. However, Jesse Hall writes, "this hope has not been fulfilled." The reason: "homeostasis requires moment-to-moment adaptive, neural, hemodynamic, inflammatory-immunologic, hormonal, biochemical, and metabolic responses within an inter-organ communication network coordinated by the sum of organ-specific differentiated function." The complexity of the body exceeds the concept of single-organ intervention. Disease is a moving target. There's something more than an organ, more than the sum of the organs. Single-organ therapy seems like horse and buggy, as though we're always a step behind; what we react to happened way before, but we're just seeing it.

Single-organ intervention may prevent early mortality, Hall writes, but in the end it "permits" an extended ICU course, eventuating in cell death in a stepwise manner and, ultimately, multiple organ damage. The restless tide.

Arnold Bardwell sleeps and wakes in the chair, his head on his chest, his arms draped on the metal stroller.

"Never apart," he says again.

"What was your day like?"

"Get up, go shopping, watch TV—we watched a lot of TV. We met in Germany, in a greeting line. She was in the air force. I was in the navy. I was an adviser to Truman."

"What are you going to do?"

"Sell the house. I don't think I'll last a year."

"You can make it. You just need to get yourself over a difficult period. You'll be okay."

"Maybe."

"Can I do anything for you? Call somebody?"

He shakes his head no. "She could be a stern woman, but she was a warm person."

"Would you like to say good-bye to her?" I ask him.

"You could do that?'

"We could wake her up and you could say good-bye to her."

"How would you do that?"

"We would stop the sedation and let her wake up and if she had problems breathing, we could sedate her again right away."

"I guess I would like that if you could do it."

"Let's wait until Dr. Fowler comes."

⋅✧⋅ ⋅✧⋅ ⋅✧⋅

They come for Fleischer. How many times has he gone and come back? His wife this time goes out with the bed, her hand on the side rail even as it goes through the doors of the unit, the way someone walks next to a coffin.

⋅✧⋅ ⋅✧⋅ ⋅✧⋅

Fowler is here to see Mr. Bardwell. It's nice that he comes. He leans down so the old man can see him. "How are you doing?"

"Terrible. She wouldn't want this."

"We can make her comfortable," Fowler says. "We can turn down the vent."

"How long will it take?"

"There's no way of knowing."

Outside I ask Fowler if he wants us to extubate her. "No, leave it in. We'll just turn it down. I don't want to see her struggling. Call me if you need to."

In the room, I take out the tampons, which don't have much blood on them, and the thin black strings taped to the bridge of her nose. Still, her mouth is a mess, blood and abrasions from the intubation. I smooth her hair back with a washcloth and run a comb through it. Take the tube out of her nose. Try to make the last picture a nice picture. I turn off the Versed and the fentanyl.

"What made you choose such a terrible profession?" I forget sometimes he's here.

"Why?"

"All this suffering." He lowers his head. "I don't know how you do it."

Those stories of some old person dying and then the spouse dying a week later—you can see why. That's what life becomes. Each other. Wake up, breakfast, walk the dog, a little shopping, TV at night, sleep. I tell him it could be a long time or not at all. Too much trauma to her system, too much sickness, down too long. But to bring them up, to say good-bye.

Her eyes open. "Mrs. Bardwell. Can you hear me?"

Her face explodes like someone drowning who's suddenly broken the surface of the water, eyes wide, blinking, startled, her mouth open in a gasp for air.

"Don't be afraid. We had to put a tube in your throat to help you breathe. You're all right. Don't be afraid. Your husband is here. Don't try to talk."

She tries to raise her head off the pillow, terror in her eyes, but then she calms. The old man stands and moves toward the bed, his face over hers. "I love you." Her eyes find his and her face softens and relaxes, not peacefully but with a sense that she understands what everything means, that she's dying. She nods slightly. Her head held in place by the tube, her eyes move around the part of the room she can see. From that first frightening moment, her features have composed themselves into bright, curious eyes and the slack, sedated flesh has found its familiar shape, like a balloon inflated. As if everything has reassembled—who she is, what has happened, what is going to happen. "Zeus misses you," the old man says. Her lips move in a small smile. Then she begins to slip. Her eyes terrified. She starts to cough, then gasp, her head rising off the pillow. He can't see this I think, and, moving behind him to the pumps, I give her ten of Versed and two hundred of fentanyl. Her eyes close.

"Did you give her some medication?" the old man says.

"I did."

"I'm going to go home."

He walks away, pushing the stroller. "Thank you."

"Zeus," he says, "is our dog."

Joyce is the respiratory therapist. Fowler had written for a respiratory rate of four.

It's sixteen hundred. Joyce makes the changes on the vent. "How long do you think?" she asks me.

"Not long."

She pulls the chair the old man had been sitting in next to the bed and holds the woman's hand, moving her thumb in a caress along its surface. Someone must have told her what Sue told me when I first came here: no one dies alone.

They call from Interventional Radiology to say they're on their way back with Fleischer, and two minutes later they come through the door. His wife is with them. Usually I tell them fifteen minutes to get them settled, but I let her in. Another drain for the abscess. It's a flat plastic bag. It looks like a flounder. The JPs are full of blood. Peggy stands in the corner of the room while we hook him up to the monitor, back on the vent. For some reason, they taped his eyes shut. He won't wake up for a while. I lower the side rail to make it easier for her to do her reading-hand-holding. I pull the chair to the side of the bed. She looks at me but we don't speak.

Mrs. Bardwell is breathing only the four breaths a minute the machine is giving her. Her oxygen has dropped to 50 percent and stayed there. As if falling, she has found a ledge to rest on. Time goes by. Joyce leaves. I stay in the room, on that ledge with her. Her heart rate picks up, compensating. Oxygen not reaching the far frontiers of her body. The heart sprinting for a goal it can never reach. She breathes over the vent. I give her more Versed and fentanyl. The wind goes out of her sails. Her breath falls to four again. There's a long pause, but her heart settles into a rhythm. Even a heart weak like hers. Being here is everything. Then long pauses on the monitor. The a-line is flat, then all the lines go flat like strings somebody out of sight has pulled tight. I print the strip. Time of death 17:10:37. I call Fowler. "Okay then," he says. The husband's number is on a blue Post-it. It rings five times. He says, "Thank you."

It feels like he's going to say something but he just says, "Thank you for calling."

Frank and I tie an identification label on her big toe, tie her hands together with gauze straps, tie bunny ears so her mouth won't slack open, and put her in the shroud and then into the death cart. I call Donor Services, and some guy named Steve tells me to hold and comes back a few minutes later to say because of her age she isn't a suitable donor. We start to leave for the morgue and discover behind the monitor two patient-belonging bags we have to itemize: a light-brown blouse with a fluffy clown collar, black pants with an elastic waist, a bouquet of flowers still bound with rubber bands, white panties, a book, *My Ántonia* by Willa Cather, a Sony cassette player, earphones, a hairbrush, lipstick, a thin robe, slippers.

After, I think about all that stuff, about how she didn't seem like someone who came to the hospital expecting to die, and that maybe we should have extubated her to see how she would do and how, after rounds, Fowler did, but none of the residents came by again.

The history of nursing is part of the history of medicine. Medicine has always been the care of strangers; nursing became the care of strangers. Nursing went from home and family to strangers, from a religious calling to a trade, from running the day-to-day of the hospital to becoming subordinate to medicine, from cleaning laundry to running codes. Science, technology, the discovery of bacteria, antibiotics, sterilization, anesthesia, the ability to diagnose inaugurated the era of cure, the ability to really treat disease. The rising tide lifted all boats.

Cure is everything. What patients want, more than anything, is not healing, or meaning, or even understanding. There is no hidden meaning, no untold story that would change things. Meaning is not inside illness like a seed in a husk. What they want is to go home, to go back to before. The trim is everything.

It's like a Venn diagram where there are two circles that overlap so there are areas that are separate and an area in common. We have common ground with medicine. We say in the ICU, "Think medically." We don't treat patients in a way different from that of medicine; we treat them medically in a different way.

8

MEDICINE AS GHOST RAIN

*Medicine is above, distant. Like what the Navajo call "ghost rain."
Ghost rain is the dark rain tendrils you see in the West that fall from
white clouds but evaporate in the dry air and never reach the ground. In
the nineteenth century, medicine thought it would be better to be mysterious, incomprehensible. A popular physician's guide advised doctors
to do tests in their office, not in patients' homes, "lest they begin to do
tests for themselves," and, to prevent them from understanding their pre-
scriptions, to "use phenicum for carbolic acid, secale cornutum for ergot,
kalium for potassium, natrum for sodium, chinin for quinia."*

*There are philosophers who study not metaphysics, knowledge, or eth-
ics but everyday life: Michel de Certeau, Maurice Blanchot, Henri Lefe-
bevre. Blanchot says that the everyday is a riddle: it is the ordinary, the
uneventful—"nothing happens, that is the everyday, yet it is the essential
ground of our existence, the source of all that is possible." The everyday
is all around us, yet it is the most difficult thing to uncover. It is where
we already and always are, but we do not see it: it is elusive, "silent, but
whose silence has already dispersed when we try to listen and that we
hear better while we chatter, in the unclamouring speech that is the soft
human murmur in us, around us." The everyday is fluid, invisible, a per-
petual becoming; it can never be something that you "know."*

*To get perspective we step back, and that distance makes us think,
"Now we see it." Certeau describes it as being like looking down on
Manhattan from the 110th floor of the World Trade Center, being able to
see the whole of New York, and thinking you are seeing the city: "To be
lifted to the summit of the World Trade Center is to be lifted out of the
city's grasp. One's body is no longer clasped by the streets . . . nor is it
possessed by the rumble of so many differences and by the nervousness of
New York traffic. . . . The elevation transfigures one into a voyeur. It puts
one at a distance. It transforms the bewitching world into a text that lies
before one's eyes. It allows one to read it, looking down like a god."*

But this "reading" of the city is a form of blindness, what Certeau calls a "fiction of knowledge." You think you're seeing the city, but what you don't see is the activity of the city, the pedestrian movements, the walkers. What is not seen is the people of the city, whose movement in fact makes up the city, who live "down below," below the thresholds at which visibility begins. The everyday escapes the imaginary totalization produced by the eye.

What is called "knowledge" is created by a spectator who withdraws from something in order to observe it, to examine it from afar and from on high but in so doing loses sight of what is actually there.

We walk out of report and there's a commotion in Lawson's room. His mother is standing outside, off to the side. She's still wearing the yellow isolation gown over her clothes. Here every night. The room is crowded. Fowler. The residents. The night nurse, Amanda. His sat is blinking: sixty-eight. Systolic blood pressure seventy-four. It looks like they're getting ready to intubate him. Every person is holding something in a hand—a tube, a needle, a syringe—like a dart they are about to throw at a board.

He had come back to the unit the night before last. He's huge, bloated. He looks almost comical, like one of those enormous figures in the Macy's Thanksgiving Day parade. Or like that comedian Martin Short, who does that fat character who interviews Hollywood stars. His eyes are wide open. They lost IV access. It would be the best thing if he were to die. But probably not this way. Diane has him today and has plunged right into the room. Everybody is wearing the yellow gowns. He has MRSA. It's a bacteria resistant to most antibiotics. It's something you get from being in the hospital, from being on too many antibiotics, from being here too long.

Amanda is on the floor on one knee holding Lawson's hand in hers looking for a vein. The neck tie has come loose from her gown, which hangs in front of her by only the elastic on the wrists like a cloud of pollen she is walking into. There is blood all over the floor. The gown is bright yellow, the blood bright red. Still crouched, she turns her head toward the door. "I'm in. Can someone get me some Levo," she says, "and then can someone get me some normal saline and some Nimbex." She says it all in a super-calm voice. Nobody really wanted him in report because there's no hope, and nobody wants to be the nurse when it happens for good. Jimmy Glick, that's the character.

Gallup is 240 miles west of Albuquerque. You drive out on I-40 past Old Town, past the newer apartment complexes, past trailer parks, old adobes, and then nothing, as if you dropped off a cliff although the road is so flat to the Arizona border they say if you look straight ahead you can see the back of your head. Past Acoma. Acoma is atop a four-hundred-foot mesa with sheer walls. The reservations here are what castles are to Europe: ancient, majestic, mysterious. Past Grants, then desert. Route 66, with its abandoned motels and shuttered single-pump gas stations, runs next to 40 like an old skin a snake has shed. Hogans. A junkyard of cars, metal flickering in the dry desert air like shattered glass. Then just before the Arizona border, Gallup.

Gallup is the largest city between Albuquerque and Flagstaff. It's sometimes called the Indian Capital of the World. It has the largest drunk tank in the United States. One year thirty-four thousand people were picked up for public intoxication. Drunk people who freeze to death are called Popsicles by ambulance drivers. In 1988 Mother Teresa added Gallup to her itinerary of forsaken places. It's in the heart of Indian land—Zuni, Hopi, but mostly Navajo. To the north and the east of Gallup, across Arizona and New Mexico and into Utah, lies the twenty-five thousand square miles—the size of West Virginia—of canyons, mountains, deserts, forests, lakes, mesas of the Navajo Nation.

The young woman is Navajo. Lena Begay. The notes say she presented to the ER in Crown Point with a peritonsilar abscess. Then left AMA—against medical advice—with an IV in her arm. Some family brought her back two days later with the IV still in; she had a fever, headache, didn't know where she was. The spinal tap indicated meningitis. The transport notes described her as alert with "flight of ideas." They intubated her to do an MRI and then kept her intubated because she was going into DTs.

Her black hair is short, with a spiky comb and sideburns that come to points like an arrowhead. She's on the vent. There are two-by-two gauze sponges taped on her arms like confetti from a parade. The night nurse had said they stuck her seven times last night trying to get IVs in. I cradle her head in my palm. Her neck seems supple. Meningitis is kind of a mystery. One of the things young people like college kids can get. The IV fluid is normal saline with vitamins and minerals like folate and thiamine that make it neon yellow. It's the IV for alcoholics. Pharmacy calls it a banana bag. Some nurses call it the bag of shame.

Mateo points to the red STOP sign on the door and asks if he needs goggles. "What kind of isolation is he on?"

"Droplet. And he's a she." The ICU is like a sewer sometimes. HIV, hepatitis C, TB, meningitis, needle sticks, sputum, feces. One of the Pulmonary fellows, who wears a jacket and tie so she looks like Charlie Chaplin, has hep C from a stick in the OR and sometimes she looks tired and pale.

In rounds, Fowler says he doesn't think it's meningitis. Everyone, though, is to take Cipro as a precaution. They order an echo for endocarditis. "We'll wait for cultures and meanwhile we'll treat her with broad spectrum antibiotics."

Before any family comes in, a woman named Karen calls from Crown Point. She says she's trying to get gas money together. The family, when they do come in, is a brother and two sisters. I tell them they can go in, but they stare through the windows and stand even farther back. They're heavy, square, thin-legged, with flat heads and black hair. They speak to each other in Navajo. The Pueblo Indians speak Keres. Keres sounds like a foreign language but familiar, like French or Italian. The sound of Sioux has been described as soft and rippling, like something you would hear through a bead curtain. Navajo is like no other language. Clyde Kluckhohn describes it as having a nonchalant, mechanical flavor, almost as if a robot were talking. A small clutch of the breath that linguists call glottal closure can differentiate Navajo words. *Tsin* means "log," "stick," or "tree," and *ts'in*—the glottal closure—means "bone." There are four separate tones for vowels: low, high, rising, falling. The Navajo language is impossible to learn.

I ask them if they know what meningitis is and then, to explain it, draw them a picture of the brain, the meninges, the different layers, how they cushion the brain, line the spinal cord, which is why you get a stiff neck, that pressure on the optic nerve causes photophobia. They're quiet. They've moved slightly farther away. They're all looking in different directions: into the room, the unit, behind me, at the drawing. Customarily, if they don't know you, Navajos won't look you in the eye. They'll look at your ear, your mouth, over your shoulder. It's because they don't want you to look at them. If you look a Navajo in the eye, it's because you're angry at them.

When Kluckhohn studied the Navajo religion, he said he was reminded of the Eskimos' description of their religion—"We do not believe; we fear." To the Navajo the world is a dangerous place. He distinguished five main formulas for safety. Formula 4 was, When in a new and dangerous situation, do nothing.

The women are wearing football shirts. One is the color of the Denver Broncos, the other barn red with a white number 13. The three of them may not be brothers and sisters in the way Anglos are. There are sixty Navajo clans. They have names like Poles-Strung-Out, Under-His-Cover, Red-Forehead, Parallel-Stream. All members of your clan and of the clans linked to yours are considered "sisters," "brothers," "fathers." That I know of, I never saw a Native American when I was back east. If I had thought about them, I would have thought they were poorer, less educated. But what they are is different from me. They prefer not to shake hands. The Navajos have names but use kinship terms instead, like "This is my oldest maternal nephew." They have more than one name. They have "war" names. They have names they acquire in life, like "Clean Girl" or "Son of the Late Silversmith." Kluckhohn writes, "Names are powers to The People. To use a name very often would wear it out, whereas if the name is kept fresh and full of strength, uttering it may get its owner out of a tight hole someday." Some nurses get angry with the Navajo because they won't donate organs. A nurse will sneer and say, "They'll take an organ, but they won't give one."

The brother and two sisters leave without going into the room or asking me to tell her anything, like they love her or they were here, the way I am used to people doing. On the back of one of the girl's jersey in big white letters is the name Warner.

From the room next to Begay's the sound of guitar music, of voices singing in Spanish. Her name is Dulce Ortiz. The curtain is open. She's tiny. She looks like a fallen leaf, dried up, brown. Her skin looks like those pictures they show when they dig up a mummy or open some pharaoh's casket in Egypt. A man is standing next to the bed with his forearms on the side rails and his head lowered. He comes out of the room.

"Can you tell me how she is?"

"You know, I'm sorry, I don't have her today, and I don't know her that well."

"It hurts. It hurts to see her like this."

"Who are you?"

"I'm her brother."

"You're close?"

"We got along great. She would call me every day. Come around the house. Between you and me, what are her chances?"

"I do know she's very sick."

"I was in that room." He nods his head toward Seven. "Meth overdose. I had a fever. I lost my teeth from Dilantin." He smiles to show me. "I had to learn how to shit again. When to eat. It changed me. I'm a better person. I used to be crazy. I live in Dixon. I go in my camper at night and I listen to the river." He moves his hand in a wavelike motion. "I want to thank you guys for all you're doing for her."

From above, medicine views the world of illness.

The new world of illness may be an undiscovered world of meaning and significance, but the ill themselves are portrayed through the lens of the medical profession as broken. The ill are destitute, shattered, incompetent, in need of guidance, of direction, of meaning.

Illness is seen as loss: a loss of wholeness, a loss of certainty, a loss of freedom, a loss of the familiar world. David Morris writes, "Illness threatens to undo our sense of who we are. Its darkest power lies in showing us a picture of ourselves—false, damaged, unreliable, and inescapably mortal—that we desperately do not want to see. It can wreck the body, unstring the mind, and paralyze the emotions."

Eric Cassell calls it "the world of the sick": "As illness deepens, connections are increasingly cut off by the symptoms of sickness and the forced withdrawal from society. . . . As he leaves the world of reality, the sick person begins to build a world of his own. To the hospitalized patient, the world shrinks to such a small place, scarcely larger than his own body. So pervasive is the helplessness that distress, pain, and weakness may appear to be the only realities. Understanding fails and sustained thought seems difficult to achieve. All control of the world is gone."

People who are ill are said to lack the ability, knowledge, or skills to interpret or understand illness when it strikes. The person who is ill, S. Kay Toombs writes, "finds it difficult to readily incorporate the experience into the mundanity of everyday life; the stock of knowledge-at-hand strangely inadequate for interpreting the existential crisis. Unable to readily fit illness into the typified schema used to organize and interpret experience, the ill find it difficult to communicate the experience to others."

Illness as lived is unreflective, incomplete. The meaning that lies in illness is not known by the ill. Illness is an experience, but an experience without knowing. It is a knowledge that is not known by those who have it.

It is to the physician that the patient must turn. Stanley Reiser said that when we are sick, we are like travelers on a voyage with an uncertain destination; doctors are the navigators who explain our voyage and relieve the anxiety and fear that perhaps constitute the main burdens of illness: "The very circumstances of sickness promote acceptance of their judgment. Often in pain, fearful of death, the sick have a special thirst for reassurance and vulnerability to belief. . . . The sick are not the best judge of their own needs, nor are those who are emotionally close to them. . . . Professional authority compensates for the often impaired and inadequate judgment of the sick."

Where before the goals of medicine were diagnosis, treatment, cure, now the goal of medicine is to understand the meaning of the patient's experience. The act of healing requires that physician and patient have a common understanding of the patient's experience of illness. So how does the physician reach it? By empathic witnessing. Empathy is the ability to experience someone else's feelings as your own. We see, we feel, we respond, and we understand as if we were, in fact, the other person by directly experiencing within ourselves the other person's feelings of desperation and disintegration.

To the silence and disorder of illness, medicine will give voice and shape. Illness becomes a "story." To make a story of illness is "to recover and to reshape the voice that illness so often takes from us." "When people have a chance to tell their stories, they're able to see the meaning of life, to see the path they've taken, and approach the whole of their death very differently." The doctor is changed as well: listening to such stories and responding to them with empathy are for the listener an equally important moral, life-changing act.

Illness is the new world. Medical care is reconceptualized. The interpretation of narratives of illness is the core task in the work of doctoring.

Understanding the meaning of illness is now the task of medicine.

Vi is standing outside her son's room. She is putting her arms through the sleeves of a yellow gown. Going in again. He is naked to the waist, a towel across his groin. He's swollen, his skin so tight it shines like a penny on a sidewalk. Thin strips of tape close his eyes. They've paralyzed him. A rolled towel lifts the tube from his lower lip and another towel is next to his head, but his long body is still at that crooked angle, his head cocked to the side. No friends visit. Two sisters a while ago. To the floor twice and back. Like he's on a bungee cord. This is his third room in the ICU.

"He had a rough time yesterday." Vi's own face is puffy. "We made him a DNR. They're going to start chemo today. Morgan is opposed to it. He's dying. If we don't do chemo, he'll die."

"This way he has a fighting chance," I say.

"That's what I think. If we don't do anything, he'll die. His head is getting bumps. It's been fourteen days since chemo."

"What do the other doctors say?"

"The oncologist wants to do chemo. I can talk to Fowler. Morgan's distant. I never see the neurologist." When she says that, her eyes get small and her mouth tightens and I can see how she got through divorce, remarriage, losing her job, how she can stay in the room day and night.

"How are *you*?"

"Okay," she says, surprised. "I'm okay."

"Still reading a lot of books?"

"My mysteries."

"I think you're right to fight for him. We think you're brave, and we say how strong you are."

"Thank you. I'm just trying to do what he would want. I believe in miracles."

"I do, too."

If someone says they think the patient sees Jesus, I say I do too. If they say they think they're already in heaven, I'll say I think they are too. I believe what they believe. I know it makes them feel better that I think so too, but I don't think it's really lying. We have Christians, Jews, Navajo Singers, medicine men, Zen Buddhists, Tibetan Buddhists, Jehovah's Witnesses, Sikhs from that commune in Española, trust fund shamans from Santa Fe, a Gypsy once, and then just everyday people without anyone else who pray on their own around the bed, their heads bowed or their arms in the air or holding hands and one person praying. I think they're all right. The poet Billy Collins says that when they die, the dead move off in all directions, each according to his or her own private beliefs. Some join the celestial choir, some stand naked before a stern judge, some are in the apartment of a female God, some squeeze into the bodies of animals; the secret is that everyone is right, as it turns out. "You go to the place you always thought you would go, the place you kept lit in an alcove in your head."

I put a feeding tube through Lena Begay's nose into her stomach. She has tattoos on her right arm: a hatted clown with a long, wide mouth and big lips. Below it the word *smile*. A small heart in the middle of a serrated lightning bolt. Inside her wrist the name Karen, with little flower blossoms around it. Her temp has spiked to 38.9. Her arms start to shake and then stop. Her stool is liquid from all the antibiotics. I have Diane help me put in a rectal tube.

"What are they telling Vi?"

"They blow smoke up her skirt. She says she's willing to withdraw if there's no hope. He's been going asystole. Twenty-second pause. His heart's trying to stop. He must have tumors pressing on his heart."

When I give them Begay's temp in rounds, Fowler orders a chest film. "We need to panculture her, send a stool for C. diff. What does she have for lines? Let's change them."

"I don't think it's meningitis," the Pulmonary fellow says. He's pulled up the X-ray. "There's a right lower lobe infiltrate. We should start her on Flagyl."

I tell Fowler she had rigors.

"She's probably withdrawing."

"It didn't look like that. It looked like fever."

"You can give her some Demerol. If she starts withdrawing, we'll put her on Ativan."

The resident Niera wants to put an a-line in even though Begay doesn't need it. Lucas is teaching her. She calls him Tony. He blushes when she does. It's femoral, which is the last place you want to put one. With all the moisture down there, they get an infection just like that. We'll take it out later and tell them it wasn't working. Niera is from India and is wearing sandals without socks and the hems of her scrubs drag on the floor.

More than half the residents are from other countries: India, Japan, Korea. My grandfather came from Ireland. He was a barber. He taught all his sons how to cut hair, just in case. Of his five sons, one was a lawyer, one the head of the Boys Club in Manhattan, one a doctor. My father went to Harvard. We lived at first in Malden. He ran for a House seat in the state legislature and lost. He opened a neighborhood grocery store.

He began to drink. We moved to the Cape. He stumbled, then fell, but before he hit bottom, the branch coming out of the wall he grabbed was cutting hair and though it didn't save him, it gave him more time.

Niera and the other residents, it's like they fly in and land on the mountaintops. Their first and lasting perspective is from above.

Begay's brother and sisters come back late in the afternoon. They still don't go into the room. The first time I told them they could go in, but I gave up on that. Each time they give a snippet of information, like a pearl they produced among themselves in the waiting room.

"She has a female girlfriend."

"Is her name Karen?" They looked surprised. "She called."

"She drinks."

"How much?"

"Two cases a day."

"She can't drink that much."

They laugh. They find my comment funny. Ian Frazier writes that Indians thought the custom of shaking hands was comical. Two Indians would go up to each other, shake hands, and then fall to the ground laughing.

Near the end of the shift, I wash up Begay with Michelle. We change her gown and more and more tattoos appear, like animals coming out at dusk: a bouquet of flowers behind her shoulder, a butterfly in the web between her thumb and index finger, and along the thumb the name Danielle. On her left forearm a spider with four long legs, the word *tsi'yam*, a lightning bolt, vines of a rosebush, a pirate's face, the word *cry*, and below her shoulder, on the deltoid, the face of the Madonna, a shawl covering her head.

My birthday is in two days. Then Halloween. Then El Día de los Muertos, the Day of the Dead, brought here from Mexico. Whole families go to cemeteries and bring food and drinks and flowers to attract the souls of the dead so they will come, and they can talk to them. They make a special bread, *pan de muerto*, of flour, butter, sugar, eggs, anise, and orange peel with strips of dough that look like bones and a small round piece of dough on top that is meant to be a teardrop. They bring tequila for the person, toys if it's a kid. They tell stories, jokes. They wear shells on their clothing so that when they dance, the noise will wake the dead. They bring pillows and blankets so the dead can rest after their long journey. Death is different out here. The graveyards are festively decorated.

Then there are the *descansos,* the roadside memorials. Most of them are where you would expect, where the road disappears around a curve, at the bottom of La Bajada, on the interstate, intersections where you could see how the accident could happen; they're like captions of a picture you can imagine. But some are on straightaways, on flat roads, and you can't imagine how it happened. There's one like that near our house.

We live near the village of Cerrillos. Cerrillos is one of three mining towns between Santa Fe and Albuquerque. Except for some upscale homes in a development called San Marcos scattered on the desert like the beginnings of a Monopoly game, the seven miles of Highway 14 before our house are prairie. The *descanso* is next to a metal road barrier on the dirt edge of the road. The road is flat. No curves. No hills. There's nothing else there. You can see the Sangres; you can see the Jemez, the Galisteo Mesa; you can see forever in every direction.

The *descansos* change with the holidays. You never see it happen, but people come and decorate. It's not just on the big holidays like Christmas but on Valentine's Day, Easter. For Halloween, there's a scarecrow figure hanging from a black metal pole with a yellow beak like a banana, a straw hat, and blue suspenders. From another pole a skeleton. A wooden Casper the Friendly Ghost stuck in the ground. He's sticking out his tongue. "BOO!" is written on his chest. A gravestone that says "TURN BACK!" What is always there, through the changing holidays, is a small evergreen spruce; for Halloween, the boughs are draped with white gauze, like fog.

The next day Lawson's name is not on the board. The unit is full, all the patient names in someone's neat printing with a black Sharpie, but it feels like something is missing. Like part of a forest has been clear-cut. The night secretary is sitting in the lounge.

"What happened to Lawson?"

"They withdrew."

"When?"

"Last night. About midnight."

"I just talked to his mother yesterday."

I found Tara, his night nurse. "What happened?"

"He bradied down. His pressure fell, and his mother decided that was enough."

"She seemed pretty determined yesterday."

"What sucked was that she wanted to wait until her father got here but Niera said they needed the bed and they couldn't wait. She made them do it."

"Did he go fast?

She snapped her fingers. "Like that."

"Where's his mother?"

"Gone."

They die when we're not here. We take care of them for days, weeks, and they die when we're not here. They die like dreams. Like dreams you have, that are vivid, that make you sweat, you wake up with your heart beating, and then you can't remember. They die while we're awake, elsewhere. Shopping at REI. Hiking the Atalaya Trail. Sitting on the Plaza. Lawson. Maestas. It's like they weren't real.

In report Maggie says, "Lawson went to heaven last night." In his room is a guy from Española. A GI bleed. "I'll take him," Holly says. "I like GI bleeds."

Begay's girlfriend, Karen, comes in the early morning. She's wearing a long white T-shirt that's sleeveless. She has tattoos on each bicep. One looks like a medicine wheel; the other is an arrow with a name on the shaft. She's wearing glasses with black rims with a sparkling stone in the corner of the rims above her eyes, which are red as though she's been crying.

"I'm her girlfriend. I have some powder the medicine man prayed over. It's the old-fashioned way."

"What is it?"

"Yellow powder." Between the fingers of both hands like a swing between two chains, she is holding a small folded paper bag, the size you would put a piece of jewelry in.

"What is it?"

"Pollen."

"What do you do with it?"

"Rub it on her."

"Can I see it?"

She opens the bag and tips it toward me. I can see a fine-grained powder the color of turmeric.

"I think it's okay." I help her gown up. At first they think it's like a coat but then they figure out you put your arms through the front. "You drove?"

"I had to find someone to watch my little girl."

"You need a mask, too."

She looks at the box of gloves on the table by the door. "I'm not going to wear those."

"Okay."

We go into the room and she walks to the far side of the bed looks down and starts to cry.

"She's going to be all right," I tell her.

"Can you hold this?" She opens the bag and lets it sit on my palm. She puts her fingers into the bag, rubs the powder between her hands, then runs her fingers through the girl's hair, then the flats of her hands down her cheeks. In English she says, 'It's Karen, bay,' then something in Navajo, back and forth, her voice sometimes rising to song. She is weeping, rubbing; "I love you."

When she's finished I ask her what "bay" means.

"Like girlfriend. Like babe."

She says she has no money, no place to stay. I call the social worker who's supposed to handle stuff like this, and she says too quickly, I think, there's nothing—no food vouchers, no housing assistance. "Only if they come emergently." Then she says there's a Presbyterian soup kitchen "across Lomas and down aways."

"Does she have to convert?" I ask her. She doesn't say anything. "I know they have housing on the campus—McDonald's something."

"They're full."

I saw a cartoon once with a Native American father standing next to a little boy. They're standing overlooking sweeping desert, mesas, under an immense sky. In the caption, the man says to the boy, "Someday, none of this will be yours."

"I'm sorry," I tell her.

"That's okay. I can take care of myself."

The Navajo are different from the Pueblo Indians scattered along I-25. The Navajo have no casinos. The Navajo were nomads. They moved their flocks to higher pastures in summer and lower valleys in winter. Anthropologists called it *transhumance*. They were unparalleled masters of the raid. The Spaniards moved the capital of New Mexico from San Gabriel on the Rio Grande to Santa Fe because of Navajo attacks. The Navajos believe their Creator placed them on the land between four sacred mountains. If they can help it, Navajos never live anywhere they can't see one of them. If you look west from I-40 you can see Mount Taylor, one of the four sacred mountains of the Navajo. The number four has great power for the Navajo. There are four sacred colors, four sacred plants, four sacred gemstones. After a healing ceremony, the patient is not to talk to anyone or have sexual relations for four days.

To the Navajo the world is a dangerous place. The Earth Surface people can be living or dead. The dead are witches or ghosts who plague the living. An intricate network of taboos protect against them. The doors of the hogan always face east. A Navajo never sleeps with his or her head facing south. Navajos will never cut a melon with the point of a knife. They never comb their hair at night. In the hogan, a Navajo must not step over the sleeping body of another. A mother-in-law and son-in-law must never look into each other's eyes. But this life is everything. The Navajo don't believe in immortality. There is an afterworld, but it is a shadowy, uninviting place, like this earth, located to the north and below the surface. A trail goes down to it. There is a sand pile at the bottom.

To a Navajo, relatives are the most important thing. The worst a Navajo can say of another Navajo is "He acts as if he didn't have any relatives." Navajo leaders will say, "Act as if everybody were related to you."

My father was an alcoholic. I would stay out late playing basketball and walk home in the twilight past the closed-up summer cottages. I would look through the window to see how much whiskey was left in the bottle in front of my father. I would try to sneak into the house, into my room. I was a child trying to sneak into hell. I used to have to touch things four times—a fork, the TV dial, a doorknob, a light switch. The world was a dangerous place.

The ID attending and a resident are here to see Begay.

"Is she awake?" the attending asks me.

"No, she's still sedated."

"She was awake yesterday," says the resident. It's not true. She looks away from me. She's wearing a lavender blouse with a wide collar and a skirt slightly longer than her white coat. She has hoop earrings, a necklace with a stone. A nice patina of makeup that makes her skin look as smooth and hard as a just-iced pond. A nice black folder for her papers. Lying about what they do must be how they get through these rotations.

"We're going to sign off," he says. "You can take her off isolation. Her cultures came back negative. It's just a pneumonia."

We need to extubate her, I think. I turn off everything, the propofol and fentanyl, to wake her up, force them to take out the tube. Half an hour later her eyes pop open.

"Don't be afraid. You're in the hospital." Can't imagine what it's like to wake up with a tube in your throat and your hands tied down, but she calms quickly.

"You were very sick. You're going to be okay. You have a tube in your throat to help you breathe. We're going to try and take it out today. Just stay calm and breathe easy, okay?"

She nods her head, but her face has a wide-eyed, feral look.

"Are you having any pain?"

She shakes her head.

"Karen was here and she said she loves you." Her eyes widen. Love. "Just breathe easy."

Morgan is the attending today. Niera had most of the unit last night. They're outside Lawson's old room. Holly has the new GI bleed. Some nurses like GI bleeds. Drinkers. Sometimes they're characters, rogues. Some nurses like vents. Some like sepsis. Everyone, though, hates quads, extubated quads most of all. That *click-click* thing they do in the corner of their mouths to get your attention.

I look into Begay's room. I have her sitting up so she can see. I see bubbles on her lips as if she was blowing them intentionally. I suction her mouth. It's full of secretions like a pool overflowing, pouring like a broken water pipe. It must feel like drowning. She twists her head back and forth, gags when the suction catheter hits the back of her throat. "I'm going to suction you. Just relax." But fear has her. This happens, but this is even more: the top of her gown, the pillow are wet, the tape around the tube loosening. She twists her head violently side to side. She has raised her arms as far as the restraints will allow like a dog on a leash, raising her head at the same time, trying to get at the tube. I hold down her hands. Who's near? "Michelle!" She comes and I tell her to push forty of propofol. Not a minute goes by and her eyes glaze as if someone has just hypnotized her.

The team is here.

"We put her on CPAP," I tell Morgan. "She did fine but got too agitated and I had to resedate her. I think we should just wake her up and pull the tube."

Morgan doesn't know her. The resident gives the history. Then they talk about staph negative cocci bacteria, H. influenza, Klebsiella chains and cocci bacteria. They talk about sensitivities. New-generation antibiotics. Finally, like a plane that was off course and got back on, the resident says, "She's got a right lower lobe pneumonia." Then he adds, "Her HIV is nonreactive."

Morgan goes into the room. He looks down at her.

"She has a good gas," I tell him. "PO2 eighty-four. CO_2 thirty-eight."

He lifts the sheet from her arms and then her legs. "It looks like she's into self-tattooing."

"Are we going to extubate her?"

"Tomorrow."

The brother and sisters never come back. I didn't think they would. Kluckhohn says that Formula 5 is an alternative to Formula 4: "*Escape*, which The People select with increasing frequency when pressure becomes too intense; safety lies in flight."

❖❖❖

End of the day. No doctors in the unit. No teams. No families. You can see through the unit as if it were a forest that has been thinned. The day is rolling to a stop. A young woman is walking toward Room Seven. She is tall and thin. Her shoulders are straight and her head sits perfectly on them. She could be a dancer. She's holding her left arm across her stomach as if it was in a sling, but it isn't. She looks in the room, then around.

"I'm looking for Timmy Lawson."

"Are you family?"

"A friend."

There's always a person who comes after, when it's over, maybe she was far away, or she heard late, usually not family, and often carrying something—flowers, a book of sayings, a religious picture.

"He died."

"When?" Her voice is soft. She looks into the room.

"Last night."

She's quiet. She's standing still, as if waiting for a bus. "Is his mother here?"

"No. I'm sorry. He died peacefully. Vi was with him."

"Thank you," she says and turns and walks down the hall toward the door out of the unit. She's cradling her left arm and around her elbow I can see the blue coban dressing they put on after you donate blood.

The Colorado River once ran free from headwaters in the Rocky Mountains south into Mexico, where it flowed into the Gulf of California. It made one of the largest estuaries in the world. An estuary is where freshwater from a river and salt water from the sea mix. The Colorado Delta covered two million miles from Sonora to Baja. It braided into a complex network of wetlands and habitats for fish, waterfowl, jaguars, beavers, deer, coyotes. It was inhabited by the Cucapa, which means "people of the river."

For six years after the construction of the Hoover Dam, while Lake Mead filled, no water flowed. The land below changed. The delta is now 5 percent of what it once was: the waters brackish; the desert pupfish, the Yuma Clapper Rail, the bobcat, the vaquita porpoise, the totoaba, and the Colorado delta clam extinct or endangered.

Medicine speaks of returning, like a prodigal son, to the world of illness. But the world below has changed. Time has passed. The world of illness is a world shaped by the absence of medicine and is a world of its own. It was science that gave rise to modern medicine. Science gave medicine the ability to diagnose and cure. Science was a train medicine caught that sped it forward, a balloon it jumped on that let it rise above, a royal robe it put on that created reverence and awe. But science was also a Rubicon it crossed, and there is no going back.

9

DYING

Qualitative research believes that people don't just do things willy-nilly, that there is a structure of rules and tacit understandings that underlie what people do. Researchers study people to try to make sense of why they do what they do, to experience what they're experiencing. They call themselves ethnographers. What they do: participant observation. The method: watching in a careful and meticulous way.

The first thing you do if you are an ethnographer, though, is scaffolding. Scaffolding is deciding where you are going to position yourself for the study. Ethnographers compare it to putting up structures alongside buildings to support workers, as you would do if you were going to clean the face of the Washington Monument. Or it's like putting up your tent for the night. You have to factor in how close you want to be, how high in case it rains, the angle of sunrise, proximity to neighbors. You have to prepare the ground, no rocks, no tree stumps. Do you want to be in the trees or out in the open? You want to be close, but not too close, not too low. You have to be able to see. Everything depends on that.

If medicine is far away and above, nursing is near. And constant. Twelve hours, if not at the bedside, then just outside the room, always in view. It's as though you tether yourself to the patient, as if you are hikers rope-tied together for an ascent, for the steep hill. If the patient slips or falls, you'll feel the rope tighten. If he or she wearies, you'll feel it slack. Nearness and constancy. Scaffolded from the beginning. A privileged proximity to the world of illness.

One thing I was unprepared for was the dying. The first day of nursing school we learned how to make a bed. The second day we learned how to make a bed with someone in it, something that so impressed Hemingway that he wrote about it in *A Farewell to Arms*. We learned you should turn patients every two hours so they don't get skin ulcers. We learned how to give medications. If you're giving both Novolin and regular insulin, you draw them up clear to cloudy, the regular first. We never learned about death. We never talked about it. In nursing school, I never saw anyone die.

The night nurse said the brother had been in the room all night, sleeping in the chair, and that he was "scary." I looked at the H and P quickly. The history said, *Tyler Nezzie, attempted hanging; length of time down unknown; asystole, epinephrine given, shockable rhythm, defibrillated to sinus rhythm*—then the progress notes—*Sedation off since yesterday morning, pupils equal and reactive, no motor response, no gag, no corneal; suspect severe anoxic brain injury.*

When I go into the room, the brother springs from the chair right to the bed, right by me, like a New Yorker walking past me on Madison Avenue. He's big, maybe six three. Black hair to his shoulders. A blood-red sleeveless shirt. A silver loop earring in one lobe. Thick arms like sides of beef hanging from hooks. But that smooth, sunset-mesa skin. He's young too, early twenties.

There's no stigmata of brain injuries. It's like the surface of the water. You can't see what's below. Tyler Nezzie's been in the unit for three days. The ligature is still there, a quarter-inch cut into a magenta bed around his neck like an arroyo. A scrunchie of thin EEG cables—blue, red, tangerine, and yellow—is taped to his forehead and drawn back over his head.

The brother now goes to the sink and splashes water on his face. He goes to the side of the bed and puts his hand flat over the young man's chest where his heart would be and begins rubbing. He starts to talk. Loud, like you would talk to someone you were walking with and it was very windy and you were trying to get your voice above the wind.

"Let's get out of here! Let's get out of here! Let's go! I'm just waiting for you, and when you're ready we'll go anywhere you want. I've got my check. I'll follow you and we'll go anywhere you want. We're gonna go. I'm waiting for you. We're gonna go. I'm going to show you everything you haven't seen. . . . I haven't seen. We'll see it together. Okay? Okay?"

He sobs for a few minutes, goes to the sink, fills his hands with water, splashes his face, and comes back to the bed.

"Get up. You have to get up. Okay? Get up. You gotta get up. The things we talked about we haven't seen, we have to go, we have to be there instead of just reading about it. Talking about it. We have to be there. I can take you to a place where we can find our roots." He's sobbing. His body is shaking. The palms of his hands are flat on his brother's chest.

Not every nurse likes neuro patients. Lori says neuro is counterintuitive. Usually, if a patient's blood pressure is high, we try to lower it. We try not to fluid-overload them; if we have to, we dry them out with Lasix. With neuro patients, it can be the opposite. We want to perfuse the brain, so we increase the blood pressure, keep them pumped up with fluids. Then there's the smell. Neuro patients have a unique smell, strong, like the scent of cut hay. It can make you gag. It's a mystery. No one knows what causes it. You can go long stretches without a neuro patient. You forget things. What it's called when the pupils constrict and then dilate to light. The difference between decorticate and decerebrate posturing.

The brother has stopped talking and is leaning with both arms on the side rail. I tell him my name, that I'm the nurse today. His name is William. I ask him if he has any questions. He shakes his head slowly. When I start to assess the young man, the brother stands right next to me like he's a student I'm training. The patient's pupils are big, five millimeters, but react. I put my palms on both sides of his face and turn his head away from me. His eyes move back toward me. I tell William it's a reflex called "doll's eyes," and that not having doll's eyes can indicate severe brain damage. I flick his eyelash, dab his eyeball with a gauze. No blink. Sink the suction catheter down his throat. No gag. Squeeze the metal edge of my hemostat until his fingernail blanches. No response. He's breathing on his own, over the set rate of fourteen. The EEG is scrolling. Every so often, under the sheet, his legs twitch like someone who's having a dream.

"Who's making decisions for him?"

"His girlfriend. She's his wife."

"Is she his common law wife?"

"With our people after four years."

"Do you have family?"

"Two sisters. They're at work. They don't have a ride down."

"Did you have breakfast yet?"

He shakes his head.

"You should get something to eat. Nothing's going to happen right now. It'll be OK. You need to take care of yourself. I'll be here."

He doesn't say anything but he extends a big arm and shakes my hand

In For the Time Being, Annie Dillard says a hospital is a hole in the universe through which holiness blows both ways in blasts. The obstetrical ward is the wildest deep-sea vent on earth; it is where people come in. The ICU is where they leave. You can die in the ICU. You can't die everywhere in the hospital. You usually don't die on the floors. Patients are admitted to the floors to get tests, treated, recover. They walk around in their own bathrobes. Jeopardy! on TV. Go to the cafeteria. It's like the mall. Some even go outside to smoke. You can die in the emergency room, but usually they'll admit them to the ICU with brain oozing out, pupils blown. So they can die. You can't die on the table in the OR. Almost never.

The ICU penetrates the world of death the way you can push your finger into the middle of a balloon. What medicine has done is slow the tempo of death. Thirty percent of the patients will die in the ICU. Ten to fifteen percent will die without leaving the hospital. Fifteen percent will die within a year. Some could die at any moment. The ICU is like a heath that smolders with a fire that never goes out and at any moment any spot could explode in flames. For all that, when they die, they die quietly. Ninety percent of patients who die in the ICU die with the decision to withdraw care.

There are two teams on Nezzie's case, Neurology and Critical Care. The Critical Care resident is a thin Asian woman. She doesn't seem to have any cheekbones and it makes her face seem flat. When she talks, she rolls her eyes up and holds them there like she's watching birds fly overhead. She tells me the family conference is postponed from today because the sisters couldn't come.

"Is he seizing?" she asks.

"Not by the EEG."

"What's his Dilantin level?"

"There wasn't one ordered this morning."

She writes a note in the chart. "Brain dead."

"He's not brain dead," I tell her. "He overbreathes. He has brainstem function. That's not brain death."

"His CT shows anoxia." She's still writing her note.

"You can't diagnose brain death by CT. You have to do an apnea test. He would breathe. You can't say he's brain dead. You can't tell the family that."

"We'll try and get them all together tomorrow. They need to withdraw." She finishes her note and leaves. It's short. The last sentence: *Prognosis: death.*

I have Mr. Fleischer again. Fowler says we need to give him a chance to get off the vent or he's going to get a trach. He turns to me. "What's he on?"

"CPAP since yesterday. Five and ten. FIO2 35 percent."

"Let's get a chest film. Do you think he could tolerate some Lasix before we extubate?"

He's not on any sedation, so he opens his eyes when you ask, shows you two fingers, stays calm with the tubes in his nose and mouth, the drains coming out of his stomach, and all the noise of the unit, the overhead pages, Code Blues, stat this, stat that. They can get delirious from just being in the ICU; lying in a bed day after day, naked under the gown, the lights always on, no night. One-third of patients who are in the ICU more than five days will develop a form of delirium: they'll get paranoid, combative, pull out IVs, Foley catheters, even chest tubes. There's a name for it: ICU psychosis. They've done studies of people who have been in the ICU, who have survived critical illness. They have more anxiety, more fear, nightmares, they don't live as long. It takes something to be awake and be so still.

I tell him we might take out the tube today, later. I have my hand in his as if I were going to shake it but I'm just holding it. He nods. People ask if it matters what someone is like, that if he's a fighter, if she's tough, does it make a difference? We always say it does, that if a person is a fighter in life, there's a better chance, and then they always say, "He's a fighter," or "She's tough."

Two women who turn out to be the girlfriend and her mother go into Nezzie's room and go right to the two chairs by the wall like you do when you get on a train or a bus. The girlfriend's skin is sallow, light brown, pocked. Her mother is tiny, her dark brown face wrinkled like a raisin. The girlfriend's name is Tayen. They look like mother and daughter. They must sleep somewhere in the hospital. They can't go back and forth. They live in Black Rock; it's about three hours west.

"Are you making decisions?" The chairs are side by side on the opposite side of the room where the brother slept.

"No, I don't want to. They already hate me and blame me. William yelled at me that it was my fault. We had been fighting," Tayen says.

The story we have is that she had gone out. He was back home with the kids calling her. She got home at five thirty and they fought. She found him later. He had tied an electrical cord around his neck. She found him lying on the bed.

She's moved the chair next to the bed and laced her fingers with his. "The other nurse said he's gone. I'm going to miss him."

"Gone? The nurse said that?" Nurses can say stupid things like that. They say things like "He's in there," or "The lights are on," or "There's nobody home."

The Neurology resident comes into the room. He's dressed in black—black shirt, black pants. He looks ghoulish. He's skinny like a junkie, a blues-playing junkie.

The girlfriend asks, "Are you taking care of him today?"

"I'm with Neurology. We're concerned with his brain. Other doctors are handling medical issues."

"Can you stick with him?" she asks. "Another doctor saw him before. It seems like there are a lot of different doctors."

"I'm the doctor on days during the week."

He touches the cornea with the tip of a gauze. He twists the man's nipple between his fingers like when you turn a key to start a car. He looks at the EEG. "How long has the propofol been off?"

"This morning. We don't have a Dilantin level."

"It doesn't matter. He's not seizing. It's myoclonic."

Outside, I ask him, "Are you going to be at the meeting tomorrow? Critical Care wants to withdraw."

"We don't want to do that. We want to wait a few days. He's not in pain."

"Are you opposed to that?"

"They're the primary team."

"Do you want to be there to express that?"

"No."

The era of modern medicine began with death. Or rather it began with pathological anatomy.

On the very first Monday of medical school, Ellen Rothman has anatomy lab. "Anatomy lab presented my first real experience with death. I faced a roomful of dead people who had chosen to donate their bodies to science. Yet my introduction to death felt backwards. I was thrust into the physicality of death without experiencing the human struggle of the dying process."

It was death that enabled medicine to see inside the body. Before pathological anatomy, death was the end of life and the end of disease. Disease, Foucault writes, reached the end of its course, fell silent, and became a thing of memory. With autopsy, medicine could see death's fingerprints on the tissues and organs. What medicine found in autopsy, it read back into life. The corpse became a text. Richard Bright correlated the symptoms of dropsy—puffy face, dark, smoky-colored urine—with shriveled kidneys at autopsy. Acute nephritis is Bright's disease.

When Marie-François-Xavier Bichat, the father of histology and pathology, said the analysis of disease could be carried out from the point of view of death, the whole structure of medical thought and perception changed: "For twenty years," Bichat wrote, "from morning to night, you have taken notes at patients' bedsides and all is confusion for you in the symptoms which, refusing to yield up their meaning, offer you a succession of incoherent phenomena. Open up a few corpses: you will dissipate at once the darkness that observation alone could not dissipate."

Fleischer's wife can tell something is different. Like one day you know fall is here, the colors have changed, the air is cooler, clearer. I think it was the way he looked at her when she came into the room. "What's going on?" she asks. I tell her we might extubate him today. They're looking at each other. The first time was maybe exciting in a way. Came in sick, treated, got better, but then he slipped. Winter, spring, then summer, but now it's winter again. They're in a season they didn't expect. "When?" she asks.

"After rounds. Eleven. Twelve."

Another woman is in Nezzie's room with the girlfriend and the mother. That makes three but that's okay. We're visitors in their lives, too. The girlfriend cries a lot, but whenever I come into the room she stops or cries sort of soundlessly. Now she has one arm over his stomach and with the other has braided his fingers into hers so they are entwined and then closed as if they are holding hands. The woman is always on her phone, or the phone rings and she answers it, and the talk is always about an appointment, some document, where they'll be when. She's a force.

"I'm not coming to the meeting. I don't want them to blame me," the girlfriend says.

The phone rings. The voice at the other end is loud, female. The woman says William is not here. The woman is quiet, listening. She looks at Tayen. Tayen shakes her head. The woman then says Tayen isn't here either. "Thank you," Tayen mouths.

"My cousin, Erna," Tayen tells me. Erna is already moving deeper into the room for better reception.

"He was good with my kids." Her voice is dreamy.

"He was? That's nice."

She starts to cry and then stops.

"So, what happened? You guys had a fight?"

"Yeah."

"About what?"

"Well. He drinks a lot and, um, he would get drunk and be gone for three to four days. It got real bad starting this year and the last time he left he didn't even tell me where he was at. And like two days after he was gone I finally called his sister and I'm, like, I'm just letting you know that I haven't heard from your brother and she's like, 'Oh, well, he's partying with my brother,' and that's what they do. They drink. And they go."

"So he does see his brother."

"Yeah. When they drink!" She laughs. "So anyway, Saturday was my birthday. I went out with my friends. One night! I have three kids and we both work weekends." She looks over at her mother. "So she comes and helps with the kids but he ended up not working Saturday night, but I didn't want him to go with me because once he starts drinking he gets out of hand. So I told her I didn't need her to come because Tyler can stay home and watch the kids. But I felt really uncomfortable about it because I don't trust him not to drink." She sniffles but doesn't cry. "It came like one o'clock in the morning and he kept calling me telling me to come home. Calling me every half hour. So I came home at five thirty."

"In the morning?"

"Yeah. And his brother was there. I could tell he had been on coke, and so I asked him, 'Are you doing . . . that?' Because he would do it a lot before. I asked him, I'm like, 'Are you doing that?' and he started getting mad about me being gone, saying I was with other guys. And he got aggressive with me, which is something he's never done. I've never been scared of him."

"The cocaine."

"Now! Now that I know. Now! I know now that's what it was. He was in my face yelling at me and he's a quiet person, you know, he doesn't—if you're getting mad at him, he just sits there, you know, and kind of takes it."

Only the times when I'm near her do I realize how small she is, probably not even five feet. But when she talks, it's a whole world inside of her that you can't see: young kids, troubles, growing up on the rez, drinking, moving someplace new, poor, always trying hard, trying to figure it out, being brave. But it's like that for most everybody. They come into the ICU. Ordinary people, and soon they tell you everything. They admit you to an intimacy reserved for a loved one, for family, without reservation, without probation of time or moral requirement, without earning it. The only time I've been snorkeling was in Costa Rica where we went on vacation in 2004. We stayed at an ecolodge and took a day trip to an island. Before we went on the island, the boat anchored offshore, and we all put on fins and snorkel tubes. The area was called Drake Bay, and the water was a dark blue-green and churned by the wind and you couldn't see below, and then I put on the mask and lowered my head below the surface and it was a whole world, a world you never see, would never have expected, schools of fish, sea turtles, swaying kelp, coral reefs, busy, beautiful, teeming.

"I don't think they understand." It's the cousin, Erna. She's standing at the side of the bed looking down at the young man. Her hand is in a fist around the phone. She doesn't look or sound like she feels bad about anything. "That he's going to be like this."

"Who?"

"The family. The sisters. The brother. The one who keeps coming in here, 'cause he keeps telling him, 'Get up, let's go.'" She imitates him a little by making her voice deeper. She doesn't like him.

"He does say that. They do need to understand, to hear from the doctors that if we take him off the ventilator, he'll die. It's tragic, but he would die."

The wife lets out a soft wail. Her head is on his chest; it rises and falls with the ventilator. Her eyes are closed. It's a sound someone who is dreaming would make.

C. S. Lewis tried to get God off the hook for all the suffering in the world by saying that we make the problem of suffering and pain worse by vague talk about the "unimaginable sum of human misery." He says that if I have a toothache and you, sitting next to me, have a toothache, you may think there is twice the amount of pain in the room. But no one suffers that: "There is no such thing as the sum of suffering, for no one suffers it." I think that's wrong. I think they do. I think suffering is like gravity; it's equal at every point. Everyone's suffering is the sum: the son losing a father, a mother losing a daughter, a sister a brother, a wife a husband. All the same. The sum.

"We understand that. He doesn't know it. He thinks he's going to be all right," the sister says.

Death was once simpler. It was an absolute, decisive point where time stopped. The night into which life disappeared. Now it has slipped its moorings. Death was once when your heart stopped. It was called "heart-lung death." But then people started to be resuscitated, breathing, hearts beating. On April 15, 1975, shortly after she turned twenty-one, Karen Quinlan went to a friend's birthday party, took some Valium, and drank some gin and tonics. She went into a coma. She was removed from mechanical ventilation in 1976. She didn't die. She lived on in a persistent vegetative state until she died from pneumonia in 1985.

There was the Harvard Ad Hoc Committee on Irreversible Coma in 1976 and then a 1981 presidential commission's landmark study, Defining Death: Medical, Legal, and Ethical Issues in the Determination of Death, and finally the Uniform Determination of Death Act. There were arguments about whole-brain death and brainstem death. Death was different state by state, like the drinking age or state tax: ten years ago you could be an intensive care patient being transferred from a hospital in Boston to one in Washington and you would be alive in Massachusetts, dead in Connecticut, alive in New York and New Jersey, and dead again in DC.

Now death is supposedly simpler again. Death is brainstem death. You can be in the ICU, on a ventilator, your heart beating, warm, getting fluid, peeing, having labs drawn, getting your potassium replaced, and be dead.

"Is Fleischer's gas okay?" Kevin is the respiratory therapist today. He nods and gives me the printout of the ABG. Kevin does some weaning parameters for Fleischer to see if he's ready. He clamps off the tube so Fleischer tries to but can't draw a breath; it shows the strength of his respiratory muscles. He checks for a cuff leak by deflating the balloon on the tube to see if air is flowing through the trachea. Kevin wears bright Hawaiian shirts. His dream is to open a bar in Belize. He's been there twice. Once he went there in the off season. He showed us pictures of him on an empty beach, him in an empty bar, the bed in his room.

"Did he get his Lasix?" It's Miller. "Has he had his chest film?"

"Everything's ready."

Kevin and I get on either side of Fleischer and pull him high in the bed to get ready. He's light, the weight of a boy. When they come to the ICU and they've been resuscitated with fluids in the ER, they can be huge, and then three to four days later they're normal sized and you wonder, were they big and lost it or were they small all along. Sometimes they balloon up when they're here and you know that's not them.

Fowler is in the room. He looks at me. "I need to ask him what he wants to do if he needs to be reintubated." I can see his wife lower her head. Fowler goes to the bed. He leans down so his face is right in front of Mr. Fleischer. "Bernie, we're going to take out the tube. I think you're going to do okay. But if we need to, do you want us to put the tube back in?"

Fleischer's scalp is an archipelago of scabs and brown spots. The tube is on the right side of his mouth. It goes down almost twelve inches to the carina, hovering just above where the lungs go right and left. It's been in for more than two weeks. We untape it and move it every day so he won't get a pressure sore on his lips. The vase has new flowers. The book next to it is *Bless Me Ultima*. He shakes his head, no.

Fowler looks over to the wife, then back. "What if it was only for a short while? If it was something we could fix?" Mr. Fleischer shakes his head again. He's saying, "Enough." Fowler looks at the wife again. Her head is still down. "Okay then," Fowler says. "Okay then."

People do fight. They fight and fight to live but what you see is, if it comes to it, at the end of the day, they don't fear death. It's a forgotten truth deep in medical experience, in the history of medicine. Osler said he could hardly remember a dying patient who was afraid of death.

I lay a towel over Fleischer's chest. Kevin loosens the tape around his neck, suctions his mouth, deflates the cuff. He's wide-eyed like a child you're lifting out of a stroller. Kevin pulls the tube and lays it on the towel. It's like in those alien movies where a slimy monster crawls out of someone's mouth. "Cough," Kevin tells him. I listen with the stethoscope to both sides of his neck. He has a little stridor, a high-pitched wheezing sound when he breathes in, like wind whistling through a narrow canyon. His trachea's swollen. Stumbling out of the gate.

"Maybe a little racemic epi," I say to Kevin. We put a face mask on him with the nebulizer of epinephrine to decrease the swelling. Wreaths of mist float around his face. "It's okay, Mr. Fleischer. Just breathe easy. You're doing good." The room is quieter without the vent. Now we wait.

At four the young man's right pupil is dilated and nonreactive: blown. It's like a black moon eclipsing the iris. I call the Asian resident for the change. She says to call Neurology. I say Critical Care is the primary. "Neuro is," she says. "Critical Care is never the primary." They do stuff like that, say they're not the primary, or they're just consulting. It's like a shell game they play with us.

I have Dana help me boost him up.

"Are they going to withdraw?" she asks.

"There's a meeting tomorrow."

"You know how in Vegas, the background music in the casinos has a hidden sound you can't hear. It says, *Lose. Lose.* We should have a hidden message, *Give up. Give up.*"

Nurses can be harsh sometimes. Before Game 7 of the American League playoffs with the Yankees, Red Sox pitcher Mike Timlin said to reporters, "The game's already been played. We just have to see who won." Because we're with the patient all the time, we know who won the game. We know if the patient is going to die. That knowledge, when doctors order more tests, write more orders—it's called "therapeutic relentlessness" when families still want everything done—can make nurses less tolerant of the families, less kind.

An ancient woman with old but beautiful clothing—a long full skirt down to her feet, which are covered with shoes that look like slippers, a knitted shawl over her bent shoulders and a kerchief over her head tied under her chin—walks into the young man's room. She walks quickly like she's floating. I often see someone like her come with Native American patients. It's usually a man who is the medicine man or the person the Navajo call the Singer and who has a piece of turquoise or a stone they touch the person's face with, or pass over the person's chest. The woman goes to the head of the bed and looks down at the young man. They gather around the bed.

The setting sun is on the other side of the hospital. The light in the room comes from the darkening sky slatted by hanging blinds, from the monitor over the bed, from the blue screen of the vent. They are dark shapes. Their heads are down. The woman is speaking. No one moves. She touches his forehead. They relax and move. When it's over, they'll take him back to the reservation the way they usually do—in the back of a pickup. Every tribe—each of them—is a sovereign nation. You don't have to call the Office of Medical Investigation, no morgue, no paperwork.

Kevin now has Fleischer on just a simple face mask. We have him sitting at almost ninety degrees to open up his lungs. His heart rate is starting to tick up. You need to relax, I tell him. You need to breathe easy. Fowler is at the door. They were all sitting, and now they stand. Peggy, a daughter, and the son. The daughter has the varied pigmentation of vitiligo. She's wearing a long-sleeved shirt. The fingers of her hands are white as though they were dipped in cream. Under her makeup the skin along her hair is a different color, like a coastline. "We're doing good?" Fowler asks. "He's on nebs, right?"

"I'm going to give you some Ativan," I tell him. "Help you relax." Trying to bridge him to the other side, to shore. I know he trusts me. I've taken care of him six, seven times. It's as if you were on a ship that was sinking and you were way below deck and you were trying to get out and had to walk down dark corridors and up dark stairs, and there was a person who you felt knew the way, you would gently hold on to that person's sleeve or the back of his shirt so lightly he would hardly feel it. I feel his hand on me like that. I stand by the side of the bed. Everyone is quiet. His heart rate comes down, his breathing steadies. Everyone sits.

The patients' beds in each room are in the middle, six feet from the walls, so I figure that Fleischer and the young man are about twelve feet apart. An old Anglo and a young Indian. A woman with each of them. Tayen has been here the whole day. I let her stay. There's no rise and fall to the day for him, no steep hill to climb, no valley, no events.

"How long have you guys been together?"

"Five years."

"That's a long time. He's a young guy. What were his troubles?"

"It's just that . . . that's what reservation life is like, you know; that's all they do down there. His parents died right before I met him from drinking. He lost his dad on Christmas Day and his mother this April. He's a really good person, you know. Sure, a lot of people are but . . ."

"Did he ever have any counseling?" I ask her.

"No, I guess I just thought it was a drunk thing that he would never take this far."

"I think it would be okay if you don't go tomorrow," I tell her.

"I mean, like . . . I been here, I went home yesterday earlier because I guess I just come to accept it. We talked with the neurologist Tuesday morning and then Tuesday night, and they told me that he's . . . this is it . . . so I guess I finally understand, and that night and the next morning I finally come to terms. So I guess that's why I left yesterday, but I'm just waiting for his sisters."

"Are they coming today?"

"One. One. She should be here tonight. I just don't understand how they cannot be here. It's just so hard for me to understand that." The cousin's cell phone rings, and she gets up and walks to the window.

"Do you think they might do it tomorrow? Stop everything."

"You know, I don't. No one has come in today, and I think it's going to take some work. Some time for everyone to agree. It might take a few more days. They wouldn't do it without letting you know, give you a chance to be here."

On the phone the cousin says, "Over here?" then, "Okay."

The cousin says to Tayen, "They want his Social Security number. They ever get it?"

The brother doesn't come back until near the end of the day. They all look at each other when he comes in, but no one speaks. He goes to the side of the bed, puts his hands on the side rails, and looks down at the young man. The cousin floats behind him, looks at me, furrows her brow, and nods her head sharply. She means: Tell him.

Still looking down, William asks, "How is he?"

"He's worse."

"Worse? How?'

"One of his pupils is dilated and doesn't react to light, and that's a sign of swelling in the brain. It means he's deteriorating. He's suffered a devastating injury. He'll never be who he was."

"Well I'm going to still believe that he's going to get better. I'm going to still believe."

"That's okay. That's okay."

And he starts rubbing his heart again. The cousin is standing by the window crying, and the girlfriend is sitting in the chair and starts to cry. Softly. The way people cry without making a sound, their faces crumpled up like a can in a trash compactor.

One of the things nursing can do is make you know yourself too well: how much or how little compassion you have. How brave you are. In a code. Under stress. Some are too emotional. Some don't care. Before I was a nurse, I had never seen anyone die. My father died in 1994, my mother in 1998, but they died like leaves on a tree that wither and dry and fall softly. People who aren't nurses have experiences of grief or loss separated by years like small towns you see from a train. The ICU is a cauldron of feelings: hope, fear, pain, guilt, blame, superstition, over-whelming sadness. Being a nurse is like being one of the Greek heroes whose punishment is to be tethered to one spot. It feels like that. You can't leave; you can't walk away. The cauldron is right there. Nursing can disclose you, show you yourself. There's nothing transformative about caring, no leaven that makes you, by being a nurse, more compassionate, beyond who you are. Nursing is like what Heywood Hale Broun said about sports: it doesn't build character; it reveals character.

"We're going to leave now," Tayen says. "Are you going to be here to-morrow?"

"No, I'm not. I'm off tomorrow. But I'm back on the weekend. If another nurse has him, that nurse would probably take him back. But if not, I would take him back."

"That would be good because I think . . . you're very . . . you know . . . you've worked this with us."

"I have."

"So, thank you."

"Okay. You take care of yourself. You and your cousin."

"Okay."

It leaves the brother and me alone. He looks better. Then I notice the sides of his head are freshly shaved and the top flows back on his head like a pelt into a long ponytail.

"Did you get a haircut?"

"Yes." He laughs. "I needed a haircut."

I think about the way that whenever I looked into the young man's eyes William would come real close and look, and I would tell him what I was doing even though everything I told him burned like acid; how much we had talked and how he had listened, and that he wasn't so much scary as scared, just a boy himself; how there was nothing to do for his brother—really all my work with them was trying to tell the truth, win trust while being the bearer of the worst possible news, watching what he does not see, which is the dying of his brother, when what he sees is him lying there as if asleep; and trying to shepherd them, to move them along to the waiting end and doing it without really a plan, without training, without any skill beyond just who you are.

We have Fleischer down to two liters on a cannula. Like he's coming down a ladder, back to earth. The feeling in the room is different, relaxed. He made it to the other side, to shore. I have Blake help me boost him.

"Mr. Fleischer," I tell Blake, "plays the cello."

"Aren't most famous cellists female?" Blake says.

"No, the most famous cellists are male." His voice is dry, cracked.

"It's a large stringed instrument, right? It has four strings? Maybe— I'm a male nurse—and the way the women sit there with their legs apart." We're done, so Blake is free to show him what he means, and he squats with his legs apart.

"I'll take him away now," I tell Mr. Fleischer. He has a little smile on his face.

But we stay in the room, Blake, Peggy, the son, the daughter. The way hikers who reach the top of a mountain at dusk stand, look around, are quiet. Then Peggy asks me if I had seen the aspens, and I said I had not. And then the son said he could see them golden all the way from Los Alamos. And they both said how beautiful they were this year and that I should see them soon. I thought it was nice their asking me that with all they had been through and how it almost did not turn out good, and I realized the other day I had looked toward the mountains that were gray and colorless now after the summer and saw the flank of one of the hills lit up by what I thought was a stray shaft of light but now realized was the glow of the aspens.

Now the day ends. Fleischer asleep. A nurse in every room. A final look. A final note. I can see William through the window. He's standing at the side of the bed. He's wearing a different shirt. Short sleeved, white. He takes a deep breath. His chest expands like a bellows. He exhales so loudly I can hear him. The way the wind will come down the chimney of our kiva fireplace and blow open the flue. He puts his hands on his brother's chest and rubs it like he's scouring a stain, then raises his arms in the air like a bird taking flight, then lowers them, then rubs his chest so hard the EKG is all artifact. His arms fly up into the air and this time stay there. He's breathing louder, like a woman in labor pushing her breath out, the sound going into the unit and people in other rooms turning their heads. I close the door quietly. He places his hands flat on his brother's chest on both sides of his heart. He inhales and lifts his hands off the chest into a clasp. He puts his hands back on the chest. He lowers his head so his lips are almost touching where the heart would be and breathes forcefully onto the chest. Inhales, clasps his hands, raises his head and eyes upward, lowers his head, spits into his hands, rubs his hands together, puts his face into his palms, inhales deeply, lowers his head to his brother's ear and blows with such force I can see spit fly.

I have to go into the room to hang some potassium. When I was a boy on Cape Cod, we would go outside during a hurricane to feel the wind that we could see from inside laying flat the beach grass and bending the trees, our hearts beating in our chests like wild birds. Going into the room was like that, like going into a storm, and I think the cousin Erna wanted him to know and now he knows. He knows now.

I think about distance. When you get above the tree line in the White Mountains in New Hampshire, you can see the summits of all the mountains of the Presidential Range—Clay, Jefferson, Adams, Monroe, Madison, Washington. The summits look close. You think, This won't be hard.

But the more you hike, the farther away they seem. When you get to what you thought was the summit, you can see beyond it the real summit.

When I needed glasses, I tried progressives, then I tried bifocals. Nothing seemed to work. The world didn't look right behind glass. My optometrist tried to explain how the difference between my eyes caused the problem. He was talking about distance, how one pair of glasses did one thing but you lost something, and with the other you gained and lost something else.

A BLM archaeologist tells Barry Lopez where he will find the intaglio of a stone horse in the California desert. When he finds it, the sight makes him hold his breath. The horse lies on a barren bajada between two arroyos. It is three times life size, a standing profile, its head to the east, brought to life with stones called desert varnish. He calculates it to be maybe four hundred years old. He spends several hours there, watching the sun flesh out the mane, the belly. "For all its forcefulness, the horse is inconspicuous," he writes. "If you don't care to see it you can walk right past it. That pleases him I think. Unmarked on this bleak shoulder of the plain, the site signals to no one."

The archaeologist had given him an aerial photograph of the horse. He says that the belief that an aerial view of an intaglio provides a fair and accurate description is untrue. In the photograph, the horse looks crudely constructed, from the ground, more deftly rendered; in the photograph, "vaguely impotent," from the ground, quivering, living. "Intaglios, I thought, were never meant to be seen by gods in the sky above. They were meant to be seen by people on the ground, over a long period of shifting light."

Asymptote means that a curve can come as close to a line as possible without ever touching it. In the ICU, nursing and medicine come as close as can be, almost touching but not quite. Nursing is not medicine. And it's not more important than medicine. Caring isn't more important than cure. But nursing has something medicine doesn't have, an unlost heritage that, not having abandoned, it has no need to return to: nearness, the view from the ground.

10

POETIC AND TRAGIC MURMURINGS OF THE EVERYDAY

There can be a different experience of the poor. In his biography of Simone Weil, Robert Coles writes of her desire to live among the French peasantry, to learn about not only their lives but also what she saw as their courage, resourcefulness, and endurance. He describes this as a common experience in the history of social observation among intellectuals who wanted to see firsthand how others live: there is the expected scene of people who are poor and struggling but who are also capable of "thoughtfulness, perseverance, of stoic forbearance, personal honor, a courtesy and civility, and hospitality."

There can be a different experience of people who are ill. Medicine now lays claim to illness as its birthright, its lost heritage. Nursing could lay claim to it. Nursing's claim would be that there is no claim. One day a patient died. There were fifteen to twenty people in the room with her and spilling out into the unit. Someone complained. Lori said, "It's all right. She belongs to them." She meant the experience belonged to them. The experience of illness, of suffering.

It's odd that we think ordinary people who are ill do not understand illness; do not understand suffering, loss, or death. That they don't know the very thing that is happening to them. It's odd that we think people become incompetent with illness when no one provides them with narrative therapy or empathic witnessing for their daily sorrows, struggles, losses, and pain. We say we "fall ill," or we "come down with something," but the poor do not fall. Illness is not a fall from a height but a neighbor in the life of the poor, a shadow at the door. They know more about illness, suffering, about tragedy, death; they know it early, and they know it throughout life.

The night nurse for Six is Dave. He's juiced up, bristling. Some of the night nurses are so wiped out you worry how they drive home, but some are so stoked up on coffee that it's like the beginning of the day for them. He's in his late forties, I figure. He says, "Cool," "Right on." He's a fist bumper.

"You ready?" he asks. "Janine Sinclair. She's thirty-nine. PCom hemorrhage. She was at work. Headache. Worst of her life, of course. Collapsed. Nine one one. She's on twelve of dopamine. ICPs are running twenty to twenty-five. It's a Codman; we're not draining. Her ventricles must be tighter than a gymnast's pussy. For greater than twenty, you give mannitol. One bag q two. She's PEARL. She deviates to the right. She withdraws only. The Swan's for her filling pressures. Her wedge is running twelve, her CVP eight. Serum osmos q six. At least it wasn't her Acom."

"Why?"

"Think personality." In a different voice, he says, "I have a drain in my head. Oh, you mean this?" He puts his hand on top of his head like he's pulling something out. "Oh, here." He sticks his hand forward like he's offering something. He puts his face into an innocent expression. He snorts.

"SIMV. Not overbreathing. Foley. I'm back," and he extends his arm and a closed fist and very gently I bang it with my own. "It's all good, bro."

After the night nurse leaves and you're alone, your heart always thrills a bit. The need to make sense of everything quickly: Are they wet? Dry? Do they need fluid? Will they herniate? It feels like in the morning you come in, sit in the group report, come out, get the bedside report, and then you draw yourself back like a bow. You're an arrow drawn back into the string of the bow as far as it will go. You are the bow and the arrow and the arm drawing back the arrow. You stay that way for twelve hours, taut, tensed, everything stretched, no slack, so if the thing that can happen does happen, you're ready.

I look at Janine Sinclair lying on the bed. Her intracranial pressure is twenty-eight, creeping up; her systolic pressure 102, too low. Some mornings you don't have time to make that sense of things; it's like getting on a train that's already moving, leaving the station. I call Mateo to do a gas to check her CO_2 before I call the resident. In the chart I see Neurosurgery ordered an angiogram for this morning.

Dulce Ortiz has been here for two weeks. I've never taken care of her. I haven't seen the brother who said he was a meth addict since that day. *Dulce.* Sweetheart? Came in with respiratory distress. She's tiny, almost like a child. Her skin is waxy, the color of beeswax. It's as if her face froze in pain, as if she died in ice and her face froze. She has scleroderma and lupus. Both autoimmune. Your own body betrays you. Makes you think

God is a trickster. The chest film this morning showed terrible lungs: bilateral infiltrates and pleural effusions. The progress notes say, *refractory pain.* "Just touch her," the night nurse had said and made her body go all tense like what Ortiz must do.

But she opens her eyes when I ask, and when I touch her she does wince and her heart rate shoots up to 120. Hate to wake them up, but you have to know. Her skin is hard and dry as a saddle and smooth as a baby's. The sutures are still in her trach; the gauze tucked under the plastic flange is stiff with dried yellow-brown mucus. Her brown hair is thin and dry as winter grass on the prairie. Her lungs, stiff and hard like her skin, sound like a train going through a tunnel. There's nothing in the room: no icon of Jesus or Mary, just a leather cord around her neck with a piece of paper the size of a stamp.

There's probably nothing we can do for her. She's like a plane that's flying, and the engine has stopped, but it keeps flying as before by momentum, soundlessly in the air, and if you were on the ground looking up at the sky, you would think, That's a plane flying, not knowing that gravity's fingers are reaching up to bring it to the ground.

Mateo hands me Sinclair's ABG, "CO_2's forty-three." When the CO_2 is high, the vessels in the brain dilate to get rid of it; the intracranial pressure goes up. I call the Neuro resident.

"Increase her rate. Keep her CO_2 below thirty-two. Is she getting a CT today?"

"She's getting an angio," I tell him.

Murphy calls the Neuro residents the Bodines. There are only five of them. One's a woman. The joke comes from the TV show *The Beverly Hillbillies.* Jethro Bodine is the son of Jed Clampett's cousin, Pearl Bodine. Jethro drives the Clampett family to their new home in California and then stays. He doesn't know what to do for a career, whether to be a short-order cook, a double-naught spy, a streetcar conductor. He finally narrows it down to either a fry cook or a brain surgeon.

They're withdrawing on Four. I took care of her when she first came in. Yolanda Perez. I had thought, This is the most alone person ever. Thirty-eight, a prostitute, found down in a motel room on Central. Cirrhosis. Hep C. IV drug use. The night nurse had said, "Rode hard and put up wet."

For some reason they didn't want to treat her. They were going to just let her go and we kind of made them intubate her, or Martha did, right away in the morning that day seeing her on a nonrebreather face mask, struggling, her heart racing, calling Morgan and saying they needed to intubate her right away and after, staring at him, saying to him, "It's not for us to decide." Even after that, it was like she fell overboard in the dark and drifted away without anybody knowing, nobody to throw her a line. Some, most, get the whole nine yards—ventilator, dialysis, transfusion, plasmapheresis. She went into a coma, her liver failed, then her kidneys, and she turned as yellow as a golden Buddha. An alone, golden Buddha.

Janine Sinclair's husband is a big man, tall, maybe six five, square chested with long hair, wavy with deep troughs like a wind-whipped sea. But like some big men, he has a soft voice and when he talks he makes himself small, rounding his shoulders and tucking his head. His name is Josh. "Is her ICP twenty-eight?"

"We're not going to treat it because she's going to have an angiogram."

"Is that bad for her?"

"No, no it's not. It'll be okay. I'll find you when she's back." They learn things quickly. What an ICP means. What's a normal blood pressure. After a day or two they ask what the FIO2 is, did her white count come down, has she had a bowel movement?

Back in the unit after the angiogram, Lori helps me hook her up. Her ICP is thirty-two.

"What else can we do?" I ask her. "I can't put her head up because of the sheath."

"I'd put her in reverse Trendelenberg. That'll get her head up."

"We should get another gas. Check her CO_2."

"I'll do your calcs for you." Lori says.

The Swan-Ganz catheter is a window into the heart. It goes through the right atrium, the right ventricle, then sits in the pulmonary artery. It has a little balloon at the tip, and when you inflate the balloon, it floats forward and wedges in a pulmonary vein, and then you get to know how much blood is in the left side of the heart; you can plumb its depths, measure its tides. A doctor named Jeremy Swan got the idea from watching sailboats with spinnakers in Santa Monica.

"Her CVP is four," Lori says. "The wedge looks to be about nine. What did they get at night?"

"Eight. Fourteen." '

"She needs volume. Let's think. Her ICP is thirty-two. Her wedge is nine. Heart rate one eighteen. BP ninety-eight over sixty-two." She looks from the monitor to the bed. "You need to fill her tank. The brain's response to hypovolemia is to vasodilate, so you'll get get high ICPs. Her heart rate is high. Some of that could be from the dopamine, or she's compensating for hypovolemia. If you give her volume, it'll lower her ICP. Can you bolus her?"

"I can give five hundred for a wedge less than ten."

"I'd give her a liter. She's dry. What else can I do for you?"

"Can you give my ten o'clock meds?"

I lift Sinclair's eyelashes. Both eyes go up and to the right, toward the bleed, like just before you were hit by it, you saw the car coming. I rub my knuckles along the little bones that rib up in the groove of her sternum. She has little bruises on her breasts where the residents pinch her to see what she does. Seven or eight, like a school of minnows. In the mornings they scream at the patients, "Show me two fingers! Show me two fingers!" so loud that everyone in the unit stops for a second like you would if you heard people having an argument.

"It's the husband," Lori says.

"It's all right. Let him in."

Josh comes in and leans on the side rails. "What do you think?"

"We're having some problems with her intracranial pressure. We're going to give her some fluid."

"She's gonna make it. She's a fighter. If anybody can make it, she can." His body shakes the way the ground shakes in a film clip of an underground nuclear test.

"The one thing in her favor is she's young. Youth is a big factor. We have to hope for the best," I tell him.

He looks down at her. "We met at a gas station called the Alamo. She was at pump number three, and I was at pump number nine. They announced overhead, 'Go ahead, pump number three.' She looked at me, and I said to myself, If she looks at me twice, I'm going over there. Well, she did, and I walked over there." He's smiling. "And I said, 'Hello, pump number three.' "

Mateo calls and says Sinclair's CO_2 is thirty-nine. "I'll go back up on the tidal volume, blow it off," he says.

Michel de Certeau describes everyday life poetically. He says that it is the "rumour of a different country." Examining it, he writes, "You had the impression of exploring the night-side of societies, a night longer than their days, an obscure sea from which successive institutions emerge, a maritime immensity on which socioeconomic and political structures appear as ephemeral islands." It is like "the snowy waves of the sea slipping in among the rocks and defiles of an established order." He describes it as a world of confused sounds, incomprehensible fragments, "innumerable lexicons and strange vocabularies." He refers to its poetic and tragic murmuring. He says it is cunning; an obscure, stubborn life; a practical world of fantasy, imagination, and remembrance.

It wasn't until the sixth day that the first person came in for Yolanda Perez, and it turned out to be her daughter. She was young, early twenties. She had three kids with her. When we told her how sick her mother was, and there was little hope, right away she said she wanted us to stop. She said her mother had a heroin addiction and was in an abusive relationship that she kept going back to. She asked if we could wait for her brother to come from Tucumcari. We told her to tell us when she was ready.

There's a lung mass on Ortiz's X-ray. The Pulmonary fellow is rounding with Fowler. The X-ray is up on the scanner. Everyone is looking at it from behind Fowler, who is sitting at the computer.

"Classic shattered glass," the fellow says. There's an odd jellyfish shape in the right middle lobe. "What are her inspiratory pressures?"

"Fifty-two," a resident says.

"How come she doesn't have a pneumothorax with pressures like that?" someone asks.

"The scleroderma. Her lungs are a cement wall," the fellow says. "Why aren't we doing a lung-protective strategy? We should paralyze her."

"In fifteen years I've never ordered a paralytic in the ICU. I have nightmares of conscious paralysis," Fowler says.

"You could do pressure control, reverse the I and E, give her a longer inspiration," the fellow says, then makes a motion to zip his mouth and closes his lips.

"Let's approach the family about a lung biopsy," Fowler says. "Any other problems? Jim?"

"She's not tolerating her tube feeding."

"Let's start her on Reglan and see how she does. Let's get a CT of her chest in the morning."

After, I look up *scleroderma*: hair loss; tight, masklike facial skin; rapidly progressing; affects kidneys, esophagus, heart, lungs. Lung problems most common cause of death. Runs in families. She has a pretty daughter who comes in.

Josh is sitting in a chair by the bed. A young man is sitting next to him. They're going through names of people, how they're going to react. "Diane. She won't be able to take it. We'll have to have Jonas tell her. Kathy'll be brave." The young man nods. He's listening hard to everything Josh says.

"This is my stepson, Nathan."

"This is your mother?"

Nathan nods. "That's where the shortness comes from." He doesn't look up.

"That's not something I would have thought about," I say. He does look like her—fair skinned, strawberry-blond hair. Southern white, working-class people, moving along the cactus belt, jobs like Dillard's, behind the counter at Allsup's, falling in love, breaking up, cobbling together lives out of low-paying jobs. He stands next to the bed. He's about five six. He rests his hands on the metal side rail, looks down and smiles at her the sweetest, kindest smile. The left side of her head is shaved. The incision is a raised crescent of staples. Darker roots of hair against pale skull skin. Tubes from her mouth, nose. It's like that movie *Shallow Hal* where Ben Stiller is under a spell and sees Gwyneth Paltrow who is obese as thin and beautiful even when the chair she sits on breaks.

As Agee writes in Let Us Now Praise Famous Men, *how he sees the lives of the tenant farmers changes. In the preface, he writes, the "nominal subject is North American cotton tenantry as examined in the daily living of three representative white tenant families." Later: "Actually, the effort is to recognize the stature of a portion of unimagined existence and to contrive techniques proper to its recording, communication, analysis and defense." Finally: "More essentially, this is an independent inquiry into certain normal predicaments of human divinity."*

Rounds are over. We're sitting by the computers where the teams usually sit.

Blake is telling Michelle, "We did two thousand vertical feet in one gear." Dana has up on the computer a slideshow of a town house she is trying to buy. "I have to pay off my credit card first." The three rooms across from me are all vents. Seven is being dialyzed. They're doing an echo on Five. Eight is getting blood. The sky is immense in New Mexico. You can be driving down Highway 14 under blue sky and just a few miles away over the Ortiz Mountains the sky is black, shot through with lightning. It feels like that, like I'm sitting under blue sky and ten feet away are raging storms.

"You're first admit," Martha tells Blake. "Do you want an aneurysm or a GI bleed? There's a trauma stat in the ER. They're going to CT and then the OR."

The one female Neurosurgical resident walks by. Sabrina something. She's thin, her skin a little rough, a dandelion-sized area of acne scars below a cheekbone.

Blake shudders and looks down. "She's such a bitch."

"She's just trying to fit in," Martha says. "She's the only woman in that group."

"She'll be a man in seven years," Blake says. "You'll walk into the men's room, and she'll be taking a leak standing up. She's so ugly."

"Do you think she is?" Lori says. "I've never really looked at her closely."

"You're afraid to."

"I'm going to look at her close," Lori says.

"A guy walks into a grocery store," Michelle says. "He buys one frozen dinner, one soda, and one candy bar. The cashier says to him, 'Are you single?'"

" 'Because I only buy one thing of each?' "

" 'No,' " she says, " 'because you're so fucking ugly.' " She hoots.

"Whatever comes first," Blake says.

At noon the gauze under Ortiz's trach is red with blood and with a clot as thick as a placenta. I suction her mouth, and the tubing frosts red, like someone had thrown a tomato at a window. She has a two o'clock blood work I do early, and the H and H comes back 6.4 and 18.6. She's bleeding somewhere. I call: two units of packed cells, check her stool for blood, recheck the H and H after.

A young man in his midtwenties and an older Hispanic man come in Ortiz's room.

"I'm George. Her son." Then he looks at the other man, "This is her boyfriend, Albert." The man is standing by the side of the bed. Hard to believe she would have a boyfriend.

"Are the test results back yet?" he asks.

"Do you mean the blood cultures? No."

"They were going to test something yesterday."

"We haven't had any positive cultures yet. But we're treating her with broad spectrum antibiotics that cover most everything."

"Has the doctor been here yet?"

"They were here earlier. They're talking about doing a lung biopsy."

"What will that show?" The other man is touching the sheet over where the compression sleeves would be on her legs.

"We should talk outside."

The son and I stand in the hall just outside the room. "It might be diagnostic, but it might not show anything. Even if something showed up it might not affect her prognosis."

"We don't want it if it's just to probe her, stick her with something."

"Who has the power of attorney? Who's making decisions?"

"My sister April and me."

"We have to ask ourselves what your mother would want."

"She wouldn't want to be kept alive by a machine." He's wearing a hip-length camouflage jacket with a small American flag sewn just below the shoulder on the right arm. The stars are toward the front so it's as though the flag is flying toward his back, like he's walking into a wind. His jeans have an ironed crease. His heavy black boots are polished to a shine and laced high. His hair is short.

"I don't think we're at that point," I say. "I think we could be close, but we're not there yet. Even if something showed up. And if we are, we could withdraw care. Do you know what that means?"

"You would stop feeding her?"

"We would stop feeding her, make her comfortable, make sure she has no pain. Everybody could be with her at the bedside. I don't think we're at that point. Are you in the military?"

"Marines. I'm stationed at Camp Lejeune."

The boyfriend comes out of the room. "Are those things on her legs helping her?"

Two residents trade out the Codman for a ventriculostomy so we can drain Sinclair. The Codman is a wire that goes under the scalp, into the brain. It just tells you the intracranial pressure. The ventriculostomy goes right into a ventricle so if the pressure goes too high you can drain cerebrospinal fluid. Like a pop-off valve.

One resident looks Middle Eastern. The resident he's talking to is from India. They map the site. The Middle Eastern guy says, "One centimeter anterior to the coronal sinus to avoid the motor strip, three point five in front of the bregma. I'm thinking of buying a rental in the Tenderloin. You could work in the city and live twenty miles away. What do you say? They capped reimbursement. But they capped malpractice too. You could marry a teacher and get a rent-controlled place."

"My wife's a pediatrician," the Indian guy says and laughs.

For the ventriculostomy, they use a hand drill like you would use to drill a screw into a stud. They go right through the skull and thread a catheter into the ventricle.

"You could go to the pier and watch the ships come in and eat sourdough with melted Monterey."

They drop the drain to the floor until yellowish drops of cerebrospinal fluid drip into the chamber.

"Where do you want it set?" I ask them.

"Set it at fifteen. For an ICP more than twenty for five minutes, drain for two. We're not going to chase it."

"We already have Neurology."

"Set it up," the Indian guy says.

I once thought when you became something like a priest or a doctor, something happened to you, someone would slip you a secret coin, whisper something in your ear, or you would open a desk drawer and find a piece of paper with a secret message the way presidents supposedly do that would transform you, like how the pope, because he's the pope, can make statements that are infallible.

Medicine talks about the mysterious relationship between the doctor and patient, how it's magically there, even if the doctor doesn't believe in it, even if it's badly used. In The Birth of the Clinic, *Foucault says the theory is this: "If, in the hospital, the doctor does not carry out theoretical experiments on the poor, it is because, as soon as he sets foot in the hospital, he undergoes a decisive moral experience. It is by entering the asylums where poverty and sickness languish that he will feel that active commiseration, that burning desire to bring comfort and consolation. It is there that he will be religious, humane, compassionate."*

But it's not true. In Time to Heal, *Kenneth Ludmerer writes, "The power of medical education is limited, particularly regarding its ability to produce doctors who are caring and socially responsible; much of the behavior of physicians reflects influence from outside medical school, such as the character and values of those who choose to enter medicine, the cultural climate of the time. Our physicians reflect the type of people and society we are, not just the efforts of academic health centers. It would not be an exaggeration to say that as a nation we ultimately get the type of doctors we deserve."*

In the first semester of her sophomore year, Ellen Rothman does volunteer work in the respiratory therapy department at Yale–New Haven Hospital. She wants to see the clinical side of medicine but what she actually does is stock respiratory therapy closets around the hospital once a week. She works with a woman named Diane. Rothman describes her this way: "I was assigned to help Diane, a terse obese black woman with whom I was never able to establish a rapport. We worked our way through the hospital filling empty bins. Every fifteen minutes she stopped for a twenty-minute coffee break. At each break she filled a Styrofoam cup two-thirds full with stale coffee. Then she grabbed ten packets of Equal sweetener and emptied them into her coffee. Then she downed the entire cup. I lasted three or four sessions before giving up on volunteering altogether."

There's blood all over the front of Ortiz's gown like a red bib. I suction her mouth and catch a huge clot like a fish on a line. She could have a fistula to the innominate artery in the trachea. Bleed out.

They come right away. "I don't think it's the trachea," Fowler says. They put a seal of what is basically glue around the trach. "Let's give her the two units of blood and see if she holds on to it." I look at her small, brown body on the bed and wonder if somewhere inside her an artery is spurting silently. Just like Sinclair's high ICPs. How much damage is it doing? Quiet destruction. Like tectonic plates sliding before the earthquake.

The catcher in the rye. Eleven hours of boredom and an hour of terror. It's what we're supposed to do in the ICU, see these things as or just before they happen, but I wonder, what if all of a sudden you just can't do it anymore. That bow-and-arrow thing. When Rich Ankiel of the St. Louis Cardinals threw seven wild pitches in the first inning of a playoff game, they said he had Steve Blass disease. Steve Blass pitched for the Pittsburgh Pirates in 1996. One day he couldn't throw the ball over the plate. He never pitched again. I wonder if one day you just can't do it anymore. You can't draw back the bow, or if you do, your arm starts to tremble. You don't see something when it happens, or you think something is okay when it's not. The philosopher Isaiah Berlin said his biggest fear was that he would reach for it and it wouldn't be there.

Now the daughter is in Ortiz's room. She wears jeans. She has lavender lips and wide, round eyes like the pools water makes in sandstone. She's at the bed stroking her mother's forehead. Long, slow strokes. She has brought in a CD that is playing Hispanic music.

I tell her I have her mother today. "What's the music?"

"The songs are called alabados. By Los Hermanos Penintentes? In Truchas? It's her favorite music." I shake my head. She smiles; there are things Anglos who live here don't know about Hispanic culture.

"How is she?"

"What do the doctors say?" I ask her.

"They don't really say anything. I haven't talked to any of them."

"They haven't told you what they think?"

"No," she says.

"She's very sick."

She doesn't say anything. Then she says, "We'd like to take her home."

"I don't know how much we can do for her."

"We just lost our grandfather. He had dementia. We know we're going to lose her to the scleroderma but not now."

"When was she diagnosed?"

"One and a half years ago. She got a stomach bleed from steroids. Then she got pneumonia. I guess she never got over that." She's silent. Then, "I don't know what to do."

"Does she have an advance directive?"

"She didn't sign it."

"Do you know what she would want?"

"No." She moves the CD player at an angle toward the bed. "We'd like to take her home by Christmas."

Sometimes it's a game in which the family will say the doctors haven't talked to them and the doctors have, or they'll say they were never told something when we know they were, and the unit will develop a kind of scorn for them for not letting go, for wanting everything done, but then you see how they pull the curtain, play music, touch them. Lori says they pray. I've never seen it. "They pull the curtain. They're quiet. They hold hands around the bed."

Sometimes it feels as though we're ahead of the family, waiting for them to catch up, to understand what's going on, for them to say, "She wouldn't want this," or "We think we should stop." We try to bring them along, show them the way. When they ask how she is, we'll say, "Worse," or "Not getting better." Try to get them to change the code status. But sometimes they know. They understand. They just want a little more time. For not really knowing her, I look into her eyes for a long time. She has her face composed in that pretty way, her eyes wide, and she knows I'm not going to tell her I know that the doctors had talked to her, and that she was lying, and she wasn't going to tell me she was lying. And that it's okay. They want one more day. They would like to go back to before. They would like to go home. Because they can't, they want one more day.

In Billy Collins's poem "Statues in the Park," a friend has told him of the code of equestrian statues: how a horse with two legs raised meant the rider had died in battle; four legs touching the ground meant the man on the horse had died of a cause other than war. He pictures his own statue:

And there was I

up on a rose-gray block of granite

near a cluster of shade trees in the local park,

my name and dates pressed into a plaque,

down on my knees, eyes lifted,

praying to the passing clouds,

forever begging for just one more day.

I have to suction her. The necklace is leather, with two pieces of cloth the size of a postage stamp. On one is a cross and below it a heart with a sword through it; the other is a picture of Jesus with his arms outstretched. It's mixed up with the ET tube. I place them on top of each other on her chest. April is smiling. "It's a scapular. One goes in the back, one in the front."

"I'll let you do it," I tell her.

The daughter of one of our patients has bought the unit a box of chocolate, one of those double-decker Russell Stover boxes with a diagram inside that tells you what's what, so you don't have to bite into a piece to find out. A note with the box says, "Thank you for taking care of our mother." Her mother is Angela Ortega. Came in with pneumonia and had to be intubated. She's morbidly obese. It was like she had no neck. They put a special trach in. But she survived. I see the daughter and the husband in the room and thank them. He's an old guy, gaunt from the smoking you can smell on the clothes that hang loose on him. Every day what happens is, the daughter brings him, stays with him, but then the old man gets upset and starts to cry, and she takes him out. The daughter looks more and more weary, sad.

"How is she doing?" I ask her.

"A little better every day. Thank you for all you're doing for her. I know that one day she's going to walk out of here and come home with us." She's small and nice-looking with one of those faces that is so kind. Kay comes in and asks me to help turn her.

"We'll leave for a while. I leave my prayer book here," the daughter says. She puts a blue folder on the roller table. "We'll go and have lunch. Thank you."

The kabbalistic rabbi Isaac Luria said that to create the world, God had to contract himself, he had to withdraw to make space for the world. The technical term for this contraction is *zimzum*. The plan was for grace in the form of holy light to flow downward to the world through ten holy vessels. But during Creation, the vessels shattered. They actually shattered into 288 sparks of holiness that are now hidden in the world, imprisoned in things. "The sparks scatter everywhere," Martin Buber says. "They cling to material things as in sealed-up wells, they crouch in substances as in caves that have been bricked up, they flutter about in the movements of the world, searching where they lodge to be set free." It means that goodness is hidden in the world. I think that's true. Goodness is hidden in the world and, in the ICU, that goodness, hidden, shows.

When I go back into Ortiz's room, there's a puddle of brown liquid on the floor like melted chocolate. I get Michelle and Kay to help me clean her up. The decubitus on her sacrum is a crater, the feces is dripping into it. Everything about her seems stiff, slowed. We turn her and the expression on her face turns slowly into pain, like the time it takes for light to appear from a star.

I tell Josh we're going to bathe his wife.

"I'll give you guys some time," he says. He usually comes in the room and stands a distance from the bed away from the electric fence of lines, tubing, drains, the metal side rails, and asks how she's doing in a half whisper as if afraid of waking her. He's been here most of the day with the boy, talking him up, giving him advice, making him feel like they're in this together for the long haul.

It doesn't take long to bathe her. In the hollows beneath her iliac crests, looking across at each other, are small tattoos of wing-open butterflies. Her breasts are small, like little ant hills. We're on either side of her. We run the washcloths along her flesh.

"She's a cutter," Lori says.

She's staring at a ladder of pale scars that run up the inside of her wrist. Like old initials carved into a tree. None of them deep enough to die from.

I leave to get a gown, come back, and Lori has combed her hair. A straight white part clean as a plowed road. A sweet thing to do. A kind of love.

"He seems like a nice guy," Lori says.

"He's very nice. He's devastated. They've only been married a year."

"I didn't know that."

"He's so in love with her."

She looks down to see who someone could be so in love with. She cocks her head. "She's cute. She looks cute, doesn't she? Like she's a lot of fun." She did look cute, the dark roots of her blond hair, pixieish, the sweetness imparted to her son.

"I don't know how you do it, all this suffering," Helen Bardwell's husband had said. I do wonder at the things we do. You tell people you're a nurse, and they say, "I could never be a nurse." Susan Overby wrote a book called *Ordered to Care*. In it, she talks about nursing as a form of labor shaped by the obligation to care in a society that refuses to value caring. That doesn't feel true. I don't feel that I'm ordered to care. Doctors aren't "ordered" to cure. But nursing does require something. When you think of the twelve hours, of what could happen at any moment, of their very life that you feel you hold in the palms of your hands, of the families, the skin, blood, urine, stool—it does require something, a devotion, a commitment.

Now I think no one is really alone. After the daughter, the brother came, then one day the father, then a friend, and now at the end there are twenty people in Bed Four. People can be either hysterical, wailing, falling on the bed or so quiet you wouldn't know they're here. Yolanda Perez's family is quiet, grieving like the way bombs are exploded in containers. A muffled sound. The box shivers. A little smoke. They're wearing yellow isolation gowns. Father Martin is here.

Sandy is her nurse today. "Is this Yolanda Perez?" Father Martin asks her. He doesn't go into the room but stands outside the door. Maybe he doesn't want to gown up over his black habit. Maybe they didn't ask for a priest, but he wanted to bless her anyway.

Father Martin is a small man. He's retiring in a few weeks and he's been speaking to me more than he had before, how he had been in the army, in the war, and was writing a book about it and how it had shaped his life. He has funny priest humor. How he has a *J* and a *C* on the soles of his feet so when they roll him into the emergency room they'll know he's Catholic. He'll look at a patient's chart and ask, "Is he one of ours?" Or how you can tell when people are Christian because their eyes are symmetrical or equidistant from their nose or something. I have no idea what he's talking about. When basketball players shoot foul shots they do a little ritual—bounce the ball to their right, spin it, flex their knees, some even make a cross or blow a kiss to a kid at home—then, just before they shoot it, tense their bodies. Father Martin did something like that.

I could see him tuck his head into his chest, tense his muscles like a rabbit before it jumps, move his hand, and then with a spiritual flick of the wrist shoot a blessing into the room. Then he was gone.

I've been watching a show on the Discovery channel called *Man vs. Wild*. It's about a former British special forces guy who parachutes into places like the jungles of Costa Rica or a volcano field in Hawaii with only a knife, a flint, and a tin cup. His name is Bear Grylls. Last week it was the Sierra Nevadas. He built a raft out of a few logs tied together with grapevines. The raft got him several miles downstream out of the wilderness before he was thrown off and the raft destroyed by the whitewater. He ate grubs he found in a rotted tree. He drank his own urine. It felt like we were gathering whatever wood we could find—a prayer here, a father, what friends she had—for the short journey out of the wilderness that had been her life.

In The Care of Strangers, *Charles Rosenberg writes that we can only imagine the feelings or experiences of those who found themselves in early American hospitals: "We have comparatively little evidence bearing directly on the antebellum hospital patient's felt experience; they were rarely consulted during their lives and remain generally mute to the historian."*

We have little evidence today. Most, if not all, of the literature on illness, the "experience of illness," is the writings of physicians who become ill and become patients. It is a genre in itself. The tone is like that of someone who fell off a luxury liner into the ocean. If illness is a country; what is illuminated is only the highest peaks; the valleys and lowlands remain in the dark. What is common in these accounts is a tone of not being understood, heard, known. Before his death from prostate cancer, the essayist Anatole Broyard wrote: "I wouldn't demand a lot of my doctor's time. I just wish he would brood on my situation for perhaps five minutes, that he would give me his whole mind just once, be bonded with me for a brief space, survey my soul as well as my flesh to get at my illness. I'd like my doctor to scan me, to grope for my spirit as well as my prostate. Without some such recognition, I am nothing but my illness." These accounts complain about no longer feeling indispensable or indestructible; the loss of plans, goals, aspirations; their sense of isolation from other physicians; the indignity of being a patient; about medicine's inattentiveness to the experience of illness or the doctor's lack of interest in their lives. Doctors who become ill want something more from doctors than do ordinary people; they complain more about medicine and hospitals. It's almost a kind of ventriloquism; the voice of illness is really the voice of medicine.

11

THEY TELL US EVERYTHING

In 1984, Michel de Certeau published The Practice of Everyday Life. *It is called a theoretical monument to the everyday. Certeau wrote that the lives of ordinary people are dominated by, submerged under political, economic, and scientific systems—schools, factories, hospitals. The grid of domination, Certeau wrote, is everywhere.*

Yet the everyday somehow escapes this. The Practice of Everyday Life *is about the resilience of ordinary men and women. Beneath the massive reality of organizations and institutions, Certeau saw unsuspected resources—creativity, inventiveness—hidden among ordinary people, "clandestine arts of the weak over the strategic and powerful projects of political, economic and scientific rationality." He called them "microresistances," "microfreedoms." He said the "resistance" of the everyday is a resistance born of "the stubborn insistence of the body, of childhood memories . . . of traditions and imaginings." He referred to the immemorial intelligence of the powerless.*

He gives as an example the way indigenous Indians subverted the Christianity of the Spanish colonizers, how they transformed the laws, practices, and representations imposed on them by force: "They remained other within the system they assimilated and which assimilated them; they escaped it without leaving it. They metaphorized the dominant order; they made it function in a different register."

Or, in one of his favorite images, the pedestrian on the city streets. The pedestrian chooses where to go, what paths to select, what to ignore. Pedestrians take shortcuts, detours. Their walking is a poetry of "use." They compose paths, they write a long poem of walking.

Patty's the night nurse. She gives report off the top of her head; no notes, she doesn't look at the chart. "Paul Lucero. He's a Do Not Announce.

The cops are investigating. The mother chose the code name: Angel. He was at a party, took some drugs, but his tox screen was so loaded, they thought maybe someone had spiked something. It was a traumatic intubation. He got tons of fluid in the ER. "

The team is four beds away. I look at the first-day progress notes: *Corneal and gag reflex absent; no response to noxious stimuli. Pupils fixed, dilated @ 7 mm, Negative Doll's;*
Impression:

1. *Anoxic Brain secondary to multisubstance ingestion;*
2. *Shock secondary to # 1: pressor-dependent;*
3. *Respiratory failure secondary to # 1: Apnea off vent;*
4. *Acute renal insufficiency w/ rhabdomyolysis;*

His lips are covered with dark flakes of dried blood. The endotracheal tube goes right through where his two upper teeth would have been. The teeth next to the tube are red as though they've been dipped in red candle wax. It's been fifteen hours since he was intubated. His eyes are open in that coma way. I snap my hand at his face just short of his eyes like I'm going to smack him. No blink. I shine the flashlight on his pupils. No reaction. His eyes float like flies drowned in a glass of water. I take a tissue from a Kleenex box, spin it between my fingers into a tip and touch it to his eyeball. No corneal reflex. I slide the suction catheter down the tube and let it sit there. No gag. I take his left nipple between my thumb and index finger and twist it. I put my pen over the nail of his middle finger and press until the skin blanches white. Nothing. From his sternum, downward across his stomach, disappearing around his back, is a livid bruise, as clean as if it had been laid down by a paintbrush. His sputum is thick, tan, the color of peanut butter.

My other patient had come in from Las Vegas yesterday. The night nurse said he had been in pain all night. He's awake. He's Anglo. He's a big man with a full head of white hair. A fierce face. He's unshaven. He's pulled his gown down to his waist. It's clenched in his hands. The hair on his chest is white like rime ice. His eyes are closed tight as though someone had said, "Close your eyes." He's alone.

"Mr. Wallach. Mr. Wallach." He opens his eyes.

"I'm Jim Kelly. I'm going to be your nurse today. How much pain are you having?"

"Through the roof." I could see his chest tense up. The words came out in a grunting sound as if you were talking while you were lifting a TV.

"Where?"

"Here." He puts the palms of his hands flat on his stomach as if to hold his intestines in. He pushes out each breath and groans every time.

"Listen, you have to try and breathe easier. If you're tense, it can cause more pain." I put my hand on his shoulder. "Easy. Easy. We'll get you some more pain mediation. I know it's hard, but you have to try and relax."

The H and P says he's seventy-seven. *Mr. Wallach moved to New Mexico from Virginia at age twenty. He worked between New Mexico and Oklahoma in the oil industry. History of asthma, COPD, diabetes, hypertension. The past three years have been very difficult to get by and he has had frequent pneumonias with extended courses of antibiotics and hospital admissions. He was admitted to Alta Vista Hospital in Las Vegas with a 3-day history of increased cough, fever, and chills. He was given intravenous steroids as well as several antibiotics. He improved. Yesterday, his abdomen became distended and in the evening he became hypotensive. He then became oliguric. C. diff on the stool returned as positive and he was started on Flagyl. With his oliguria and hypotension, he was started on dopamine. I was called at 12:59 a.m. to accept his transfer. The patient arrived here at 5 a.m. by helicopter from Las Vegas.*

When I come back, the wife and one son are in the room. They're in chairs facing the bed. The TV is off. They get up when I come in like when you're waiting at the DMV and they finally call your number. When she stands the wife weaves and reaches out and puts her hand on the son's arm. Being in the ICU must be like your first day on a cruise liner when you lose your balance when you walk on the deck because it's water and not solid earth under you. They ask what's going on. "We'll round soon and we'll get a plan. I'll be able to tell you more then. I'm going to give him some pain medication now."

"I've been in a motel room for ten days," the wife says. "My son is going back to Pecos to get my pills. Will that be okay?" Her cell phone rings. She steps into a corner of the room.

"You're from Boston," the son says, smiling. "My mother can understand you. She's from Lynn. She pahks her cah in Hahvuhd Yahd."

She comes back cupping the phone in her hand. "It's my daughter in Pennsylvania. She doesn't know whether she should come." She looks at me. She does look like someone from New England. Direct. Hair that she has let go white. Firm in the way living through winters makes you tough. Proper. Maybe a librarian.

"I don't think she needs to come right now. I don't think there's any imminent danger of anything bad happening."

Lucero's mother is standing over the bed. She's reading aloud from a book with a sky-blue cover. She's reading very fast, but in a clear, strong voice. She looks young. Forty. A necklace of turquoise stones. She has several bracelets on each wrist, some just silver, some with single stones. And a ring on almost every finger. Her long black hair is down. She's wearing black jeans that taper to above her ankle. Glammed up. She stops reading when I come into the room. She's smiling. "I'm Sophia. I'm his mother. How is he?"

I could tell her he's dead. It's as though I can see into a future she can't or that we're on different points in the continuum of time. I'm in a future she doesn't know. I could reach out and bring her into this future. This is the way the world is now. In a moment it could be a completely different world. A world she would look back on as a never-will-be-again. I could open the door, and she would walk through into this future.

"Not very good."

"I'm not going to think that. He's going to be all right." She looks down at him. "I need you to spend time with me. Come back to me. We need you to stay with us. You're a fighter. You were the best kid ever. Stay with me. I need you. You have a calling. You're a conqueror."

In rounds they say the problem is that we can't do the tests for brain death because he has methadone in his system, and it takes eight to fifty-eight hours to clear.

"We can talk to her about code status though," Murphy says. He dispatches a resident into the room. A minute later, a scream: "My oldest child. He was the one. My rock. My rock." I look into the room. She's pulling the sheet up to his neck and then smoothing it flat. "You're a rock, Paul. You're a rock."

Debbie the monitor tech comes in and asks if we can increase the gain on his EKG. It keeps alarming at the nurse's station. I look at the screen. The EKG waves—the P wave, then the QRS—are small, like cut grass, as though someone had run a scythe over it. The gain is as high as it will go. They gave him tons of fluid in the ER. There must be a sea of water between his heart and the surface of his skin. The levee broke. Fading out before it reaches the surface. A pillow over the bell of his heart. I touch his skin. It's like cement.

I get a better picture of Wallach in rounds. They think it's COPD exacerbation with a left-lower-lobe pneumonia, C. diff, which you get when you take too many antibiotics, then sepsis, then hypotension, then renal failure.

"We need to rule out a surgical abdomen. Let's get a CT, and let's get a renal ultrasound," Murphy says.

"He's in a lot of pain," I tell them.

"How much is he getting?"

"Fentanyl drip. It's at fifty."

"We don't want to intubate him. We'll never get him off the vent." They say that all the time about COPDers: "Never get them off the vent."

They leave a long list of orders: abdominal X-rays, renal ultrasound, bladder scan, a rectal tube to decompress his abdomen, a nasogastric tube to suction, aggressive hydration, a CT of the abdomen.

Lori has the Sinclair woman today. She's just back from CT.

"I hate traveling right away in the morning."

"How is she?"

"Not good. Her stroke's worse."

"Worse how? Did she rebleed? Infarct?"

"Infarct."

"She'll never be who she was."

"No."

"Have they talked to her husband about withdrawal?"

"They started to talk to him about palliative care."

"He really loves her."

"Bad deal."

"Let me help you. You chart and I'll hook her up." The tubing of the ventric, the a-line, and the Swann are tangled next to her head like a bird's nest. The paralytic is off. No more pressors. The storm is over. This is who she is.

The man coming toward Lucero's room extends his hand to me, "I'm her pastor," he says. He's a large man with a barrel chest and a goatee and a small ponytail like a paintbrush. He could be a biker. He could easily have pulled up on a hog parked outside. When he walks into the room, the mother moves closer to the bed the way animals protect their young. An older man is standing behind her.

"Your son, Paul?" the pastor says.

"He has a calling," she says. She talks loudly, like you would if you were singing, or in those churches where the preacher says something and the people are standing, and they say something back like, "Praise the Lord."

"It was prophesied that he would be a preacher," she says. "He's in the wilderness. He's coming out of it. We're going to believe." She's standing over the bed, her arms passing over her son's body as though smoothing a blanket.

"Amen," says the pastor. "And he gave his life to the Lord?"

It's a question.

"No," she says. "Not in that way. He was raised in church."

"Amen. I spent time with his parent before coming. Do you understand?"

"I do. Do you want to pray over him?"

"Bless this world," the pastor says.

"Father, come to pass," says the mother.

"Lord, we know you in time. I ask you to heal his body and mind. Raise him up."

"Amen."

The other man in the room has closed his eyes and raised one hand over his head.

The pastor has put his hands, fingers wide, just above the boy's chest. "We bind you up."

"Amen," they all say.

"We bind you up."

Outside, he says to me, "How is he?"

"Dead," I say.

He frowns at me and makes a shushing sound. Then he nods and flattens his hand, palm down, in a finished gesture. I don't but I want to ask him what "We bind him up" means.

Wallach's blood pressure is dropping. His oxygen saturation is eighty-seven. He looks paler, fading. His wife is in the chair knitting with a big yellow ball of yarn. I call the resident.

"What's he on?"

"Dopamine at twenty."

"What's his heart rate?"

"One twenty-five."

"CVP?"

"Twelve."

"Add vasopressin. Wean the dopamine. Let's try and get his heart rate down. Is he making any urine yet?"

"None."

"Put him on a nonrebreather. And let's get him to CT."

Lucero's mother roams the unit on her cell phone. It's like she's mad, possessed, talking on the phone, reading aloud. I wonder how people bear these things, a son who will die. Her skin has a smoker's hue like a light shining through a lampshade in the daylight. She wears bright lipstick. Her face is expressive. She never stops. When she's not talking, her lips are moving or she's praying or reading. When she's not in the room, she leaves the blue book on the table next to her chair. It's bound so you can add pages. The leather cover is softened by touch and smoothed like the handle of a cane. The text is handwritten. On the cover is written, "Activation As God's Official Legislator and Law Enforcement." Inside, on the left page, are simple bold-faced sentences like "I come," "I effect and enforce," or "I place upon myself," but most say, "I decree." And on the opposite, there's scripture. One says, "I decree," and you look to the right and the scriptures are from Isaiah, Colossians, and Ephesians. "I decree and declare that the Spirit of the Lord is upon me. The Spirit of wisdom, understanding, divine counsel, supernatural might, knowledge of and the utmost fear of Jehovah. As I advance, I am divinely empowered and increase in skill and understanding." One says, "I place upon myself," then, on the opposite page, "The armor of light and of the Lord. The shield of faith to defensively and offensively cover my body." And she does seem lit up, ready for battle, ready for this fight.

When I need to tell her not to talk on her phone in the unit, I touch her arm slightly, say, "Sophia," softly; whisper, "You need to go outside." I like her. I feel she's a kite flying high and wildly in this sudden storm, and I can help by pulling the string taut once in a while so she doesn't lose the wind and fall or get caught up in it and blow away.

When medicine turned its gaze to illness, it discovered it knew very little about suffering. Eric Cassell said the relief of suffering was considered one of the primary ends of medicine by the public but not by the medical profession. He blamed this on the "reductive" methods of science, which inevitably led away from an understanding of suffering: "The central assumptions on which twentieth century medicine is founded provided no basis for the understanding of suffering; for pain, difficulty breathing, yes; for suffering, no." He says that to understand the nature of suffering is now the goal of medicine. But they're not sure what suffering is. Cassell describes how he first looked in literature but couldn't find much: "The search for an understanding of suffering led to an exploration of the plays of classical Greece, Russian literature, suffering in other cultures, and the place of suffering in various theologies." But the search found neither a comprehensive nor a final definition of suffering or its components.

Medicine sees suffering as hidden; that suffering cannot be seen on the surface because we hide our suffering to disguise our vulnerability. Suffering needs to be drawn out, to be made to speak.

To nursing, nothing is hidden. Everything is revealed. What unfolds in a room, over days, is the tableau of the family: suffering, conflicts, regrets, fears. Life maybe framed by an end. Even if patients are sedated, unconscious, families talk to them. They talk to each other. They talk to us. They tell us who they were, what they did, their struggles, what kind of son or father or mother they were.

Everything is revealed: so much that, for all the watching, nursing is also a looking-away, to let them pull the curtains to pray, to let them sit in a chair next to the bed and say they are sorry for something, or "Remember when," or "When you get out, we'll . . ."

There's something happening with Lucero. The monitor and the vent are both alarming. He's desatting. His oxygen is in the seventies. His tidal volumes have dropped to two hundred. I call Mateo. We stand and look at the vent. The pressure to deliver a breath is climbing: thirty-eight, forty-two.

"He's going to pop a lung," I say to Mateo.

"Hear the machine?" he says. It's whining like a truck laboring uphill. "It can't deliver the breath. It's the pressure in his chest on the tube. I'll change him to pediatric mode." We watch for a minute, like watching to see if something you glued together will hold. His volumes come back. "Buy him a little more time," Mateo says. His body is weeping so much the air feels wet like July humidity back in Vermont. Warm, with texture, like walking through a room of silk scarves brushing your face. And sweet like a field of wildflowers. It's a body weeping plasma, weeping itself.

I go outside and find his mother in the waiting room. She's on her cell phone.

"Sophia, we need to discuss code status."

She starts to cry loudly. I put my hands on her shoulders. "We're going to come to a fork in the road."

"I want everything. I don't want you to stop." She shakes her head side to side. "I don't want you to stop. Nope."

Wallach's labs come back. The creatinine has climbed to 2.8. The Renal doc is here. "Tell me about him." He says this without looking at me. He has his thumb under the progress note section. He's not a cowboy; he's from Philadelphia, I think, but he wears a cowboy hat, cowboy boots, a vest, a bolo tie. "All hat, no cattle," Michelle says when he's in the unit. I have it down: "Pneumonia, antibiotics, C. diff, sepsis, acute renal failure. Do you want to talk to his wife?"

I bring him into the room. He talks to her about putting in a temporary catheter to do hemodialysis. When he says kidney failure, she blinks. Even though he says that most people in this situation regain kidney function, I could see her change in that instant. It was like looking at a lake just as a cloud passes over the sun and the lake darkens and the air cools. It moved right over her, head to toe.

Outside the room, he says he'll call Surgery to put in the Vas Cath. It's a special catheter that goes in through the subclavian or jugular vein to just above the right atrium. It's for dialysis. He sits down to write a progress note. "You guys are working hard for no reason." He looks toward the rooms.

"You mean Two and Three?" I ask him. Three is Ortiz.

"And Five."

Five is a GI bleed with maybe hepatorenal syndrome. My expression must look like I'm not getting the punch line of a joke.

"They're not breaking in the right direction." He moves his hand like the prow of a ship and then suddenly off to the side. "All this work for no reason. It's like taking care of vegetables."

They think of them that way. *The House of God* is a novel by Samuel Shem, a pseudonym for the psychiatrist Stephen Bergman, about being a medical intern. Shem goes home after a day in the ICU. His wife, Berry, asks him how it had been. He says he was shaken by the horror of ruined life. It was different, he says, high powered, like being part of a manned space program, but it was also like a vegetable garden, only the vegetables were human.

Ellen Rothman is looking for the moment when she knows she's become a doctor.

Near the end of her second year, in a chapter titled "On My Way," she describes how she suddenly recognizes her transition to the medical mentality. "Now I looked at everyone as a patient." The man on the subway with a blond tuft in the middle of his hair has Waardenburg's syndrome. She now looks through medical eyes, "no longer clouded by the oblivion of the layperson."

She becomes involved with one of her classmates, Carlos. They get engaged, move in together. At the end of the second year they leave Boston for a ten-day trip to Greece. While in Greece she learns she has a contract to write White Coat. *They return to Boston, she writes, "tanned, relaxed, and, if not quite ready to start again, at least curious about what lay ahead." She gets better at diagnosing, explaining treatment options, discussing death, but, she says, "I still felt impossibly far from being a real doctor."*

She doesn't like surgery: "I hated the atmosphere in the OR." A month into the rotation, she learns she has passed her boards: "I had proved to myself that I had mastered the first two years and was now ready to move and become a doctor." But at the end of the obstetrics rotation, the novelty of working in the hospital has worn off, and she has a new and unsettling experience of self-doubt.

People come into and go out of Lucero's room, so many at first you don't know who they are, but after a while it's like a merry-go-round with all the horses in place so you recognize them when they come around.

Three women. "We're his sisters. This is our grandmother. He raised both of us."

They're full of questions. "What are those lines?" "What's the white one?" "Is that good?" "What should it be?"

The sisters are both short, chubby. Smooth brown skin. One is wearing a red sweat suit with matching top and bottom. The younger one a sleeveless white shirt. She has a string of pointed stars tattooed beneath her collarbone like a Christmas ornament. They stand on either side of the bed, their heads barely above the top of the side rails, and then sit on chairs, watching. Like a little class.

The older one asks, "Is he a guinea pig?'

"No, he's not a guinea pig. We're waiting for a test, a certain test to see if he can breathe on his own. He's in a coma."

"If he comes out of the coma and wakes up, he wouldn't be able to breathe? Is the machine keeping his heart going?"

"No, his heart is beating on its own."

"What side is your heart on?'

"The left. You can feel it." I put my palm flat on my chest to show them.

A man by himself. "I'm his father. How is he?"

"Not good. He's had a severe injury to his brain. We have to wait for definitive tests, but our opinion is it's not survivable."

He sinks his head.

"Were you close?"

"Not really. I tried to help him out. I got him an apartment. I know he had a rough time recently. He lost his job."

"You've been divorced for a while?"

"Eight years."

Josh is standing in the doorway. Lori is bent over, dumping the urine. She nods and mouths, "He knows." He's alone. Except for the boy, he's always been alone. They're like spores blown in the wind from hardscrabble towns in Texas, Arkansas; landing in a new place, Albuquerque, Phoenix, Tucson, far from home, far from friends.

"I'm sorry, Josh." His body shakes.

"I've been in jail. I had a bad drug habit, and I dragged her into it. Meth. I was doing twice what people do. I was doing sixty to seventy units a day. I was clean for two years. My marriage broke up. I went back into it. She just used recreationally until she met me. We got to where our families wouldn't have anything to do with us. We had a little window, and we saw we had to get out of there, so we came out here." He starts to cry. "That was ten months ago. I haven't had anything stronger than a diet soda in ten months. She's the kindest, sweetest, most beautiful person you could ever meet."

"Where's her son?"

He straightened up. "He's gone. He lied and now he's gone."

"Where?"

"He had a deal in Arkansas. There were warrants for him, and they agreed to drop the charges if he left the state. His girlfriend is still there, and he's gone back. I got home from the hospital, and there was a note saying he'd left."

They tell you everything. Medicine sees the world of illness as a silent world. There are books like How to Talk to Patients, The Hidden Dimensions of Illness. *In* The Healer's Art, *Cassell cites a notion of the Spanish medical historian Pedro Lain Entralgo on the origin of the lack of communication between doctor and patient. Entralgo said the Hippocratic physicians were "so eager to separate themselves from the superstitious and popular medicine they superseded that they disavowed the spoken or sung charms, chants, and incantations that were formerly the primary modes of treatment. The use of the word in treatment was suspect." In* The Silent World of Doctor and Patient, *Jay Katz writes that the practice of silence "was part of a long and venerable tradition. Explanations would reveal the uncertainties in the art and science of medicine and create a state of mind inimical to cure."*

They tell you things. One woman was sitting in the room of her brother. I was going in and out doing things. The brother had had a stroke. I was in the room a long time. I was facing away from her, taking vital signs off the monitor. She said aloud, "I killed a child once. My sister's. I was leaving her house. They were waving good-bye. I didn't see her run behind the car. It was the softest sound." She spoke in a very calm voice. "I started to drink. I give talks now. I volunteer."

You learn things about them. She's a twin. He likes to bowl. She volunteers with Kitchen Angels. It's an intimacy they give you. It's a gift. Richard Titmuss said in his book The Gift Relationship *that nursing is a "stranger relationship," a kind of creative altruism that allows nurses to be free to choose to give to unnamed strangers.*

But they give to us too. Their telling is a gift.

Traveling out of the unit to MRI or CT you feel like you're an astronaut floating in space on a fix-it mission, outside the ship, drifting, connected by only a thick cable. I give him an extra fifty of fentanyl and two of Versed before we leave the unit. It seems to quiet him down.

It happens before we transfer him to the scanner, when he's still on the bed. Suddenly he's as wet as if he had just got out of the bathtub. White as porcelain. I rub my knuckles along his sternum. "Mr. Wallach." No response. The heart rate on the transport monitor says forty-three then thirty-seven, but it's all squiggly. He's breathing little shallow breaths. Get him back to the unit or call a code? The room we're in is the smaller of the two CT rooms. I can see through the wired glass window into the room where the techs sit and run the scanner. The window on the other side of that room opens to where they do the MRIs. The people in the room are all wearing blue hospital scrubs. It's as though they're the crew of a submarine surrounded by a strange underwater world. I'm in that world. It seems like they're all moving slowly. One of the techs, Ramona, is at the foot of the bed. She's looking at me.

"Push the code button," I tell her. "We need the crash cart." People appear at a code like a squall. They appear as if they were there all the time and popped up like a rake you stepped on. The techs are all in the room.

An ER nurse is kneeling on the bed. "I don't feel a carotid."

An ER doctor is standing over his head. "Is he breathing? Do we need to bag him?"

I know what happened. The fentanyl stopped his breathing. I know what I need. "I need Narcan," I say. Narcan is an opioid antagonist. I give him .4 and just like that his eyes open, numbers come up, his color back. Everyone stops to see if it holds. "I need to get him back to the unit."

We're traveling fast. There are five maybe six of us; I can't tell: respiratory, two transport guys, a CT tech, a nurse who came when we called the code. It's a jigsaw path back. Go past the backside of Admitting, the cath lab offices, through double doors, past elevators, along a Med-Surg unit, past the waiting room where his wife is standing in the door.

He's screaming, "I'm going to die! I'm going to die!" Screaming it.

I'm at the head of the bed. "You're not going to die. You're going to be all right." But I'm kind of yelling it at him.

Then he screams, "Don't lie to me!" We're through the doors and in the unit. Now he's screaming, "Mother! Mother!" Murphy and two other residents are waiting. The vent is outside the room. It's completely covered in plastic like an outdoor grill.

"I want an ABG," Murphy says. "I'm going to make the fentanyl prn. Go easy on it." He looks at me. "Do that art of nursing thing."

We hook him up, give him some Versed, and he quiets. No more screaming. I'm thinking we're going to have to intubate him. Mateo is kneeling on the floor for the ABG. He has an index finger on the wrist where the artery should be. In his other hand, he's holding a small syringe, the needle pointing at Wallach's skin like a bird waiting for a fish to come to the surface. What did his wife think when we went by? Was it like standing on the shore and seeing someone you love being swept down a river? Someone has to talk to her.

His pH comes back 7.13. His CO_2 is 65.

"I want to try him on BiPAP," Murphy says. He's been in the unit, hovering. "I'd like to avoid intubating him."

His wife comes back, walking slowly, her arms a little outstretched, like someone walking in the dark in a strange hotel room. I tell her he had an event in CT. "He didn't stop breathing but his breathing slowed down. We corrected it right away."

What's it like out there in the waiting room, wondering what's going on, a scary page like Code Blue overhead, not knowing what you're going to hear when they come back to the unit? I tell her we're going to put him on a breathing device that will help him get rid of his carbon dioxide. I wonder if she knew that page was for her husband.

We strap the BiPAP mask on tight against his face to get a good seal. Now he's not responding. Narcan lasts only thirty minutes. I give him another .4 and then another.

Mateo finishes tightening the mask. "You were good with him. Telling him he wasn't going to die. I think that helped him." But we both know that the thing is, everyone in the hospital who says that, who says they are going to die, dies.

⬧ ⬧ ⬧

"Have you been outside?" Martha says to me. "They have a Crock-Pot. It's like a picnic."

She means the mother, Sophia, but I find her in the room.

"Where are your daughters?"

"Can I bring in some healing music on a CD? They went to get a CD with a song he dedicated to me."

The girls come back. They have a small CD player. They play it, and the song starts off with something about a "ho."

"That's not it," the mother shrieks and the girls put their hands to their mouths. "It's number twelve. It's by Nelly," she says to me.

The song starts. It's a rap song. The girls move their bodies. The mother hands me the lyrics. She's smiling. Her eyes brighten. The song is called "Luven Me."

Ay yo ma, how you doin, it's ya son now

And I picked up the mic and put the drugs down

Now I'm tryin to do some things that'll make you proud

Instead of everytime I call it's to bail me out

Oh why didn't I listen to things you used to tell me

Knowin that everything that you said would ever fail me

Don't stop ever lovin me

Uh, uh I said whatever you need

Don't stop ever lovin me

Uh, uh, I said you don't have to work no more.

She's clapping her hands and moving like they do at those New Age churches and she's saying loudly, "Let's go. Let's go." And they're all clapping their hands, and Nelly on the CD player is rapping, "*Uh, uh, uh 'cause ya son will be there for you.*"

Certeau says ordinary people are "unrecognized producers, poets of their own acts, silent discoverers of their own paths in the jungle of functionalist rationality. . . . In the technocratically constructed space, they circulate, come and go, their trajectories form unforeseeable sentences, partly unreadable paths . . . neither determined nor captured by the systems in which they develop."

We think that medicine is truth, and in the hospital the facts of science meet the superstitions of ordinary people, a sort of myth meets the monitor. But it can be the other way around. It is ordinary people who have a metaphysic, and science is the myth: the myth of cure, the myth of brain death. We say they deny death when I think they know; we keep the truth from them, we say they won't understand, when they do understand. It's just that they have their own sense of time. I think Sophia knows. Somewhere. I think April knows. Fleischer wasn't afraid to die. They have ways of working things out we maybe can't understand. And reasons. This life is everything. Billy Collins said that the dead wish they could come back and learn Italian or see the Pyramids, or play golf in a light rain. They wish they could wake up in the morning like us and stand at the window looking at winter trees, at the tracing of snow on the branches. We wish they could too. We wish they were here with us. When they're gone, never again. They may believe the person is going to heaven, they may think they are already with Jesus, but you can tell that they know this life is everything, being here is everything, that this life, this person is once. So it's okay with me what they do, if they don't look you in the eye, or say the doctor hasn't talked to them, or pull the curtain and pray, or if they dance.

A new woman is in Lucero's room. She's next to the ventilator, leaning on the rail. "Is his mother here?" she asks me.

"She's out in the waiting room."

"She's one of my best friends." Her hair hangs in long black coils. She's wearing black Chuck Taylor Converse sneakers like the kind the Celtics wore and we wore in high school. High-tops with white laces not laced all the way up. A dress of uneven hem. Her lipstick is bright red. She looks like a Gypsy. "We had our first at the same time. I think of my own kids when I look at him. How is he?"

"Very bad. There's a test we can't do because he has drugs in his system, but we think, and other tests indicate, he's brain dead and brain death to us is death. At some point something is going to happen. His heart will stop. We won't be able to ventilate him. An event. We'll have to decide. Are we going to do everything? Shock him? Pound on his chest? Give him drugs? Or just let him go."

"You think he's suffering?"

"At some level. It's tragic. He's a young man. Don't tell Sophia because I know she doesn't want to hear it."

I can see Father Perrini outside the room. The first day I met Father Perrini was when he came to see a mother who was T-boned at an intersection. Her two babies died. He walked in with the family. Father Perrini was wearing a brown woolen robe with a hood, a rope belt, and sandals over socks. I thought maybe it was something he wore that day but he wears it every day. When he sees me, he blesses me. He does the hand thing. I might nod and smile and say, "Thank you, Father." Sometimes I say, "Bless you, too, Father Perrini." He thinks I'm Catholic. I let him think it. My last name is Kelly, I'm from Boston. He gets a huge kick out of my accent.

"How's the mother?" He peeks into the room.

"She doesn't believe it. She thinks it's going to be okay."

"I knew a father once whose daughter was in a car accident, and they said she was brain dead. They wanted her organs and her father said, 'Why would they want that? She'll need them when she wakes up.' Could they be wrong? You hear stories of people waking up. Even years later."

"They're not wrong. That never happens. He's never going to wake up. He's dead."

He nods his head. "Can I go in and give him the sacrament of the sick?"

The Gypsy woman is still here. "I'm going to leave now." But she stays where she is, next to the bed.

"It's going to be hard for her," she says.

The soft blue book is still there. The CD player. A picture of Jesus on the pillow next to his temple. Father Perrini is next to the boy. His Bible is open. I can see his lips moving.

The woman looks at me. "I lived in Oregon. The pastor denounced me as a witch because I could prophecy. I got divorced. I was depressed for years. I wanted to die. I had a vision. I saw an opening. A hole. People around it. They said, 'It's not your time.'"

She looks over to the bed where Father Perrini is holding a Bible and moving his hands in the air. "I don't go to church anymore. I don't have the gift. I miss it."

By the end of the shift, he's grotesque. I can't open his eyes. His lips are huge and his tongue sticks out, swollen like a dead animal's. Like he's being strangled, like invisible hands are locked around his neck. The emerald tip of a bite block in a pool of water in his mouth; water in the hollows of his eyes. Those eyes swollen shut. His chest is puffed up like the chest of a bird when it's mating, but his breath sounds are like the sound you would make blowing out a match. His genitals are huge. All that fluid, like a monsoon flooding an arroyo. Blake and Frank help me change his sheets.

"If they donate his organs, I want his prick," Frank says.

"You'll have to walk around with it in a wheelbarrow," Blake says.

His skin is weeping everywhere, a sweet, sickly odor in the air like a mask over your face. There are ICU smells: sweat from pain, fear, from GI bleeds, infected wounds, from pus, that neuro smell, dialysis patients, stool. This is different. Astronauts say space smells like hot metal or fried steak. This is what it must smell like inside the body.

I have to call again and again for Wallach. I have to call because his creatinine is up, then because his CO_2 is up, and then his pressure is down. We start him on Levophed. He's working so hard to breathe, he's sweating and the BiPAP mask keeps slipping, the seal breaks, the alarm sounds. It feels like water rising.

They don't really do evening rounds; they sort of walk through the unit. Outside Lucero's room, I tell Murphy, "We're not going to code him. We'll just call you overhead." It's seven o'clock. Martha comes by for report. His pulse pressure is narrowing. "I think he's tamponading," I tell her. We say blood flows downhill. Across the circulation, blood flows from areas of higher pressure to lower pressure. Downhill. Tamponade is when fluid accumulates in the pericardium, the sac in which the heart is enclosed. All that fluid pressing against his weak heart. Every time his heart beats it's like opening a door and water coming in. Eventually all the pressures become the same. No more downhill. No flow.

Leaving, I walk out past the waiting room. The mother, the daughters, some men are there. The table is full of food: chips, salsa, plastic soda bottles, plates. A Crock-Pot is plugged into the wall.

The mother sees me. She calls out, "James." My badge says "JAMES." "Do you want some spaghetti?"

"No, I'm going home. Thanks." I walk to her and we hug.

"I'm not back tomorrow, so good luck."

She puts her cell phone into her bag. "I think things are going to be okay."

Agee lives with the Gudger family for three weeks. He sleeps in a room next to George Gudger; his wife, Annie Mae; her sister Emma; and four children. Agee is under no illusion that the tenant farmers are poor. He says Annie Mae "is of that tribe who seem to exhaust rather than renew

themselves with sleep, and to whom the act of getting up is almost un-endurably painful." That the intellects of the children "died before they were born; they hang behind their eyes like fetuses in alcohol." That they live in a steady shame and insult of discomforts, insecurities, and inferiorities. He imagines their thoughts: "In what way were we trapped? where our mistake? What, where, how, when, what way might all these things have been different, if only we had done otherwise? How did we get caught? Why is it things always seem to go against us?"

But even though they are poor, crippled almost at birth, without any real hope, they don't seem to want for anything; uneducated, they have an innate wisdom; trapped, they are not without pride. Agee begins to see in their lives dignity and beauty. In the end, he thinks them holy, divine.

Illness is a kind of poverty. The fullness of life drained. The patients and the families can't close themselves up, can't draw a curtain. Invisible people made cruelly visible. Their lives filleted open, you can see their hearts beating. They do a thousand things: they leave work early, come on their lunch break, after work, leave scapulars, crucifixes, CDs, cards, notes, stuffed animals. They wipe their foreheads, clean their mouths, their eyes, whisper to them, read to them, sing to them, pray. They sit for hours in the rooms. Sleep overnight in the waiting room. They are told unimaginable things: "If we take him off the ventilator, he won't survive." "She's suffered a devastating injury to the brain." "Too sick to operate." "Never recover." But there is no weight that crushes them, no word that silences, no truth that paralyzes. They go on; every day they come and go, leave their life and come to the hospital, leave the hospital to go back to their life, making their own way in the hospital, weaving their way around us.

12

CAN THEY HEAR?

Michel de Certeau says that people know things, that everyday life is full of know-how, judgments, acquired instincts, competencies: "People know everything. . . . They know it somewhere. Somewhere: but where? . . . Their practices know it—moves, behaviors, ways of talking or walking, the everyday arts of cooking, cleaning, sewing."

Edmund Burke calls it a practical wisdom, "a knowledge of the concrete, of ready application in the emergency; it engages the mind in a steady course of wisdom and virtue, and does not leave the man hesitating in the moment of decision, skeptical, puzzled and unresolved." This knowledge, though, is invisible, unrecognized. Certeau describes it as hidden, as "obscure, silent, invisible, cunning, ancient."

In Doing-Cooking, Luce Giard speaks of her "refusal to denigrate a mass culture . . . a will to turn one's eyes toward contemporary people and things, toward ordinary life, a will to accept as worthy of interest, analysis and recording, the ordinary practices so often regarded as insignificant, a will to consider fleeting and unpretentious ways of operating."

Giard turns her eyes toward the work of cooking a meal at home, long considered just a household task without cultural significance, devoid of mystery and grandeur. She finds, instead, that it "unfurls in a complex montage of things to be done according to a pre-determined chronological sequence: planning, organizing, and shopping; preparing and serving; clearing, putting away, and tidying up." It requires skills: "In cooking, one always has to calculate, both time and money; one has to evaluate in the twinkling of an eye price, preparation, flavor; one has to know how to improvise, what to do when fresh milk 'turns' on the stove; one has to remember that someone had pasta when they visited last, that someone does not like chocolate cake, one has to choose a wine to match."

Giard writes that "doing-cooking" is an everyday labor that unites the present moment and past memory, imagination and tradition, life and tenderness; that it is rooted in the fabric of relationships to others. The

everyday art of cooking, she says "shows a subtle intelligence full of nu-
ances and strokes of genius, a light and lively intelligence that can be per-
ceived without exhibiting itself, in short, a very ordinary intelligence."

"Joseph Martinez. Motor vehicle accident. Unrestrained. They found him in a ditch in Española. He's like Hannibal Lecter. Let me show you." Amanda leads me into the room. She means the bed. It's a TriaDyne bed that rotates side to side. The patient is strapped on to it. It's for spinal injuries.

"To stop it, you have to take hold of the handles to disengage it. Like you were steering a big yacht. Push in this pin. This is how you get to his bottom." She's down on one knee, like a mechanic looking under a car. "It's a true poop-chute." Standing up, she looks at the sheet where it sticks up where his genitals are. "He's got some priapism going on."

He's a stocky, fleshy young guy. Twenty-one, Hispanic, gang-banger look, shaved head, chin whiskers. I squeeze his trapezius muscle to see what he does, and his right arm raises and then flops and then kind of extends, his hands curling out like when you do the breaststroke. I open his eyes. His pupils are small, not quite pinpoint, dysconjugate: the right pupil sitting in the middle of the sclera, the left eye looking down, half-buried like the sun below the horizon. His head comes out of the Miami-J cervical collar like a flower in a vase. The only marks on him are scratches on his face, his temple, forehead. Little ones like a cat would make. The thing is his skin. Soft, smooth, young. Almost like baby fat. He's flat, strapped on the bed, which is tilted, his feet down, head up, just like that scene in *Silence of the Lambs* when they roll Anthony Hopkins in to meet Jodi Foster for the first time.

I look at the progress notes from the day before:

Impression:
1. *Closed head injury; unresponsive. Diffuse axonal injury; doll's eyes +*
2. *Spinal injury: ? level ? completeness*
3. *likely splenic injury*
4. *left pneumothorax, rib fracture*

They're not sure of the level of paralysis. But he can breathe on his own. That means it's not above the fifth cervical nerve. C5 goes to the diaphragm. C5 keeps you alive.

My other patient is Jennifer Montoya. Someone is in her room almost all the time. One of the four daughters or the husband. Sometimes they're like a vise, the families, tightening around you. The morning daughter is in the room. She slept in two chairs pulled to face each other with hospital blankets and a pillow. She's stripped them and put them back so it's not a bed anymore. "I'm going home now. My other sister will be here." Her hair is short and wound into tight corkscrews the way women with thin hair do, and you can see her scalp the way you can see through a forest when the leaves fall. She writes down everything. I asked her once what she was writing. "Everything that happens. So when she gets home she won't have missed anything." They're like scribes. Historians of their own suffering. They write things down. They leave notes everywhere, on the cork board, on the roller tables, taped to the pillow like prayers Jews leave in the crevices of the Wailing Wall. A secret genre no one knows.

She kisses her mother on the forehead. "Bye, sleepyhead. I'll be back soon. You're gonna be in charge. Whatever you want, you'll get. You'll be the boss. Whatever you say, you'll get. Just say the word."

She was the one who found her unconscious, who did CPR. In the ambulance, the paramedics shocked her twice and got her back to sinus rhythm. Her history was that she had non-Hodgkins lymphoma and was treated with chemotherapy, then with Adriamycin. But it affected her heart. It caused cardiomyopathy, which was probably what made her susceptible to an arrhythmia. Her ejection fraction is now 21 percent. They put her on amiodarone as an antiarrhythmic, but then she went into liver and then renal failure. The last progress note says, *Needs cardiac catheterization and implantable cardioverter defibrillator if survives. Very poor prognosis. Cath postponed indefinitely. Situation explained to family.*

She doesn't respond. To voice, to pain. She had been awake last week. She's a small woman but her belly is huge, with shiny pregnancy scars. Her limbs are like a rag doll's. Her breathing is erratic. Fast, then rides the vent, then fast again. A halo of moisture on the pillow around her hair, which is short and stylish. Two of the daughters wear it the same way.

A resident is writing new orders. She's a white woman. She has a slight build, but she is loud. She's always saying she's from New Jersey, that's she's a Jersey girl, that she's from back east. She's always going into your room and turning the sedative drips down or off, and then you find the patient awake, crazy, or their blood pressure up. She had long hair and then one day she came in and it was cut off. It looked like she did it her-self; it was cut straight across. Lori said she could see her doing that, just getting hot and cutting it off.

"She's unresponsive. She doesn't move. She's flaccid," I tell her.

"It's a puzzle."

"Was there an event? Does she have an anoxic injury?"

"CT didn't show anything. We're going to stop all sedation."

She gives me the chart. "We're ordering a CT of the abdomen."

"Why?"

"Her enzymes are down, but her bili's up. There's something growing in her lungs. We're going to start her on Zosyn."

In rounds, Morgan says they're taking Martinez back in two days to fix his neck. One of the residents asks about prognosis. Morgan says that it's how they are when they come in and at seventy-two hours. "Remem-ber that gal in Ten, the MVA from Pecos? Her dog was in the car? She woke up. Remember that guy in Seven? Paralyzed? He's driving around. They have that thing. Young brains. But the first bounce of a ball is the highest, and he's had his bounce." He talks about the pros and cons of steroids, the loss of rectal tone, and, as he leaves, he turns to me and says, "You need to do digital stimulation for twenty minutes," which makes the team laugh.

The first visitors aren't his parents but a mother and daughter. They stand back from the bed as if they were looking at something in a cage at the zoo as it rotates away, then toward them. "How is he?" the mother whispers.

"He's suffered a devastating injury to his brain." I whisper, too.

The girl is crying and standing back near the ventilator. She has a rosary in her hands, hiding it as if it were a small bird she's protecting. She's sliding the bead through her fingers. When she feels me watching she stops. The sides of the bed rise and fall slowly, like the sway of water in a bathtub.

Lori told a story one day about how she and a friend passed an accident at the bottom of La Bajada. La Bajada is between Santa Fe and Albu-querque. It means "the descent" in Spanish. It's considered the terminus of the Rocky Mountains. Before I-25 was built, it was the old Route 66.

It consisted of twenty-three hairpin turns so steep that cars drove up in reverse. Lori told how her friend said a little prayer, and her friend's eyes teared up. "And I said a little prayer too, but I'm a nurse. It didn't upset me."

In a chapter titled "Too Much" Ellen Rothman writes about her trauma rotation. She has a patient whose spinal cord is severed at C6 in a head-on collision. His name is Richard. He is married with a young son. Rothman is watching her preceptor write a note in the chart. "I felt the sting of tears forming behind my eyes. He might never regain full use of his arms or hands, but he would not be a complete quadriplegic." Later, when she helps transfer him from his bed to a gurney, she sees his wife on a cot in a shadowy corner of the room. "I saw tears silently course down her cheeks and drip off her chin as she watched us struggle to move her husband." She's happy to leave the trauma rotation. "For the first time," she writes, "I understood what it was like to care for hospitalized patients and become emotionally invested in their care. The pain was more overwhelming than I ever imagined it would be. I never thought I would believe I knew too much, had seen too much."

S. Kay Toombs writes that, in medicine, empathic understanding is a fundamental requirement for the full development of clinical knowledge. Nursing theorists claim that nursing, practically alone among the human service professions, deliberately tries to train its young in empathy, sensitivity, and compassion. Empathy means you can project yourself into the private inner experience of another person and fully understand it. This is different from sympathy. Sympathy is "I and you"; empathy is "I am you."

But you really can't walk into someone's life. You can get close to it, you can see it, but you can't feel it. Empathy isn't a bridge. Illness is a closed world you can see but not enter. The closer you are to it, the farther away you see that it really is. Illness is more like an island than a country. An island you may or may not be on, may never be on. You can visit the island. You can go to the island and come back but you don't live on the island. You can never know the island like the people who live on the island.

In the movie Things to Do in Denver When You're Dead, the characters played by Andy Garcia, Jack Warden, and Christopher Lloyd have all been in prison. Now, out of prison, they meet in a diner, and when they say good-bye they place the palms of their hands together because in prison, when someone visits you, you say good-bye by pressing your *palm to the window separating you, and the other person presses his palm on the other side of the window. Nursing is like that: you touch but you don't touch.*

Even though he's paralyzed and probably a quadriplegic, his feet move. When I run a hemostat along his soles, his toes flex down. The little guy Mitchell is the Neurosurgical resident. He says it's a reflex arc, it doesn't go to the brain. "It synapses in the spinal cord. But he's got DAI," he says. "His CT is relatively normal; there's no blossoming yet, but he has punctate hemorrhages in the cortex and the corpus callosum." There's something about the Neurosurgical residents. They're a smaller team. They're close. And it's not that they're cocky, but they seem really confident. I heard Mitchell once say that if he didn't pass the boards, he would just go to law school.

Mitchell is here when the parents come in. They look young, frightened. He tells them being paralyzed is the least of their son's problems. "DAI means diffuse axonal injury. It's like the way twisting an orange shreds the fibers"—he twists his hands in opposite directions—"the transmission in the brain is never the same. Ninety percent never wake up. We'll schedule the surgery to fix his spine, and then we should go ahead and put in a tracheostomy and a feeding tube." They're quiet. People walk into the ICU and just stare as if they never imagined a world like this. It's not like walking into a bank, a school, a grocery store and your mind knows what goes on in there, that there are people at desks, walking down aisles, buying things, closing at five or nine.

A different daughter and Montoya's husband are in the room, sitting in chairs. He has Parkinson's. When I first met him, his arm shook constantly, as though he was getting ready to roll dice, hoping to get lucky, to change the way the game was going. Now that he knows me, his arm moves less and he talks more, but everything is Parkinson's—his soft weak voice, tremor, mincing steps. He stands up and goes to the foot of the bed. He is subdued. "Not doing good today." She's seventy-four. He's seventy-eight. He had told me how long they were married, fifty-six and a half years. When he said "a half" he had bounced up like a jack-in-the box, like the half was special or that it meant he would get the other half. You have to wonder why that long isn't enough.

Long enough. Can't let go. It's this once. Never again. Never the same. Life's not long enough. He sits in the chair next to his daughter. Her name is Jill; she's the nicest one. The TV is on. They're watching *To Touch an Angel* on the station that shows old shows. Always somebody here. It's like their mother is not the one clinging to life. She's a piece of driftwood they're clinging to. If they, especially the one daughter who stays at night, were to loosen their grip for a moment, or lose sight of her, it is they who would drift away, they who would disappear.

Susan Sontag, for one, said there was no meaning to be found in illness. "The purpose of my book was to calm the imagination, not to incite it. Not to confer meaning, which is the traditional purpose of literary endeavor, but to deprive something of meaning. To cleanse illness of all meanings and to reduce it to a scientific, biological fact so that someone would not have to suffer more from thinking about his illness than from the illness itself." The book is Illness as Metaphor. *Sontag had cancer twice before she was diagnosed with a particularly virulent form of blood cancer, myelodysplastic syndrome. She wanted to persuade people "to regard cancer as if it were a disease—a very serious one, but just a disease. Not a curse, not a punishment, not an embarrassment. Without meaning." She blames "doctor-writers" for this myth of illness as "an epic of suffering and the occasion of some kind of self-transcendence."*

Martinez's parents have questions. They want to know about the tracheostomy.

"It goes here?" the father asks. He points to his neck.

"It's not therapeutic," I tell them. "It doesn't do anything for what's wrong with him. It will just make it easier to suction him. It'll reduce the risk of infection."

"Should we stay overnight?" the mother asks. "We stayed last night but woke up every half hour."

"I wouldn't. You need to conserve your strength, take care of yourselves. You need to rest. This is going to be a difficult process. I don't think anything will happen to him. He's in the ICU. He's critical. But he's young. And he has a strong heart."

We're standing not in the room but in the open doorway. I haven't seen them ever sit. They always stand close to each other but both of them with their arms over their own chest as if they're cold. Sometimes you want to rescue them from medicine, before everything gets in motion—trach, PEG, rehab, nursing home—to save them before the thing happens that if they knew before what it was, they would never want, no matter how terrible the decision.

"We should discuss code status. If something were to happen to him, if his heart were to stop or if he were to have a life-threatening arrhythmia, would we do anything? Would we—like you've seen on TV—do chest compressions, shock him?"

"He wouldn't want that," the father says.

"It doesn't change how we treat him. We treat him as if he will leave the hospital someday"—I almost said walk out—"but if something were to happen we would not intervene. It would mean it was his time."

They're silent, holding themselves. "Just something for you to think about. You don't have to decide now."

They leave, and all afternoon a series of people drift in—always only two, some of them older, grandparents, older friends. They are all from northern New Mexico, Española, Velarde, La Puebla. Rural, poor, Hispanic. The Española valley is crisscrossed with *acequias* from the Spanish times. It's where lowriding began. It's the heroin capital of the United States. Driving up north from Santa Fe, past Tesuque, the Santa Fe Opera House, past the new Cities of Gold casino, it's like going back in time, and that's where the joke comes from: What did Jesus tell the people of Española? Don't do anything until I come back.

Two men. One is wearing a worn leather bomber jacket. Black, stringy hair to his shoulders. He puts an arm around the other man, who is younger but older than a boy.

"I was his godfather," the man says. He speaks very slowly. "His grandfather and I were best friends. He was like my brother. It was an honor to baptize him. All his spiritual brothers are here." His right eye is brown but the other eye is pure blue, robin's-egg blue.

A man is pushing a wheelchair into the room. I can see a woman rise from the chair. She walks slowly to the side of the bed. The man stands beside her but not close. This man too has a thin face and lank, greasy hair. They stare at the boy. The woman wears a red shawl with tassels. She could be in her thirties. Her black hair is loose and wild around her face. It's hard not to look at her. Her eyes never leave the boy.

"My prayers are with you." Her voice is a wail but songlike. "The Virgin Mary is waiting for you. We're going to miss you. I'm going to miss you. We're going to hand you over to God. So you won't suffer anymore."

A woman and a young girl come in.

"Joseph Martinez?" the woman says.

"I hope you're twelve," I say to the girl.

"No," she says. "Thirteen," and smiles.

The mother is wearing a blue polyester sweater with big buttons. She stands in front of the girl like a shield. She has her hands behind her back and the girl is standing behind her and has entwined her hands with her mother's in a weave of fingers. You can tell they are close in life. The girl is wearing blue jeans that end in a slit at her calf. On both ankles are multicolored bracelets. When the bed rolls to the right, the mother goes up on her tiptoes to peer over the rising edge and the girl moves with her.

They are all gracious, quiet in the room, staying briefly, thanking me, even shaking hands when they leave. The room hushes them: the grotesqueness of the bed, the crucified look. The naked body. Some of them leave behind rosaries sparkling like tinsel on the metal truss.

I have to clean up Montoya. The daughter who stays at night is back.

"Do you want to step out while I clean her up? Just a few minutes," I say.

When I suction her, she grimaces but opens her mouth wide. It's a terrible expression. How can they not see it? Her skin is moist, her heart rate up. I give her fifty of fentanyl and two of Ativan. Her tooth comes out. A top one. It's sitting on the back of her tongue. I grab it with my fingers. I'll have to tell the daughter. I put it in a denture cup.

The daughter's not upset at the tooth. "We'll put it back in when she gets home." She writes something in the book.

Martinez's father has come back with his daughter. The daughter is tall, almost as tall as the father. They have very dark skin, dark hair. It's their culture out here. The only license plate in the country that has *USA* on it. Everything written in the hospital is in English and Spanish—the menus, the signs—English on top, Spanish below. Whatever they announce over the intercom they say again in Spanish. The housekeepers speak to each other in Spanish. One of the house managers calls everybody "mi hijito." The state government building is the Montoya building. Vigil is the state treasurer, the name of a DUI arrested last night, the kid who scored the winning goal in the soccer tournament.

"He wouldn't want this," the father says to me. It's as if the hour since we talked hadn't happened, as if time had stopped.

"We can talk outside."

Lori says I have speeches. I never thought of them that way. But I do have a "fork-in-the-road" speech, a "prepare yourself for the worst," a "he'll never be who he was." I once played Prospero in *The Tempest*. At the end, Prospero is talking to Ariel and he is getting ready to release everyone from the spell he has over them. He says, "My charms I'll break, their senses I'll restore, and they shall be themselves." Being yourself is what you most want and what people most want you to be. Once I told my father-in-law how a family had asked me how their mother who had a massive subdural was doing and I told them she would never be who she was, that they should prepare themselves for the worst. He looked at me in disbelief, "You said that?"

And the "window" speech. The "window" speech means that here, in the ICU, is the only opportunity—the window of opportunity—we will have to let them die.

We go outside the unit to the door by the OR. The daughter squats on the floor and folds herself up with her legs against her chest and her arms around them so her knees are almost level with her chin.

The daughter is looking down at the floor. I talk to the father. "Tomorrow, some doctor will tell you, 'Let's wait. There's hope.' They'll put in a tracheostomy to help him breathe and a tube into his stomach to feed him. But he'll never be who he was. He won't be able to care for himself, feed himself, control his bowels. His life as he knows it is over."

"He would be so angry," the daughter says.

"I know this is a lot for you. To hear this. I want you to know that we're doing everything we can for him as if someday he'll leave the hospital. But you have a choice, you can say no to things like these. There is actually a window of time when we can withdraw support on somebody, on somebody who has suffered a devastating injury like this. If they go ahead and trach and PEG him, if they wean him off the ventilator to where he can breathe on his own, you won't be able to do it. There are things we can do here that they can't do in a nursing home."

"Is he on life support?" the father asks.

"He is. If we took him off the ventilator, he would breathe on his own, but with difficulty. Do you want me to tell you how we do it?"

He nods.

"We take out the tube. We put them on a morphine drip so they won't suffer."

"We don't want him to suffer."

"We make them comfortable. And everyone can be here. If God wants to take him, we would not intervene. We would let that happen."

They're quiet. You can hear pages overhead. For doctors. For some family member who's lost, to go somewhere. A female voice says, "Catch a falling star, thirty-two twelve." A patient has fallen.

"I have a child," the daughter says. "If it was my daughter, I would want to wait."

End of shift. I walk the unit. Some of the rooms are dark, some lit, some with families, some with one person, some empty. The patient on a bed like an actor alone on a stage. The one thing you can see in all the rooms, above the blankets, resting on a pillow, is a face. Different odors. Feces, C. diff, renal. Like different temperate zones. TV voices flow out of the caves of the rooms and weave in the air. The Spanish station Univision. ESPN. CNN. García like a bug on its back, arms and legs flailing. His penis disappeared into his scrotum like a tree disappears in its own leaves. Still, a long, slow climb out of the depths. Three surgeries. A friend holding his leg and kneading his calf. His wife, Lakota, calls every day. "I don't drive." She sounds drunk. Says things like "I pray for all of you. Be patient with him. He didn't finish high school." A CD playing in his room. Mark Knopfler and Emmylou Harris. *All the Roadrunning*. Sanchez's family talking to her. "Fruta. Fruta." The loving daughter. Carson. Like he's on fire. Heart rate 143. Pressure 188 over 104. They've tried everything. Rate of thirty-five on the vent. Reversed the I and E. A healthy guy who got the flu. He's like one of those California wildfires they say is 70 percent contained or 40 percent contained. Pneumonia. Then kidney failure. Billy Collins has a poem about sitting on a train and seeing speed lines on people. It's like you can see the flames. He's 0 percent contained. Even the doctors, running out of ideas. They paralyze him, then stop the paralytic, then paralyze him again. I had him once. Early. His wife like a schoolteacher. Asking a lot of questions. A soft woman. Warm. Friendly. One day I had to call her for consent to give him blood, and the voice message mentioned what the male nurse had said today about how he was doing. She meant me. Trying to understand.

"Life changes fast," Joan Didion wrote. "Life changes in the instant. You sit down to dinner and life as you know it ends." Every day now she seems harder or denser or more focused. Friendly still, but like a child losing her baby fat. She's early fifties growing up before our eyes. They put a Vas Cath in for dialysis. Wallach is intubated. All the terror and work of breathing over. His wife sees me and smiles. I smile back. I think what García and Carson have missed. Daylight savings time. The World Series. Halloween. The first snow in the Sangres.

In The Birth of the Clinic, *Foucault writes about the origin of the teaching hospital, the change in disease theory, the rise of the medical profession. The first question, Foucault says, in looking at a profession, is, "Who is speaking? Who has the right to speak? Who is qualified to do so? Who derives from it his own special quality, his prestige?" In medicine, doctors speak. They speak mostly to each other. They have rounds, conferences, teaching sessions. They have their own jargon. They don't speak to nurses.*

In A Not Entirely Benign Procedure, *Perri Klass's description of Harvard Medical School, she writes, "One of the ways that doctors learn to be doctors is by learning that they are not nurses and must not stoop to nurses' work." During her first week in the hospital she asked who was responsible for evaluating her performance. She was told, "Everybody." "Everybody? You mean interns, residents, and nurses?" The reply was, "Well, not nurses, of course."*

They don't speak to patients very much. The first chapter of Jay Katz's book The Silent World of Doctor and Patient *is "Physicians and Patients: A History of Silence." When doctors do speak to the patient, we are there. We're there when they speak to families. We're sometimes there when they speak among themselves. We know what they say. But they don't know what we say to the families. They don't know what families say to us. If you asked a doctor what is the one thing almost every family asks us, they wouldn't know. The one thing every family, at some point, will ask is, Can they hear?*

Someone has been in the room all the time. A daughter. The husband. Whenever I do anything, suction, blood glucose, a turn, I say her name. "Mrs. Montoya," I tell her softly, "bright light," "little stick." Every day

I end my first note with "All procedures and interventions explained to patient and emotional support given throughout." I am faithful to it.

Now there is no one here. I think she feels the peace too. Like we've been at a wedding or a festival dancing to music for a long time and can now rest. The husband's crossword puzzle book is on the chair. The lettering jagged, coming out of the little boxes. He can hardly write. Fifty-six and a half years aren't enough. He wants more. He doesn't want it to end. Being here is everything. The clocks were turned back weeks ago and at five thirty it is night. Out the windows, tall hooded lights illuminate the parking lot. Above them stars. Thanksgiving is in three days, the city quickening with visitors. Sons and daughters coming home. Maybe dying is like the effort in pulling back the string of a bow but the moment before the release is a kind of stillness. Once you're back, you just hold it, everything taut, and all the runs of V-tach and breathing fast are the quivering of that holding, harbingers of release, and then *whoosh*, you let go. Her eyes are closed. The room is as dark as the outside. I take her hand and rest it in mine. I do something I almost never do. I call her by her first name, "Jennie, it's all right. You're all right." Because when they ask, what we tell them, the answer is, yes, they can hear.

Rarely, almost never, if they leave, do they come back to the ICU to see us. I think maybe twice it's happened. And you never see them outside the hospital, shopping, at a gas station. If you do, it's odd, you don't recognize them, and the reason is because they're standing. We know them by their face. The one thing you always see in a room is their face. The side rails are up, they have gowns, sheets, blankets on, but the face is always there, not covered, floating above whatever ruin or chaos rages below, within.

Levinas says it is the face, the face of the Other, that calls to us. Naked, defenseless, the face means all by itself. "The face speaks." It is a silent and imperative language. It says, "Do not leave me in solitude." "Do not kill me." The human face is a moral summons; it comes with an intrinsic "ought." It is a reminder that the Other is my fellow human being. "I am responsible for the Other without knowing if the Other will reciprocate, without knowing how it will come out."

13

LEAVING ENDS THE LOVE

Agee writes about three families on a hill: the Gudgers, with whom he stays; the Woods family, whose daughters are Emma and Annie Mae; and the Ricketts family. During the three weeks Agee and the photographer Walker Evans live with the Gudger family, they see them and the others intimately and constantly, going to sleep, waking, undressing, eating meals, rolling cigarettes.

Let Us Now Praise Famous Men *has been described as a deeply felt examination of what it means to suffer, to struggle to live in spite of suffering. Yet Agee is haunted by failure. He feels he cannot know the sharecroppers, describe them or their world. One problem was that they actually existed: "In a novel, a house or person has his meaning, his existence, entirely through the writer. Here, a house or person has only the most limited of his meaning through me; his true meaning is much huger. In that he exists as an actual being. His great weight, mystery and dignity are in this fact."*

He writes about the difficulty of conveying the "dignity of actuality." It is never the case that he stands over them in superior understanding or empathic knowing. Their reality is greater. Years later, Agee would write to his friend Father Flye about Let Us Now Praise Famous Men, *"I made a try. I felt it was a failure. The lives of these families belong to people like them."*

Maria Sandoval had been moved to a room with a window. There's a study that actually says that a window in the room increases survival in the ICU. On the corkboard on the wall are pieces of paper stuck there with pushpins. One has the names of doctors: Dr. Fowler, Dr. Morgan, Dr. Cohen.

The other is in Spanish:

Para las semanas que entran

1. *Sacar el tubo de respiración*
2. *Sentarla una silla*
3. *Preguntas posibles cosas para preguntar a María*
   Tiene dolor de cabeza?
   Le duele el tubo?
   Quiere dormir?
   Tiene calor? Tiene frio?
   Mama—todos sus hijos y amigos esperan que se recupere pronto
   para que pueda estar con nosotros otra vez, si Dios quiere

There's a kindness to the Spanish language. If you look at it long enough, a word will tell you what it means or you'll get a sense of the sentence. *Sacar* means "take out." Take out the tube. *Una silla* means "a chair." Sit in the chair. Do you have a headache? Are you hot? They all want her to get better so she can be with them again. *Si Dios quiere.* If God is willing.

The night nurse said they were having a family meeting tomorrow. "They have a lot of questions. They keep asking how this happened. They don't understand. It's all iatrogenic. She had meningitis, was treated, had a stroke. Then she got peritonitis. They're sad. They have tears in their eyes. 'Me escuchas?' they say. It's important to them that she can hear them. They revere her. They're heartbroken."

She's from Mexico. Juárez. She had taken a bus to Denver to see her children. She had kids in Albuquerque, Colorado Springs, and Denver. Lori calls it a border story. They come up I-25 and settle in big cities just off the interstate. Quick on, quick off. Two days after she gets there she has abdominal pain, fever, chills. Then a headache and neck pain. They decide to take her back to Juárez, and on the way she gets worse. She gets admitted here, and it turns out she has meningitis. She goes into afib and goes on Coumadin to prevent clots. She's on the floor, getting better. Then one day goes flaccid on her left side. The MRI shows a bleed of the left occipital lobe. From the Coumadin. Then congestive heart failure from the afib. She gets trached and pegged. Somehow the PEG migrates, perforates her bowel, and she gets peritonitis and they have to do a laparotomy to clean her out and they leave her belly open. Everything in her body failed like the way you stand up a deck of cards on their edges and one falls and then they all fall in a row, softly. The meningitis long gone in the past like some big bang that started it all and is over but everything goes on and on.

"Abra los ojos," I say but I have to lift her lids with my fingers. Her right pupil is bigger from the stroke. "Está bien, señorita. Está bien. Tranquilo. Mueva dos dedos." She doesn't do anything. She doesn't blink to threat. "Tiene dolor?" She stares. From her mouth next to the tube is a slow ooze of thick, muddy saliva. Sometimes they're frozen like ice—on the vent, sedated, fentanyl and Ativan drips, still, quiet—then they thaw out, wake up pulling at lines, talking, eating. She's something in between, a slurry; not day or night but twilight.

Melissa has my other patient, a thirty-eight-year old white woman, Carolyn Oakley. "She had come to the ER not feeling well, was sent home, called a neighbor and said she couldn't breathe. She was found down and intubated by EMTs. CT showed a right upper lobe pneumonia. The EKG showed a prolonged QT so they're questioning an anterior MI. She's on a heparin drip. Her third enzymes are in the lab. I replaced her potassium. Her tox screen was negative. She's got a psych history. Her husband's here."

A medical student is presenting on her. Next in line. They look at the CT. "The apices suggest fluid," Fowler says, "more than atelectasis. No holes to suggest chronic lung disease. If she had been lying in bed, she could have aspirated."

The student says her QT is 520. The QT interval is a moment in the electrical cycle of the heart. If it's too long you can go into a life-threatening arrhythmia. Sudden death.

"Did she get Haldol? Moxacillin can cause prolonged QT. We should correct it for heart rate. What's the QT corrected?"

The student doesn't know. "Divide by the RR interval," says Kristen. It's like her motor is always running. Her hair is a little longer. She's wearing a skirt, black shoes. They're nearing the end of the rotation in the ICU.

"Let's get an echo," Fowler says. "Does she have a chest X-ray? Let's get one. Has anyone looked at her back?"

No one says anything.

"We have to make sure she doesn't have rhabdo. We should think about a spiral CT. And let's get a Psych eval."

The morning orders for Sandoval are two pages long. She has a fever again. They want all her lines discontinued and the tips cultured, her Foley changed. Sometimes what they do is start from scratch, like a blackjack dealer in Vegas asking for a new deck. Fowler said the CT shows some infarcts by the pons. "She could be locked in. Everything—touch, taste, smell, pee—all goes through an area this size." He had held up his thumb. "It would be like having one bridge into New York City." He told them they should read *The Diving Bell and the Butterfly*, about a French journalist who had a stroke and woke up and could move only his left eyelid. "We don't know what's going on in there."

Christmas is in three weeks. There is a small tree next to the secretary's desk. It has a few ornaments but mostly lilac and blue tinsel. Martha is doing a Coats-for-Kids drive. You can give her thirty bucks, or you can buy a coat for a kid. There's no other choice. On the roofs of all the buildings around the Plaza—the Territory of the Governors, the Catron building, the Ore House—are luminaria like a ring of light, so if you sit on one of the benches you feel you're down in a well looking up at a circle of stars. The trees are laced with a dark web of wires of small white Christmas lights the size of eggs.

By the *descanso* near our house the plains are covered with a layer of snow thin as a moth's wing. It's light in the morning when I come to work, dark on the way home. The *descanso*'s small tree is threaded with orna-ments and stuffed animals—a monkey, a frog, a teddy bear. It's topped with a gold star. On the metal guard rail, a snowman, a long red scarf looped around his neck, wears a red knit hat and mittens. His black eyes are turned upward and his mouth is rounded in the shape of song. He holds a sign: JOY.

The unit is quiet. Three rooms are empty. This happens around the holi-days. The only thing going on is Bed Seven. An old woman had come down from the floor last night in respiratory distress and was intubated. They were going to wait seventy-two hours, but she's end-stage renal and the family decided to withdraw. I can see them. It's a quiet scene. They're Native American from a pueblo near Taos. Not the big Taos Pueblo, but a smaller one.

Lucas is talking to them. He's talking to several women and a few men. The man he's mostly talking to must be the son. He's thin, with a long, gray-streaked ponytail. He's wearing a short-sleeved shirt and along the length of his arms are tattoos that look like birds all connected flying up his arm. He has a baseball hat on backward. Lucas is speaking. They seem comfortable with him, trusting. He looks older, more relaxed. As different as he looks in the circle of brown faces, with his white coat, the light twinkling off his glasses, his short hair; it could be a powwow.

The Pulmonary fellow comes by holding Oakley's X-ray in front of him like it's a shield. "Her chest film looks good," he says. "No more fluid."

"Where did it go? We didn't give her any Lasix."

He shrugs his shoulders, "Redistributed? I'll come back at four. Maybe we'll extubate her."

Her husband is here. He wears a faded denim shirt over a big gut, a baseball hat with a Colorado Rockies logo, and scuffed, ankle-high work boots. His jeans are blotched with paint. He stands at the foot of the bed and looks down at her.

"I feel like I'm caught between lost and found." He looks sad. He puts out his hand, "Jack. Jack Oakley."

"How long have you been married?"

"Twenty-two, no, twenty-four years. She started having problems about six years ago. Started thinking I was trying to poison her. She tried working at a bar, but she would tell people off. She could be hateful. She would take off for a month every couple of years. One year she went to Indiana. One time she talked a man into thinking she was being abused, and he gave her money for an apartment, but she couldn't make it on her own and came back."

"You took her back."

"Divorce isn't something I would do. Maybe being Roman Catholic. What would I do?" He looked at me. "Leave her on her own?"

Two Cardiology residents come into the room. The woman, I remember her saying she was from Turkey.

"She's young to have such a problem," the guy resident says to the husband. "How are her lipids, her cholesterol?"

"Ain't been checked," the husband says.

"Does she smoke a lot?"

"Used to until it got so expensive. Now she goes through a can of Bugler a week." The Turkish woman frowns. I make a rolling motion with my fingers. Then, because she's still frowning, bring a hand to my mouth and inhale. She finally nods.

"Does she do any drugs? Cocaine? Meth?"

"Just marijuana."

"Does she have any problems sleeping?"

"I go to bed and hours later she goes to bed. She hardly sleeps at all. Sometimes I have problems sleeping, too. It's like my own breathing wakes me. I work around chemicals, so I worry what I'm breathing in sometimes."

"Well," the guy resident says, "we're going to run some more tests."

I don't see the journey in White Coat. *I don't see the "physicianhood." Rothman never seems to arrive. The milestones seem not to be medical. At the end of the medicine rotation, she and Carlos spend the weeklong break in California and get engaged. She wonders a lot about when she will become a doctor. She goes on vacation to Europe. She and Carlos are married in Rochester, New York; graduate; and then honeymoon in Ireland for two weeks.*

Near the end of her last year of medical school, she writes, "Finally I was on the verge of becoming a real doctor. I belonged in this world, and I had worked hard to earn my legitimacy." When she applies for internship and residency, Rothman thinks, "I would be a doctor soon." And at the end, "After four years, my white coat finally feels familiar on my shoulders. Do I feel like a doctor yet? I'm still not sure."

The women in Sandoval's room look like they're from not just a different place but also a different time—long dresses buttoned up like a nun's habit and laced black shoes. One of them is reading from a little book. I ask her what it is. "Cat-o-li-co," she says. They're from Mexico. They seem different to me from the Hispanics here. Gracious. Quiet. Something regal about them. They walk processionally, as if they're carrying something sacred. Come here and make a wall around themselves and then passageways for others. An ancient grace sealed and kept pure.

One of the women goes to the bed. "Mi abuelita. Escúcheme. Abra los ojos."

"Soy enfermero. Me llamo Santiago."

"Christine."

"Habla ingles?

She shakes her head.

"Un poquito?"

"Nada."

"Por qué no?" I smile.

"Burra. Burrita." She laughs and makes like horns coming out of her head.

"Esta mejor?" She looks toward the bed.

"No mejor, no peor. Tiene problemas de los pulmones, una infeccion secondaria. Tiene calentura."

"Infección?"

"Sí. Muchas complicaciones."

"Sí. Gracias."

Let Us Now Praise Famous Men *begins with sixty-one photographs by Walker Evans. The photos are of the farmers, their children but also of their beds, bureaus, stoves, dining tables, porches, shoes, gravestones. They are black and white, untitled, uncaptioned.*

William Stott said of Walker Evans that what he found of interest in the poor, in "simple people" was the visibility *of their lives: "They and their lives are wholly exposed. They are 'there,' unhidden; complexities and all, visible."*

In his book The Look of Distance *Walter Slatoff says that Evans's photos "reveal a poverty so awful and so awful an injury in the eyes and mouths of most of the people that one wonders by what right one looks at the pictures."*

But in the photographs, the farmers and their children are serious, dignified. Evans saw the sharecroppers not as simple, feeble, or limited, but as complex, strong. What shows through is not just defeat but also pride and affection, and "these people's sense of form, balance, symmetry and their fierce hunger for order."

Two Native American girls with the woman in Seven are asking Sara for a Bible. They seem annoyed when she says we don't have one. They look sixteen, seventeen. Surly teenage faces. Martha interrupts and tells them she has already received a blessing from the priest. Then one of them asks Sara for a note for her boss saying she was here and that's why she missed work. "I don't know why he thinks I would lie about my grandmother being sick." Sara starts to say we don't usually write those when Martha says she'll write it.

"What's your name?" Martha asks her.

"Angela."

Martha says aloud what she writes: "Angela has been unable to work because her grandmother is critically ill in the ICU. If you have any questions, please call the intensive care unit at this number." Martha looks at her. "Do you want a raise? I'll write, Please give Angela a five-thousand-dollar bonus." She pretends she's going to write. "How about more vacation time?"

Both of the girls try not to, but smile closed-mouth smiles.

The resident comes by and says to put Oakley on CPAP and turn off the sedation. It's the Jersey woman.

"Do you want parameters?"

"No," she says, "Her film looks good. Just see how she does."

Jack Oakley has been here all day, just sitting in the room. No TV. Not reading. He says again he's worried about a cough he's been having, about an "upper resatory" infection. A trickle of family comes in. Two daughters and a little girl carrying a drawing on coarse paper of a stick figure that must be her that she leaves on the supply cart in the room. She's wearing a tank top and flip-flops and pants that are cotton with animal designs and look like pajamas.

I've lowered the sedation. The daughters are talking to each other. The woman must recognize their voices because she wakes up and starts pounding on the bed with the palms of her hand and then kicking her legs.

"We'll come back," one of them says.

It takes a half hour to put a Foley into Sandoval. Michelle is helping me. We have to turn her back and forth to get at the drains and look at the decub on her coccyx. She's like a pile of wet laundry or that slinky toy that when you move it one way it goes back to how it was. Her pannus covers her thighs. Everything is wet—the chux, the sheets, her gown from her weeping skin. The room is like a rain forest. She's like Montoya. Their bodies don't work anymore. Heads on a stick.

We push her legs out and lift the pannus, which is dimpled and stiff like leather. We spread her labia to find the urethra. It's like trying to find a ring in swampy water. Feces is leaking from the rectal tube, mixing with the betadine and moisture from her own skin. The smell is sweetish and stinging even through the masks. Michelle puts in the catheter but no urine comes out.

"She doesn't make much urine. But we should get something. Right?"

"Right." We're sweating in the yellow precaution gowns. I have to change gloves. We start over. Michelle hoists her leg off the bed. I see a small hole. "That's it, right?"

"I think so. It's supposed to wink at you" She lowers her head to not laugh. She touches a hole with the tip. "That's the vagina." She inserts the catheter.

"Aim up," I tell her.

No urine comes out but it's deep in. I inflate the balloon. "I think it's in the bladder." We watch as yellow-tinged fluid doesn't flow but begins to coat the inside of the Foley like frost on a window.

Alastair Campbell wrote that what the caring professions offer is moderated love. It is not the love you have for a relative or for a friend: it lacks the depth, the passion of that love. It's a kind of spiritual love because it's opposed to suffering and death, but it's not the love like in Corinthians that endures all things, hopes all things, that never ends.

He takes the idea from the role of the moderator in the Presbyterian Church who keeps order in the Assembly. The moderator has no status in himself; he is a "first among equals"; he serves for only one year so he can't accumulate power or prestige.

Campbell says the power and influence of medicine and nursing are limited. We shouldn't idealize them; we shouldn't think of doctors as gods or nurses as angels, and neither as heroes. They are human and fallible. It's "work" they do. He says we should think of medicine as brotherly love, and nursing as companionship. Companionship is a chance meeting; it is closeness, but it is less than friendship. It suggests a journey. The good companion helps with the journey, travels along for a while, but then the journey ends and the companions part ways.

When I think of the things we do, the time we spend with them, trying to relieve their pain, their suffering, trying to bring them back, I think nursing is a kind of love. That it is love that enables us to do the things we do. Love that makes you want them to get better. But it ends when they leave. Leaving ends the love.

Sara waves her arm for me to come. "Help me." She's been in the ICU less than a year. There are two visitors in her room. One is an old woman who came into the unit in a wheelchair but is now standing next to the bed, leaning close to the patient, holding her hand. They're looking at each other. She's speaking Keres. Twice the woman on the bed nods her head.

The old lady stands up and walks toward her wheelchair. "She says she's ready."

"I told them I need ten minutes," Sara says. "What do I do?"

"Do you have drugs?"

"Not yet."

"Ask for morphine five to ten q thirty, ask for ten milligrams times one and may repeat times one if necessary. That way you give thirty right away. And stay in the room."

"You stay too."

Before we extubate her, we change her gown, put a clean top sheet on, a clean pillowcase. Withdrawing support is like firing a pot: you get one chance at it and it's done. Maybe an hour more on the earth, I think. Her arms are untied and, free, rise up. "Sorry, sweetie," Sara says. Her hair is a snarl. I comb her hair; wet, there seems almost nothing of it, the teeth of the comb scraping against her skull. We finish with her sitting up, her arms resting on pillows.

Martha is bringing extra chairs into the room. She looks at the patient and then she looks at Sara. "She looks good," Martha says.

Mateo is at the door. "Ready?"

The room is full. Everyone is wearing a yellow gown. It looks like a garden of chrysanthemums. The man with the ponytail and tattoos is standing next to the bed near the patient's head and behind him a boy who looks like his own son. The man holds in his arms a little girl who herself has a photograph in one hand and a stuffed pony in the other. He lifts her up and leans the girl over the bed above the woman's face. "Here's your baby," someone says. The photograph is of the girl. She goes to give it and the woman tries but can't raise her hands, so several hands lift hers and at the same time let the picture fall into them. She seems to be crying. Her sats are eighty-one. Pulse 124.

Sara has lowered the sides of the bed and everyone standing there has a hand on the woman as if their arms were oars to keep her flowing straight and not drift to the shore. I turn down the monitor screen so it's blank. A woman with gray-streaked hair standing behind the others says, "Give her permission, Robert. Tell her it's all right to go. Tell her."

Her eyes are closed, her breathing shallow and rapid. The room is quiet. "You did it, Ma," Robert says. "You accomplished everything. You should be so proud." His hand is on her forehead. Her gown has slipped down so a crescent of flesh is showing. She is breathing more rapidly. A man says, "Thank you for being my aunt." Two women stare at the monitor and even put their faces close to it and at an angle, as though they'll be able to see behind the curtain of darkness.

Most people expect the person will die right away as if death is right at the door, and we take away "life support" and open the door and death comes right in. I move over to the gray-streaked lady and whisper, "She might not die for a while. If anybody wants to leave, say good-bye, they should feel it's all right." She repeats this aloud. No one leaves. Martha walks by and whispers, "Sixty-four over twenty."

A man begins to speak. "Give us this day our daily bread." They all join in. His voice is deep and as beautiful as song. When he finishes they fall silent again. One woman in the back is crying and takes off her glasses.

Voices in the unit behind me. "They're already on Flagyl." "Tell them I need to go to CT." "I think I've diagnosed my mother. She has Munchausen's." Laughter.

It looks like she's stopped breathing. I've been watching a small area of brown skin just below the right clavicle rise and fall, rise and fall. I can't see it move. I look at Martha. She shakes her head, but it means yes and makes a slashing motion across her throat. Lori is laying six-second strips of flatline on the counter. I should have told Sara but I forgot, so I say for them all to hear, "She died. Just this moment."

They wash their hands in turn as they leave. The red hazard container overflowing with yellow gowns. Sara stands at the door, and if they look at her she says, "I'm sorry for your loss." The last two are Robert and his son. Someday he will do for his father what his father did for his mother. Give him permission. Tell him it's all right to go.

I find orders to start Zosyn and to increase the PEEP on Sandoval. There's someone in the room sitting in a chair in the corner. It's a small chair like a chair in a schoolroom. The room is dark, but she has a book open, resting on her thigh, and she is very still. Like if you were in Iowa and were driven to your basement by a tornado, you would have your child do something normal like read *Goodnight Moon* while the winds were clawing at the roof of your house.

"Hola," I say to her.

"Hola."

She stands up. She's wearing a maroon satin blouse with a wide-lapel collar and a black skirt midcalf. And black boots. She's older. You can tell she's Mexican. That way of moving, a quietness, courtesy, a lost royalty.

"Cómo está ella?

"Lo mismo."

She's standing next to the bed, reading silently from the book.

"Está frío?" She's uncovered.

"No. Calor. Fiebre."

"Gracias," she says.

"Tiene preguntas?"

"No. Gracias."

I leave and she says, "Gracias. Es un buen hombre."

"Gracias."

One of the residents calls and asks how Oakley's CPAP trial went. I tell him she was wild, agitated. "Okay, we'll keep her vented overnight."

Oakley's daughters come back this time without the little girl and say they're going to leave for the day. They'll be back tomorrow. We have men at home, one says. They're cute. They're chubby, bouncy. It's like this is no big deal, a bump in the road. They've cleaned up somewhere. They have on different clothes. They don't stay very long. She's back on a rate, sedated, eyes closed. One of them cocks her head and says she looks comfortable. The other goes and kisses her on the cheek and says, "Bye, Mom." Then she asks if they should take her teeth home.

Agee came to see many things in the tenant world. He saw dignity, holiness, complexity, but most of all, beauty. Their houses, the land they live on, the clothes they wear, their motions, their speech seem beautiful beyond anything he knows. Their homes, in their bareness, cleanness, and sobriety "were among the serene and final, uncapturable, beauties of existence." He compares them to Doric architecture. It is a beauty

inseparable from their poverty, "inextricably shaped as it is in an economic abomination, is at least as important a part of the fact as the abomination itself."

But he realized they themselves were unaware of this beauty. There appears to be almost no such thing among the members of these three families as a "sense of beauty:" "To those who own and create it, this 'beauty' is irrelevant and undiscernible." It is, however, seen by others who are outside it by virtue of economic advantage or class privilege. But those who do see this beauty "have only a shameful and thief's right to it."

14

THE HORIZON

Visible, silent, unaware. Holiness, beauty, dignity. They rarely speak. How does Agee convey the lives of the tenant farmers? By description. Their lives are there; nothing hidden that needs to be interpreted, woven into a narrative, elevated into meaning. Their discourse is the physicality of their lives, their gestures, the things they own, how they arrange them, the clothes they wear, the structure of their homes. As poor as they are, the little they possess, they imbue with value, meaning, care beyond telling. "All they touch," William Stott writes, "and all that touches them, is permeated with their being. Whereas the prosperous attenuate their selfhood through many possessions and roles, the poor condense theirs in a few. Their world and everything in it bespeaks them." Agee experiences beauty, dignity, complexity but he writes about them as things: as the grain of wood, as odor, as the spacing of furniture, hats, clothing, gestures.

"David Chrisman. Fifty-eight. History of ankylosing spondylitis." Amanda takes a deep breath. "Long night," she says. She opens the chart to look for the green tab where the history would be. "Bizarre. He was admitted for neck pain from an MVA. He was on the floor. Going for an MRI. They had him in a soft collar and apparently his head flexed; he became apneic. They bagged him, brought him back, and brought him to the ICU. He's in a soft collar attached to a traction bar with ten pounds of weights like . . . you'll see. You can't adjust him. His spine is curved. He says he can see the horizon." She pronounced *horizon* as though it was a question and looked up at me as if I should tell her what that meant.

The chart is still open to the H and P. The first entry isn't a hospital note but is from a pain clinic:

This gentleman is 59 years old, brought here by his wife. He states he was involved in a motor vehicle accident where he was side-swiped, and since then has had neck pain, shoulder pain, and the flexion deformity of his head has deteriorated. He subsequently went to the ER for worsening pain for which he received a referral here. He has suffered from AS since the age of twenty-four which has changed the contour of his spine in a way that much of the time his neck is 90 degrees to his thoracic spine and he has compensated walking so that basically he looks down on the floor. His wife feels his neck is flexed forward another 10–15 degrees. None of the X-rays are available. We suggest that he have his wife take him home, put him to bed until we see these X-rays which are presumably on their way by courier. After we review them, we plan to probably admit him to the hospital, attempt a period of limited traction. This is potentially a serious problem for him.

The next note is a progress note, handwritten hastily by a resident, with some words underlined, scribbled additions in the margin: *T-bone 10 days before admit; no med attention; neck/back pain; MRI; Bone scan not done; soft collar taken off—went apneic; OR Monday for trach; q6 hr ABGs, call PC02 > 50; upper extremities spastic; was globally sensate @ 1200; still quad.*

"Mr. Chrisman. My name is Jim."

"Hello, Jim."

"How do you feel?"

"I've got nothing."

He spoke without opening his eyes and hardly moving his lips. His head is stretched over his body like you were on the second floor of a mall leaning over and looking down at the food court. He's lying in the kind of traction bed they use for broken femurs and that we never see in the ICU. It looks like something jerry-rigged. Two sand-packed leather bags hang from a hook at the end of the bed and are attached to a single rope that runs up the footboard like a vine to one pulley, then along the length of the bed like a clothesline to another pulley, and then directly over his head, drops like a plumb line. The rope ends in the pad in which his head lies, heavily, like a melon in those mesh bags with a handle that people carry groceries in. Only one arm is visible, limp on the almost-flat white sheet, under which there scarcely seems a body. His head seems held in the air above the bed like a captured prey in the talons of a hawk.

He can move his arms, but only his elbows away from his body like a penguin. His arms start to shake and the shakes grow into a riotous tremble like water simmering then boiling furiously and then fall back to his side. I lean away from the bed out of his sight and move my own arms as if to remind myself how arms should move.

"Can you move your fingers?" They lay still. It was like he hadn't heard me but he had. I pull the sheet down. His limbs look like twigs scattered randomly on the forest floor. Like pickup sticks. "Your legs? Can you feel me touching here?"

"I can feel pressure."

"Sharp or dull?"

"Just pressure."

"Here?" I spider my fingers along the muscle of his calf, the soft inside of his thigh, then out over the bone of the hip, stopping to pinch his flesh. It's soft.

"Here? You can feel everywhere. That's good. Do you remember what happened?"

"I was going for a test. They put me in a soft collar. I stopped breathing. I lost everything."

"How long have you had spondylitis?"

"It began thirty years ago. It was progressive. The angle kept getting smaller until eight years ago. Then it stopped. I can see the horizon."

"What do the doctors say?"

"I compressed my spinal cord."

"Will it come back?"

"They don't know. Jim, could I have some water?"

In nursing you know only what you've seen, and you know best what you've seen before. Medicine knows that. Teaching hospitals institutionalize that. Patricia Benner, in *From Novice to Expert*, says you can't get ahead of your experience. You walk ahead in darkness, the light on your forehead showing the way is only as bright as what you've seen; it doesn't have batteries; it has memories. A patient reminds you of another patient. Like vases in your brain that tip and the ashes fall out and float like petals of flowers on the rivers of your blood and you remember. The first quad I took care of was during my first year in nursing in the Trauma-Surgical ICU when I was training. He was a twenty-one-year-old Navajo, stabbed in a fight in Gallup. I was three months out of Castleton State College, one month in the West, and still wearing my white student uniform the color of fresh drywall. He had a stiff Miami J collar around his neck and his arms were on pillows and his hands were curled around rolled-up washcloths as if they were resting on the arms of a chair. Scotch-taped to the far wall at the end of the bed in his line of sight between the crosshairs of his motionless feet were two photographs. One was of two babies propped side by side against each other on a blanket. The other was of the same two babies with the patient and a woman who looked like, not the babies' mother, but the patient's mother. He had a look of fear and sorrow I had never seen before. As though he was looking at something. Not the photographs, not something in the room, something I couldn't see.

He was awake almost all the time, and he cried silently and often. He was a small man, his body still normal. His muscles still lifted his skin, contoured his body. Like a flower that was killed by a morning frost but still held its color and shape. On his chest, over where his heart would be, were marks the color of ash and seemed to have been drawn with a single finger like the trace a finger would make on frosted glass. We were under two admonitions from his Navajo family: not to wash off the marks and not to tell him he was paralyzed. To tell him would be to wish it upon him, to cause it to be. As if it had happened but had not happened.

From outside the room I can hear Chrisman talking.

"Who are you talking to?" I ask him.

"I'm talking to my God."

"What did you say to him?"

"I asked him to take me to his side. And to take care of my family."

Certeau dedicated The Practice of Everyday Life *to "the ordinary man. To a common hero, a ubiquitous character, walking in countless thousands on the streets. This anonymous hero is very ancient. He is the murmuring voice of society. In all ages, he comes before texts. He does not expect representations."*

Certeau believed everyday life could not be represented; there could be no theory of it; it could not be known. "We fail to connect with the everyday when we make it an object of 'scientific' knowledge." To attend to it is to lose it. We cannot help but miss it if we seek it through knowledge. He described the everyday as "the unmanageable, polyphonic excess of life," an originary plenitude of unmanageable heterogeneous voices that never really shows itself directly and in full.

Theories of the everyday are "obsessed by this rumour of a different country." But it is a country they cannot enter; "Analyses concerning culture border on a silent immensity. As they walk along these shores of the inaccessible, they discover their irreducible limitation. The theorizing operation finds itself at the limits of the terrain where it normally functions, like an automobile at the edge of a cliff. Beyond and below lies the ocean. I have to recognize that no text or institution could ever control the place of innumerable lexicons, strange vocabularies."

The people who are ill and their families are across a border, across an ocean, on an island, a rumor of a different country, their voices a tragic and poetic murmuring. There is a border between us and them; between medicine and nursing and the ill. No passport gets you across. Not empathy, sympathy, or even love.

Certeau saw his work as not so much as something in itself, but as driving a wedge between such representations and the worlds they seek to describe: "Our speech designates the space created by the distance separating those represented from their representations. It is essential, and at the same time it is nothing. Our speech is moving outside social structures, but to indicate what they lack, that is, the adhesion and the participation of their subjects." Illness is the greater reality, unfathomable to us; fathomable to them.

Nursing and medicine are essential but not more significant, not more important, like the Presbyterian moderator. Because we are close to it, the world of illness can become visible through us, but not by what we say about it or say about ourselves; instead, more like the way Simone Weil spoke of how God is able to see the world: "But I can easily imagine that he loves that perspective of creation which can only be seen from the point where I am. But I act as screen. I must withdraw so that he may see it."

They said in report that Montoya had been extubated. Lori has her. I go into the room. Lori is asking her questions. Mrs. Montoya whispers, "Albuquerque," then says, "November" but that's okay, it was November when she came here.

Whoever has Wallach is buried. He's getting blood, dialysis, the vent constantly alarming, runs of V-tach. His face is swollen, his arms charred from steroids. His wife sees me. We've grown close to her.

"How's he doing?" I ask her.

"He's on the edge. It's up to him. Baby steps."

"What's his creatinine?"

"Three point four."

"That's high."

"That's high. Baby steps." She stands aside, and a young woman is standing there. "My daughter."

She stands squarely facing me, with perfect posture, brownish hair to her jawline, straight shouldered. "Jim was his nurse the first day." She extends her arm, and she shakes my hand with a nice firmness. "Thank you for taking care of my father."

Later I hear Chrisman singing. I don't need to ask him the song. It's "Amazing Grace." He sings softly but with fervor, "a wretch like me." He has a beautiful voice.

He belongs to a barbershop quartet. He's also a photographer, a potter, a woodworker, and an avid hiker. The father of two children. He works fifty hours a week as a claims adjuster. He drives all over northern New Mexico in his Jeep Cherokee. When he had the accident he had sat on a curb and called his wife from his cell phone and said he was fine. His wife told me all this. She arrived midmorning and sat in the computer chair by his bed and held his hand. "I'm here." They both had a calmness like if you're braced for it, the collision you see coming doesn't affect you as much. It is as if they were braced for this. His time had been full, but they both knew it had always been borrowed.

The morning passed. I helped him urinate, moistened his mouth with swabs. I asked him how he felt "Angry. Very angry." Then he apologized, that he didn't mean me. I told him I never take it personally and that he had every right to be angry. Later his wife told me he didn't mean it. "He's not that kind of a person."

The horizon. Early on, when he realized his body was betraying him, folding up on him, he must have picked an object in the far distance, like a man who knew he would be lost if he did otherwise and decided to move toward only that. Driving, getting in and out of cars, sleeping, being stared at, and all the while working, singing, being a father, a husband. Watching them talking to each other quietly, her leaning on the bed rail, his eyes closed, his life in all truth over, maybe days to live, if not hours, and that realization slowly descending on them, I thought of how hard they had worked to build a life, to not just overcome a disability but to triumph, and that they would end it the same way they had lived it, straight on, fearless.

A Neurosurgery resident comes by. He looks at the chart and goes to look at X-rays. He talks to Chrisman and his wife in the room but leaves without writing a note or saying anything to me.

Mr. Chrisman tells me. "He said they could stabilize my neck. Put some rods in. He said it was a risky procedure, and he would talk to his attending. He couldn't guarantee anything." His eyes were not just closed but the skin was tight around them as though he was trying to focus on something, watching something behind his lids that was more important than what was happening outside.

By twelve o'clock he can't feel anything below his waist. The color of his skin has taken on a grayish cast. His sats are eighty-four. "I don't think I'm getting enough oxygen. I need more juice." He has moments of panic, as if he's driving a car without lights through a tunnel. He looks exhausted. His breathing labored. "I can give you something to help you relax. Some Ativan."

Someone is at the secretary's desk talking to Carol. It's Ortiz's daughter, April, and at her waist I can see the head of a young girl. April smiles, then gives Carol a card and at the same time the little girl reaches up with her hands and puts something on the counter. It looks like something baked. Then April looks past Carol for a second into the unit like you would look at something for the last time. They turn to leave. The little girl is tallish and thin. Coltish. April looks like she looked all those days she was here, when she would come every day and her mother was alive and there was hope. Maybe just being able to come here and see her and be able to touch her and stroke her forehead and her hair and talk to her was enough, was almost a life. Her not knowing what to do was just to keep us quiet, keep that life going for a few more days. Only once.

I watch them as they leave. The girl is holding April's hand and play-walking stiff-legged. April opens the heavy door and lets the girl duck under her arm, and in the space of the open door she stops and turns her head and finds me right away where she knew I was and looks right at me, her face not sad, that same pretty look, and smiles just a small smile, but I can tell, kind. She turns and leaves, and the door closes, and I think I saw her every day I worked for weeks and will probably never see her again, and I think it must have ended okay for her, and that look was maybe a way of saying that.

I don't think nursing changes you. It does affect you. Sometimes when the day is over, it can feel like when you've driven a long way in the heat—like the time Loren and I drove from Salt Lake City to Fresno in one day—and you finally stop but it feels as though you're still going, and the car metal is so hot it's ticking with a sound like glass breaking.

Going home, the city thinning behind you to motels, the big chains, a Best Western, La Quinta, then smaller, local ones, a last gas station, and then only a lake of light in the distance, the hard night sky overhead, you do feel, for the time you were there, the twelve hours, that more than any other time in your life, you were at the heart of things.

But it's not a journey. It doesn't feel heroic. It does feel special, though. The way Agee said he was being made witness to matters no human being may see.

I almost never think about a patient afterward. It's as if what we see and hear is so much the inside of their lives that we aren't meant to remember it. It happens to them. But it does affect you. I once read that there was something different in the last stories of Donald Barthelme, a tone of modesty, of generosity, a kind of tenderness toward existence. It feels something like that.

Coming back from the lab, I see Joseph Martinez's parents by the elevator. He's still in the hospital. The father and I shake hands. "How's he doing?" I ask. The mother, I forget her name, is holding herself with her arms crossed over her chest and her hands on her arms.

"He's doing better," the father says. The wife is pale, almost with a hospital pallor. "He's trying to talk to us."

"When they cap the trach, he'll be able to talk."

"Do they take it out?"

"They will eventually. You've seen people with a little scar here." I touch my neck. "But they'll cap it first. He can't talk because the air isn't going through his vocal cords."

Angela is her name. She's standing as you would huddle yourself against a wind.

"Do they say how they think he's going to do?"

"They don't really say. They don't really talk to us." Angela shakes her head no as well. "They're talking about sending him to Denver."

"The spine rehabilitation center. This must be hard on you."

"It is." Now I remember his name, Tony. "But we're doing all right. With God's help. We're letting him guide us. We trust in him."

"It's the hardest thing. Changes your life."

"It does."

"What will you do if he's in Denver?"

"We don't know yet. His insurance ran out. They're trying to get him on Medicaid.

"I'll be thinking about you guys."

"Thank you for everything you did."

They must forget or maybe they didn't see it that way, as my telling them to let him die, that it would be okay, would be for the better. They look numb, though, and maybe all they remember was that I talked to them and that I was kind. I don't know. But what I told them could happen, that they wouldn't want to happen, that thing has happened.

We shake hands again. I put my hand on his back. It's hot, like an iron.

Chrisman's son and daughter are in the room. It's the first time I've seen him smile. The wife and daughter sit near the bed, heads down, facing each other like two people studying a chess board, their knees, under the wife's neat blue jeans and the daughter's lemon calf-length slacks, almost touching, the mother on the stool. The son is standing near the far wall. I come in at the end of a joke. "What did Youdi say?" "No such thing as 'try,'" the son says. They all smile at this. They seem to have their own language. The wife seems calm, like a flutist in an orchestra able to relax while the violinists have their turn. Her head is low, her face in a half-smile at this father-son game. The son is standing with his back against the wall almost straight the way you would stand when your parents would measure you at the top of your head with a ruler as you were growing up. He's a young man, twenty-five, dressed in clothes that aren't quite a uniform but seem related to work. A white buttoned shirt, sturdy shoes.

The rooms in the ICU never allow much light, and the overhead fluorescent is off. The unit behind me is brightly lit. A team, not ours, is gathered outside Lori's room hunched over a chart. An X-ray tech is leaving the unit, pushing her machine in front, looking side to side at each room she passes like a vendor. Phones ring. An overhead page. In here it feels like evening. Like the end of the day. They talk softly and then fall quiet as if whatever happened, happened earlier and is now over. Like a picnic, a softball game, lunch with friends. The other side of anticipation. They're like people gathered around a fire at dusk, talking quietly, falling into a silence that stirs a memory. I hear fragments of those memories like embers carried by a breeze outside the circle: "Best birthday," "We didn't get home until four hours later," "You told me not to tell Mom," "I thought when he said four he meant four hundred."

It is still light when I get home. From the top of La Bajada, I can see white, mountain clouds above the Sangre de Cristos. I had driven home thinking about distance. I looked away to either side where the flat desert runs away to the caldera, to the holy mountain of the Navajo, where the rocky hills, the ragged edge of the piñon cover, meet the sky. Where the sky meets them. I tried to see that meeting, that seam. It was like trying to see the air.

I brought an old *Webster's Unabridged* from New England to New Mexico. It's as thick as two phone books and the spine soft as pulp. Years ago I started reading it from beginning to end. Between the pages beginning with *deck chair* and ending with *decorum*, there is a corner of the *Boston Herald* from September 15, 1994. Each word appears first in boldface then descends into a whisper of smaller print, a definition, a second, a third, the nuance, literal meanings, figurative meanings, obsolete ones. What something means is not so simple. Then an example of usage from poetry or prose brought in as a last-ditch effort to save the day: *Horizon.* "An apparent junction of earth and sky; (1) the fullest range or widest limit of perception, interest, appreciation, knowledge, or experience; (2) the range or limit of hope or expectation or a visible and seemingly attainable end. 'The horizon of the world has widened wonderfully in the last 100 years.' "—C.W. Eliot.

We live south of Santa Fe on a low mesa off Route 14, the Turquoise Highway, where the city hasn't reached yet. People who have traveled all over the world say there is nothing like the morning and evening light in New Mexico. Filmmakers traveling through on trains from one coast to the other would stop in New Mexico, get out, look around. I can walk a circle from outside my front door and see, like a mural drawn on the inside of the sky, the Sangre de Cristos, the Jemez to the west, the Ortiz to the south, the Galisteo wave above the basin, even the gray tips of the Sandías. Between the sky and the mountain line is a band the color of watermelon.

In medicine there are names for things that don't exist. The pleural space. The difference between the meninges. They're like mythical islands in the real sea of the body; they don't exist but they help you navigate. Imagining them creates possibilities where without them there might not be any. The horizon seems to be created by everything there is without being any of them. To see it you have to not see everything else, everything that's easy, pleasant; everything we take for granted.

I think it must be a kind of gift to see the horizon.

EPILOGUE

This morning I was still in bed when a storm came up from the south, from Albuquerque, a direction storms don't usually come from. Not with the antiphon of lightning then thunder but a steady growling sound just like a train that grew and grew and when it arrived seemed to turn back time, turned the morning into night again. On the prairie, there were skirts of snow below the piñon on which the low sun cast shadows sharp as knives. The peaks of Baldy and Truchas were white.

The residents had come by late last night just before the end of the shift. It was the last day of their rotation. Lucas shook my hand. "What's cruisin'?" he said. He asked how Montoya was. When I said, "Good," he gave me a thumbs up. He had a little swagger, but I didn't mind. I felt a mixture of wonderment, puzzle, pride, and happiness for him. He had been so inept and timid the first weeks and now was the resident in charge, supervising the central line, telling the intern she couldn't miss, blushing when she called him Tony. His sideburns cut sharply into little arrowheads and his hair was slicked down. It's as though he began here a boy, went on a trip around the world to Morocco, Barcelona, Sydney and came back grownup, worldly. They had that last-day-of-school look. The young woman Kristen and Miller maniacally pointing their fingers at each other. She went the opposite way—came in with a hard attitude that faded into her real self that wasn't so bad and even a little endearing. Maybe being so small her whole life she tried to make herself tough. "Great working with you guys," Miller said. His green scrubs were loose at his ankles and frayed from dragging on the ground. He had rounded his shoulders and folded his hands in front of his chest as if he were a monk praying, then rubbed them together rapidly with a wicked, gleeful smile. "Two weeks of radiology, two weeks of vacation in San Diego. Then GI. Just consults." It felt odd. As if we had all been shipwrecked but only they got rescued. But it didn't feel bad like that. They were happy in their way, going on. And we're happy in our way, staying.

Everyone brings a little of the winter air in with them, so the report room is cool. On the lower corner of the board in a red Sharpie is a note: "12/22 Mr. Fleischer went home today. Mrs. Fleischer called to thank everyone for all they did."

Grace is the night charge. "Bed One. Bed One is . . ."

NOTES

Introduction

xi *"philosophy is a struggle"* Walter Benjamin, *The Origin of German Tragic Drama* (New York: Verso, 1992), 37.

xii *"Illness is a source"* Jean Shinoda Bolen, *Close to the Bone* (New York: Simon and Schuster, 1996), 19.

xii *"One unintended outcome"* Arthur Kleinman, *The Illness Narratives: Suffering, Healing, and the Human Condition* (New York: Basic Books, 1988), xiv.

xiii *"unrecognized producers"* Michel de Certeau, *The Practice of Everyday Life* (Berkeley and Los Angeles: University of California Press, 1984), 34.

Chapter 2

24 *"depraved and miserable of our race"* Charles E. Rosenberg, *The Care of Strangers* (New York: Basic Books, 1987), 15.

31 *"Everything valuable"* Paul Starr, *The Social Transformation of American Medicine* (New York: Basic Books, 1982), 33.

41 *"I desire no other epitaph"* William Osler, *Aequanimitas with Other Addresses* (Philadelphia: P. Blackiston's Son 1914), 407.

Chapter 3

42 *"generally weak, divided, insecure"* Paul Starr, *The Social Transformation of American Medicine* (New York: Basic Books, 1982), 7–8.

42 *"They cure many times"* Starr, *The Social Transformation of American Medicine* (New York: Basic Books, 1982), 48.

45 *"clear picture of what it takes"* Ellen Lerner Rothman, *White Coat* (New York: Perennial, 2000), Chicago Tribune review on cover.

45 *"They wake like sleepwalkers"* Annie Dillard, *An American Childhood* (New York: Perennial, 1988), 11.

49 *"She had been admitted to the ICU"* Joan Didion, *The Year of Magical Thinking* (New York: Alfred A. Knopf, 2005), 67.

Chapter 4

52 *"Medicine went from a relatively weak"* Paul Starr, *The Social Transformation of American Medicine* (New York: Basic Books, 1982), 4.

55 *"3 years a patient"* Charles E. Rosenberg, *The Care of Strangers* (New York: Basic Books, 1987), 38.

55 *"Society reconstructed itself within the hospital"* Rosenberg, *The Care of Strangers,* 39, 41.

55 *"More than one more day"* Joan Didion, *The Year of Magical Thinking* (New York: Perennial, 2005), 68.

55 *"I first thought of applying"* Ellen Lerner Rothman, *White Coat* (New York: Perennial, 2000), 8–9.

56 *"first imagined becoming"* Audrey Young, *What Patients Taught Me* (Seattle: Sasquatch Books, 2004), 5.

63 *"that so freezes"* James Agee, *Let Us Now Praise Famous Men* (Boston: Houghton Mifflin, 1988), 87.

63 *"I am being"* Agee, *Let Us Now Praise Famous Men,* 120.

Chapter 5

67 *"medicine has lost its way"* Bernard Lown, *The Lost Art of Healing* (Boston: Houghton Mifflin, 1996), xi.

67 *"Modern medicine is too devoted"* Eric Cassell, *The Nature of Suffering* (New York: Oxford University Press, 1991), viii.

67 *"That vision looked inward"* Charles E. Rosenberg, *The Care of Strangers* (New York: Basic Books, 1987), 7.

67 *"in a world of sounds"* Stanley Joel Reiser, *Medicine and the Reign of Technology* (Cambridge: Cambridge University Press, 1988), 43.

67 *"move away from involvement"* Reiser, *Medicine and the Reign of Technology,* 38.

68 *"compared with the sharp images"* Barnard Lown, "The Commodification of Health Care," PNHP: Physicians for a National Health Program, http://www.pnhp.org/publications/the_commodification_of_health_care.php.

68 *"What is the matter with you?"* Michel Foucault, *The Birth of the Clinic: An Archaeology of Medical Perception* (New York: Vintage Books, 1994), xviii.

68 *"all mudgy"* Joan Didion, *Blue Nights* (New York: Alfred A. Knopf, 2011), 102.

72 *"signaled our medical affiliation"* Ellen Lerner Rothman, *White Coat* (New York: Perennial, 2000), 2.

72 *"It masked my youth"* Rothman, *White Coat,* 3.

72 *"When I become a physician"* Rothman, *White Coat,* 60.

79 *"A strong presumption"* Ira Byock, *Dying Well* (Thorndike, ME: Thorndike Press, 1997), 62.

79 *"a little while"* Kahlil Gibran, *The Prophet* (New York: Alfred A. Knopf, 1951), 95.

80 *"O nobly born; Fear not."* The Tibetan Book of the Dead; or, The After-Death Experiences on the *Bardo Plane, According to Lama Kazi Dawa-Samdup's English Rendering,* compiled and edited by W. Y. Evans-Wentz, with a new foreword and afterword by Donald S. Lopez Jr. (New York: Oxford University Press, 2000), 109.

80 *"Let virtue and goodness"* The Tibetan Book of the Dead, 209.

80 *"true poetry of life"* William Osler, *Aequanimitas with Other Addresses* (Philadelphia: P. Blackiston's Sons, 1914), 423.

80 *"the country of the ill"* David B. Morris, *Illness and Culture in the Postmodern Age* (Berkeley and Los Angeles: University of California Press, 1998), 21.

80 *"Illness is not something"* Morris, *Illness and Culture in the Postmodern Age,* 5.

81 *"the rot will continue"* Barnard Lown, *The Lost Art of Healing* (Boston: Houghton Mifflin, 1996), xiii.

81 *"As we briefly trace"* Eric Cassell, "Illness and Disease," *Hasting Center Report* 6, no. 2 (1976): 27–37.

Chapter 6

82 *"almost every woman"* Florence Nightingale, *Notes on Nursing: What It Is and What It Is Not* (Mineola, NY: Dover, 1969), 3.

82 *"the very elements"* Nightingale, *Notes on Nursing,* xii.

82 *"Nursing is recognized"* Nightingale, *Notes on Nursing,* xi.

82 *"To keep the air"* Nightingale, *Notes on Nursing,* 12.

82 *"nursing is by definition"* Charles E. Rosenberg, *Our Present Complaint* (Baltimore: Johns Hopkins University Press, 2007), 151.

87 Terry Mizrahi, *Getting Rid of Patients: Contradictions in the Socialization of Physicians* (New Brunswick: Rutgers University Press, 1986).

87 *"Alyssa is beautiful"* Ellen Lerner Rothman, *White Coat* (New York: Perennial, 2000), 30, 34, 36.

87 *"ER around here"* Rothman, *White Coat,* 24–26.

89 *"voyagers in the ordinary"* Michel de Certeau, Luce Giard, and Pierre Mayol, *The Practice of Everyday Life,* vol. 2, *Living and Cooking* (Minneapolis: University of Minnesota Press, 1998), xxxix.

90 *"We know poorly"* Certeau, Giard, and Mayol, *The Practice of Everyday Life,* 256.

151 *"You had the impression"* Michel de Certeau, *The Practice of Everyday Life* (Berkeley and Los Angeles: University of California Press, 1984), 41.

151 *"the snowy waves"* Certeau, *The Practice of Everyday Life,* 34.

151 *"innumerable lexicons"* Ahearne, *Michel de Certeau,* 155.

152 *"nominal subject"* James Agee, *Let Us Now Praise Famous Men* (Boston: Houghton Mifflin, 1988), x.

152 *"Actually, the effort"* Agee, *Let Us Now Praise Famous Men,* x.

156 *"If, in the hospital"* Michel Foucault, *The Birth of the Clinic* (New York: Vintage, 1994), 84.

156 *"The power of medical education"* Kenneth M. Ludmerer, *Time to Heal: American Medical Education from the Turn of the Century to the Era of Managed Care* (New York: Oxford University Press, 1999), xxi.

156 *"I was assigned"* Ellen Lerner Rothman, *White Coat* (New York: Perennial, 2000), 10.

158 *"And there was I"* Billy Collins, from "Statues in the Park," in *The Trouble with Poetry,* by Billy Collins, copyright 2005 by Billy Collins. Used by permission of Random House, Inc.

159 *"The sparks scatter"* Annie Dillard, *For the Time Being,* (New York: Vintage Books, 1999), 51.

162 *"We have comparatively little evidence"* Charles E. Rosenberg, *The Care of Strangers* (New York: Basic Books, 1987), 43.

162 *"I wouldn't demand"* Thomas Graboys, *Life in the Balance: A Physician's Memoir of Life, Love, and Loss with Parkinson's Disease and Dementia* (New York: Union Square Press, 2008), 60.

Chapter 11

164 *"clandestine arts"* Ben Highmore, *Everyday Life and Cultural Theory* (New York: Routledge, 2008), 147.

164 *"the stubborn insistence"* Highmore, *Everyday Life and Cultural Theory,* 148.

164 *"They remained other"* Michel de Certeau, *The Practice of Everyday Life* (University of California Press, 1984), 33.

171 *"The central assumptions"* Eric Cassell, *The Nature of Suffering* (New York: Oxford University Press, 1991), vii.

171 *"The search for an understanding"* Patricia Stark and John McGovern, eds., *The Hidden Dimension of Illness: Human Suffering* (New York: National League for Nursing Press, 1992) 2.

173 *"Now I looked"* Ellen Lerner Rothman, *White Coat* (New York: Perennial, 2000), 105.

173 *"No longer clouded"* Rothman, *White Coat,* 106.

173 *"tanned, relaxed"* Rothman, *White Coat,* 111.

173 *"I still felt"* Rothman, *White Coat,* 123.

173 *"I hated the atmosphere"* Rothman, *White Coat,* 124.

173 *"I had proved"* Rothman, *White Coat,* 125.

175 *"so eager to separate"* Eric Cassell, *The Healer's Art* (New York: Penguin Books, 1979), 56.

175 *"was part of"* Jay Katz, *The Silent World of Doctor and Patent* (New York: Free Press, 1984), 3, 7.

175 *"stranger relationship"* Richard M. Titmuss, *The Gift Relationship* (New York: New Press, 1997), 282.

178 *"Ay yo ma"* Nelly, "Luven Me." Words and music by Albert Hudson, Carl Wheeler, and Dwayne Wiggins. Copyright 2000 Songs of Universal, Inc., Perk's Music, Universal—Polygram International Publishing, and Tony! Toni! Tone! Music. All rights for Perk's Music controlled and administered by Songs of Universal, Inc. All rights for Tony! Toni! Tone! Music controlled and administered by Universal—Polygram International Publishing. All rights reserved. Used by permission. Reprinted by permission of Hal Leonard Corporation.

178 *"unrecognized producers"* Certeau, *The Practice of Everyday Life,* xviii.

181 *"is of that tribe"* James Agee, *Let Us Now Praise Famous Men* (Boston: Houghton Mifflin, 1988), 78.

182 *"died before they were born"* Kenneth Seib, *James Agee* (Pittsburgh: University of Pittsburgh Press, 1965), 53.

182 *"In what way were we trapped"* Agee, *Let Us Now Praise Famous Men,* 70.

Chapter 12

183 *"People know everything"* Michel de Certeau, *The Practice of Everyday Life* (Berkeley and Los Angeles: University of California Press, 1984), 71.

183 *"a knowledge of the concrete"* Edmund Burke, *Reflections on the Revolution in France* (New York: Penguin Classics, 1986), 84.

183 *"obscure, silent"* Ben Highmore, *Everyday Life and Cultural Theory* (New York: Routledge, 2008), 108.

183 *"refusal to denigrate"* Michel de Certeau, Luce Giard, and Pierre Mayol, *The Practice of Everyday Life*, vol. 2, *Living and Cooking* (Minneapolis: University of Minnesota Press, 1998), 155.

183 *"unfurls in a complex montage"* Certeau, Giard, and Mayol, *The Practice of Everyday Life,* 158.

183 *"In cooking"* Certeau, Giard, and Mayol, *The Practice of Everyday Life,* 200.

183 *"shows a subtle intelligence"* Certeau, Giard, and Mayol, *The Practice of Everyday Life,* 158.

187 *"I felt the sting"* Ellen Lerner Rothman, *White Coat* (New York: Perennial, 2000),160.

187 *"I saw tears"* Rothman, *White Coat*, 161.

187 *"For the first time"* Rothman, *White Coat*, 167.

189 *"The purpose of my book"* Susan Sontag, *Illness as Metaphor* (New York: Farrar, Straus and Giroux, 1989), 102.

189 *"to regard cancer"* Sontag, *Illness as Metaphor*, 102.

189 *"an epic of suffering"* Sontag, *Illness as Metaphor*, 125.

194 *"Life changes fast"* Joan Didion, *The Year of Magical Thinking* (New York: Alfred A. Knopf, 2005), 3.

194 *"Who is speaking?"* Michel Foucault, *The Archaeology of Knowledge* (New York: Pantheon Books, 1972), 50.

194 *"One of the ways"* Perri Klass, *A Not Entirely Benign Procedure* (New York: G. P. Putnam's Sons, 1987), 158, 160.

195 *"The face speaks"* Emmanuel Levinas, *Ethics and Infinity* (Pittsburgh: Duquesne University Press, 1982), 87.

195 *"I am responsible"* Elder Lindahl, "Face to Face," *Pietisten* 17, no. 1 (2002), www.pietisten.org/.

Chapter 13

196 *"In a novel"* James Agee, *Let Us Now Praise Famous Men* (Boston: Houghton Mifflin, 1988), 9.

196 *"I made a try"* James Agee and James Harold Flye, *Letters of James Agee to Father Flye* (New York: George Braziller, 1962), 114–15.

201 *"Finally I was on the verge"* Ellen Lerner Rothman, *White Coat* (New York: Perennial, 2000), 321.

201 *"I would be a doctor"* Rothman, *White Coat*, 315.

201 *"After four years"* Rothman, *White Coat*, 335.

202 *"simple people"* William Stott, *Documentary Expression and Thirties America* (Chicago: University of Chicago Press, 1986), 273–74.

202 *"reveal a poverty"* Walter J. Slatoff, *The Look of Distance* (Columbus: Ohio State University Press, 1985), 246.

202 *"these people's sense of"* William Stott, *Documentary Expression and Thirties America* (Chicago: University of Chicago Press, 1986), 276.

204 *"first among equals"* Alastair V. Campbell, *Moderated Love: A Theology of Professional Care* (London: SPCK, 1984), 84.

207 *"were among the serene"* Agee, *Let Us Now Praise Famous Men*, 117.

208 *"inextricably shaped"* Agee, *Let Us Now Praise Famous Men*, 178.

208 *"To those who own"* Agee, *Let Us Now Praise Famous Men*, 178.

208 *"have only a shameful"* Agee, *Let Us Now Praise Famous Men*, 178.

Chapter 14

209 *"All they touch"* William Stott, *Documentary Expression and Thirties America* (Chicago: University of Chicago Press, 1986), 275.

212 *"the ordinary man"* Michel de Certeau, *The Practice of Everyday Life* (Berkeley and Los Angeles: University of California Press, 1984), v.

212 *"We fail to connect"* Michael Sheringham, *Everyday Life* (New York: Oxford University Press, 2009), 21.

212 *"the unmanageable"* Ben Highmore, *Michel de Certeau* (New York: Continuum, 2008), 71.

212 *"obsessed by this rumor"* Jeremy Ahearne, *Michel de Certeau: Interpretation and Its Other* (Stanford: Stanford University Press, 1995), 159.

212 *"Analyses concerning culture"* Ahearne, *Michel de Certeau*, 159.

213 *"Our speech designates"* Ahearne, *Michel de Certeau*, 158.

213 *"But I can easily imagine"* Simone Weil, *Gravity and Grace* (New York: Routledge, 2002), 41.